Good Pharmacovigilance Practice Guide

Good Pharmacovigilance Practice Guide

Compiled by the Medicines and Healthcare products Regulatory Agency

London • Chicago **Pharmaceutical Press**

Published by the Pharmaceutical Press
An imprint of RPS Publishing

1 Lambeth High Street, London SE1 7JN, UK
100 South Atkinson Road, Suite 200, Grayslake, IL 60030–7820, USA

© Crown Copyright 2009

Medicines and Healthcare products Regulatory Agency
Market Towers 1 Nine Elms Lane
London SW8 5NQ
Information on re-use of crown copyright information can be found on the MHRA
website: www.mhra.gov.uk

Published by the Pharmaceutical Press on behalf of the Medicines and Healthcare
products Regulatory Agency (MHRA)

(**PP**) is a trade mark of RPS Publishing

RPS Publishing is the publishing organisation of the Royal Pharmaceutical Society of
Great Britain

First published 2009

Typeset by J&L Composition Ltd, Filey, North Yorkshire
Printed in Great Britain by Cambridge University Press, Cambridge

ISBN 978 0 85369 834 0

Contents

Foreword   xii

Acknowledgements   xiii

Feedback   xiv

Introduction   xv

Abbreviations   xvii

**1   Qualified Person Responsible for Pharmacovigilance in
     the European Economic Area   1**

1.1   Appointment of the Qualified Person for Pharmacovigilance   1
1.2   Notification of details of the Qualified Person for
         Pharmacovigilance   3
1.2.1   Checklist for the detailed description of the
         pharmacovigilance system   3
1.3   Who can be a Qualified Person for Pharmacovigilance?   5
1.4   What are the responsibilities of the Qualified Person for
         Pharmacovigilance?   6
1.4.1   Overview of the pharmacovigilance system   6
1.4.2   Preparation of reports   9
1.4.3   Requests from Competent Authorities   10
1.4.4   Ongoing safety monitoring   11
1.5   What other tasks might the Qualified Person for
         Pharmacovigilance perform?   13
1.5.1   Points to consider   14
1.6   Examples of inspection findings   14

2   Management of Pharmacovigilance Data   17

2.1   Terminology   17
2.2   Information collection and collation   20
2.2.1   Reconciliation   20
2.2.2   Duplicate reports   22

2.3	Access to pharmacovigilance data	22
2.4	Preparation of reports	23
2.5	Requests from Competent Authorities	23
2.6	Use of computer systems	23
2.6.1	Checklist of requirements for computer systems	24
2.7	Use of paper based systems	25
2.8	Examples of inspection findings	26

3   Spontaneous Case Processing   29

3.1	Sources of suspected adverse reactions	29
3.1.1	Medical information enquiries	30
3.1.2	"Contact us" emails and website enquiry forms	30
3.1.3	Product technical complaints	30
3.1.4	Medical representatives	31
3.1.5	Published literature	32
3.1.6	Reports from Competent Authorities	32
3.1.7	Contractual partners	32
3.2	Recording Individual Case Safety Report information	33
3.2.1	Date of receipt	33
3.2.2	Methods of recording information	33
3.2.3	Coding	33
3.3	Follow-up of adverse events	34
3.3.1	Information to validate a case	34
3.3.2	Information relevant for case evaluation	35
3.3.3	Reports of drug exposure during pregnancy	35
3.3.4	Reports of overdose, abuse and misuse	36
3.3.5	Additional considerations regarding follow-up attempts	36
3.4	Case assessment	37
3.4.1	Seriousness assessment	38
3.4.2	Causality assessment	39
3.4.3	Expectedness assessment	39
3.4.4	Upgrading and downgrading of cases	40
3.4.5	Deletion/deactivation of cases	41
3.5	Expedited reporting	41
3.5.1	What to expedite	41
3.5.2	Additional information to expedite	44
3.5.3	What not to report	45
3.5.4	When to expedite	45
3.5.5	How to expedite	46
3.6	Compliance monitoring	46
3.7	UK requirements for "specials"	46
3.8	Examples of inspection findings	47

4 Literature Searching   49

4.1   Identification of Individual Case Safety Reports   49
4.2   Requirements relating to Periodic Safety Update Reports   50
4.3   Risk–benefit assessment   51
4.4   When to start and stop   51
4.5   Where to look   52
4.6   Database searches   52
4.6.1 Precision and recall   53
4.6.2 Search construction   53
4.6.3 Selection of product terms   53
4.6.4 Selection of search terms   54
4.6.5 "Limits"   54
4.7   Handling search results   55
4.7.1 Record keeping   55
4.7.2 Outputs   56
4.7.3 Review and selection of articles   56
4.7.4 Follow-up   57
4.7.5 Day zero   57
4.7.6 Translations   57
4.7.7 Reporting   58
4.7.8 Duplicates   58
4.8   Contracting out literature search services   58
4.9   Examples of inspection findings   59

5 Periodic Safety Update Reports   61

5.1   Who is responsible for producing Periodic Safety
       Update Reports?   61
5.2   When should Periodic Safety Update Reports be
       submitted?   62
5.3   Submission dates for Periodic Safety Update Reports   63
5.4   Renewals and Periodic Safety Update Reports   64
5.5   Data selection and inclusion   64
5.6   Combination products and differing formulations of the
       same active substance   67
5.7   Special patient populations   67
5.8   Reference Safety Information   69
5.9   Review of cumulative data   69
5.10   Quality control   70
5.11   Examples of inspection findings   70

6   Evaluation of Safety Data   73

6.1	General considerations for signal detection	73
6.2	Methods of signal detection	74
6.2.1	Individual case review	74
6.2.2	Systematic review of multiple case reports	75
6.2.3	Periodic Safety Update Reports	77
6.2.4	Other sources of information	77
6.3	Investigation of potential signals	78
6.4	Follow-up of potential signals	79
6.5	Communication of potential signals	80
6.5.1	Direct Healthcare Professional Communications	81
6.6	Counterfeit medicines	82
6.7	Examples of inspection findings	83

7   Risk Management Plans   85

7.1	Purpose	85
7.2	Content of the European Union Risk Management Plan	86
7.2.1	Safety specification	86
7.2.2	Pharmacovigilance plan	86
7.2.3	Risk minimisation	86
7.3	Key assessment issues	87
7.3.1	Safety specification	87
7.3.2	Pharmacovigilance plan	88
7.3.3	Risk minimisation	88
7.3.4	Other information	88
7.4	Examples of issues	88

8   Reference Safety Information   91

8.1	Types of Reference Safety Information	91
8.2	Uses of Reference Safety Information	91
8.3	Availability of Reference Safety Information	92
8.4	Consistency between different types of Reference Safety Information	92
8.5	Updates to Reference Safety Information	93
8.5.1	Triggers for updates	93
8.5.2	Labelling committees	93
8.5.3	Points to consider	93
8.6	Timelines	94
8.6.1	Timelines for periodic review	94
8.6.2	Timelines for updates	94

	8.7	Introduction of new labels and patient information leaflets following approval of changes	95
	8.8	Considerations for herbal products	95
	8.9	Examples of inspection findings	96

9   Quality Management System   99

	9.1	Written procedures	99
	9.2	Training	101
	9.3	Quality assurance	103
	9.4	Record retention	105
	9.5	Examples of inspection findings	105

10   Interactions between Pharmacovigilance and Other Functions   107

	10.1	All personnel	107
	10.2	Medical information	109
	10.3	Sales and marketing	110
	10.4	Regulatory affairs	111
	10.4.1	Safety variations and urgent safety restrictions	112
	10.4.2	Responses to requests for information from regulatory authorities	112
	10.4.3	Post-marketing commitments	112
	10.4.4	Periodic Safety Update Reports	113
	10.4.5	Product labelling	113
	10.4.6	Worldwide marketing authorisation status	113
	10.4.7	Preparation for marketing authorisation submission	114
	10.5	Non-clinical staff	114
	10.6	Product quality	115
	10.7	Legal department	115
	10.8	Human resource department or those responsible for training	116
	10.9	Senior management	116
	10.10	Information technology	117

11   Contracts and Agreements   119

	11.1	General considerations for contracts and agreements	119
	11.1.1	Points to consider for contracts and agreements	120
	11.2	Outsourcing of pharmacovigilance activities	121
	11.2.1	Points to consider for outsourcing agreements	122
	11.3	Third party distributors and manufacturers	123

11.4	Co-licensing/co-marketing and co-promotion of products	123
11.4.1	Points to consider in co-licensing/co-marketing/ co-promotion agreements	124
11.5	Other types of contracts and agreements	124
11.5.1	Agreements with local affiliates	124
11.5.2	Transfer of a marketing authorisation	125
11.6	Examples of inspection findings	125

12   Requirements for Solicited Reports   127

12.1	Relevant terminology	127
12.1.1	Trial/study definitions	127
12.1.2	Other definitions that may clarify safety reporting requirements	128
12.1.3	Summary of study categorisation	130
12.2	Safety reporting for non-interventional studies	131
12.2.1	Expedited reporting of adverse reactions	131
12.2.2	Ongoing safety evaluation	132
12.2.3	Periodic Safety Update Reports	132
12.2.4	Annual Safety Reports	132
12.2.5	Final study reports	132
12.3	Interventional clinical trials	132
12.3.1	Causality assessments	133
12.3.2	Investigator's brochure	134
12.3.3	What is a SUSAR?	135
12.3.4	Reporting requirements for investigational medicinal products	136
12.3.5	Reporting requirements for non-investigational medicinal products	138
12.3.6	Electronic reporting	140
12.3.7	Considerations for blinded trials	140
12.3.8	Annual Safety Reports	142
12.3.9	Safety monitoring boards	143
12.3.10	Safety reporting to ethics committees	144
12.4	Post-authorisation Safety Studies	144
12.4.1	Progress reports from Post-authorisation Safety Studies	145
12.5	Investigator-led studies	145
12.6	Registries	146
12.7	Examples of inspection findings	147

Annexes **149**
1 Introduction to pharmacovigilance inspections 149
2 Relevant legislation and guidance 159
3 UK pharmacovigilance offences 163
4 Safety reporting requirements for clinical studies 175
5 Pharmacovigilance initiatives 187

Glossary 189

Index 199

Foreword

The primary objective of the Medicines and Healthcare products Regulatory Agency (MHRA) is to ensure that medicines and medical devices work and are acceptably safe.

Over recent years there has been an increasing public awareness of safety issues relating to medical products. The recognition of the importance of pharmacovigilance has also grown, and both regulatory agencies and pharmaceutical companies seek to ensure that emerging safety information is reported and appropriate action taken to safeguard public health.

As we look to the future, the recent proposals from the European Commission to strengthen and rationalise European Union (EU) pharmacovigilance are a positive step forward, and should serve to simplify and clarify the roles of all stakeholders involved in pharmacovigilance, which will not only benefit Market Authorisation Holders and regulators but also the public. Importantly, the establishment of the concept of Good Vigilance Practice in European legislation will standardise the conduct of pharmacovigilance across Europe.

Since the voluntary programme of pharmacovigilance inspections commenced in October 2002, followed by the statutory programme in July 2003 onwards, the pharmacovigilance inspectors within the MHRA have acquired a wealth of experience about different pharmacovigilance systems in operation, including examples of both good and poor practice. Similarly the Pharmacovigilance Group within the Vigilance and Risk Management of Medicines Division has accumulated extensive experience of assessment issues and pharmacovigilance standards. It is hoped that the benefit of this knowledge and practical advice can be shared with professionals involved in pharmacovigilance.

While this UK guide does not replace existing documents on the subject, it does offer valuable practical guidance on good vigilance practice and will also serve to complement the new EU legislation and guidance that comes out of the Commission's review.

We commend this useful reference to you as the MHRA and Marketing Authorisation Holders work together to further benefit public safety.

Gerald W. Heddell
Director, Inspection, Enforcement and Standards Division
Dr June Raine
Director, Vigilance Risk Management of Medicines Division

Acknowledgements

With regard to the writing of this guide, prepared under the auspices of the MHRA, particular thanks should go to the Pharmacovigilance Inspectorate of the Inspection, Enforcement and Standards Division, who devised and reviewed the guide as well as authoring many of the chapters, and to the authors and reviewers within the Vigilance and Risk Management of Medicines Division and the Clinical Trials Unit, without whom this guide would not have been possible.

Feedback

Questions or comments on the content or presentation of this guide are encouraged and will be used to develop further editions. Your views are valued and both the MHRA and Pharmaceutical Press would appreciate you taking the time to contact us by post, telephone, fax or email.

Pharmacovigilance Inspectorate
Inspection, Enforcement and Standards Division
Medicines and Healthcare products Regulatory Agency
Market Towers
Floor 18
1 Nine Elms Lane
London SW8 5NQ
www.mhra.gov.uk (Home/How we regulate/Medicines/Inspection and standards/Good Pharmacovigilance Practice)
Email: info@mhra.gsi.gov.uk
Tel: 0044 (0)1707 299 130
Fax: 0044 (0)20 7084 3519

For general enquiries about pharmacovigilance
The Pharmacovigilance Service Desk
Tel: 0044 (0)20 7084 2550 (Marketing Authorisation Holders A–L)
0044 (0)20 7084 2318 (Marketing Authorisation Holders M–S)
0044 (0)20 7084 3730 (Marketing Authorisation Holders T–Z)
Email: pharmacovigilanceservice@mhra.gsi.gov.uk

For general enquiries about the MHRA
The Information Centre
Tel: 0044 (0)20 7084 2000
Fax: 0044 (0)20 7084 2353
Email: info@mhra.gsi.gov.uk

Introduction

The MHRA has identified the need for creating and publishing a guide to good pharmacovigilance practice (GPvP). Similar guidance documents exist for other areas of GxP (The Guide to UK GLP Regulations, Rules and Guidance for Pharmaceutical Manufacturers and Distributors). Publication of Volume 9A in January 2007, and the subsequent update in April 2007, saw a number of changes to pharmacovigilance practice and the MHRA felt it was pertinent to produce a guide to address practical issues in response to this.

The guide relates to pharmacovigilance of medicinal products for human use. It is intended that this guide will complement currently available EU legislation and guidance and provide practical advice to key stakeholders, in particular Marketing Authorisation Holders, about achieving an appropriate system of pharmacovigilance. The guide is aimed at any organisation involved in pharmacovigilance activities (e.g. Marketing Authorisation Holders), as well as consultants, contractors and service providers, but it does not include guidance on the pharmacovigilance activities performed by Regulatory Authorities.

This guide applies to herbal medicines; however, there are certain practical issues specific to such medicines arising from the implementation of Directive 2004/24/EC on traditional herbal medicinal products. Supplementary information about the application of the guide to herbal medicines within the UK is available on the MHRA website.

Pharmacovigilance is not confined to one department within an organisation, and so the guide aims to take a holistic approach, considering the specific requirements defined in legislation and also other activities that impact on pharmacovigilance in a more subtle way.

The programme of statutory pharmacovigilance inspections in the EU is relatively recent in comparison to the inspection programmes of other GxPs. For many organisations, the expectations placed upon them by regulators are not fully apparent and it is hoped that this guide will help to address this issue.

The two key pieces of legislation that underpin pharmacovigilance expectations in the EU are Regulation 726/2004 and Directive 2001/83/EC (as amended). Additional legislation and guidance documents are detailed in Annex 2. It is important to note that the guide is not intended to replace the existing legislation and guidance and it does not act as a single reference document for all requirements. Also, the guide does not address vigilance issues for medical devices nor pharmacovigilance of veterinary products.

It is recognised that there are differences in terms of structure, organisation, resources and philosophy between large and small pharmaceutical companies, innovative and generic companies, conventional pharmaceuticals and herbal products. In general, the legislation does not differentiate between types of company and as such it is not possible to have different sets of expectations for different types of organisation.

However, the way in which companies achieve an appropriate system of pharmacovigilance varies immensely; what is appropriate for one company may be hugely unrealistic or unnecessary for another. It is not possible to address all scenarios within the guide or to provide information that will satisfy the requirements of all individual organisations. Where possible, we have tried to provide advice on how different types of organisation may achieve compliance with the requirements.

This guide is the result of collaboration between different groups within the MHRA, including the GPvP Inspectorate, the Pharmacovigilance Group and the Clinical Trials Unit. With a combined experience of over 200 inspections of UK Marketing Authorisation Holders, the MHRA GPvP Inspectorate team has encountered many models for conducting pharmacovigilance and also many examples of both good and poor practice. It is hoped that by highlighting the areas of common inspection findings and providing specific examples of good or poor practice, the guide can assist organisations in developing effective pharmacovigilance systems.

With the ever-changing regulatory environment, it is inevitable that aspects of this guide will not remain current, although the general principles of GPvP will always be relevant. The MHRA intends to revise and update the guide at appropriate time points and, in particular, after updates to EU pharmacovigilance legislation are adopted.

The MHRA's mission is to enhance and safeguard the health of the public by ensuring that medicines and medical devices work and are acceptably safe. We aim to protect, promote and improve public health, and it is hoped that the information provided within this guide will contribute to these aims by assisting organisations in developing and maintaining appropriate and effective pharmacovigilance systems.

The content of external websites referenced in this guide is not the responsibility of the MHRA.

Information given is general guidance and must not be treated as a complete and authoritative statement of the law.

Abbreviations

AE	Adverse event
ASPR	Anonymised Single Patient Report
ASR	Annual Safety Report
BROMI	Better Regulation of Medicines Initiative
CAPA	Corrective Action, Preventative Action
CCDS	Company Core Data Sheet
CCSI	Company Core Safety Information
CHMP	Committee for Medicinal Products for Human Use
CIOMS	Council for International Organizations of Medical Sciences
CV	Curriculum vitae
DCDS	Developmental Core Data Sheet
DCSI	Developmental Core Safety Information
DDPS	Detailed description of the pharmacovigilance system
DHPC	Direct Healthcare Professional Communication
DLP	Data lock point
DSMB	Data safety monitoring board
DSUR	Development Safety Update Report
EEA	European Economic Area
eMC	Electronic Medicines Compendium
EMEA	European Medicines Agency
EU	European Union
GPvP	Good pharmacovigilance practice
HBD	Harmonised birth date
HCP	Healthcare professional
IB	Investigator brochure
ICH	International Conference on Harmonisation
ICSR	Individual Case Safety Report
IMP	Investigational medicinal product
IT	Information technology
MAH	Marketing Authorisation Holder
MedDRA	Medical Dictionary for Regulatory Activities
MHRA	Medicines and Healthcare products Regulatory Agency
MSSO	Maintenance and Support Services Organization
NIMP	Non-investigational medicinal products

PASS	Post-authorisation safety study
PIAG	Pharmacovigilance Inspection Action Group
PIL	Patient information leaflet
PRR	Proportional reporting ratio
PSUR	Periodic Safety Update Report
QA	Quality assurance
QC	Quality control
QPPV	Qualified Person for Pharmacovigilance
RMP	Risk Management Plan
RMS	Reference Member State
RSI	Reference Safety Information
SAE	Serious adverse event
SAR	Serious adverse reaction
SPC	Summary of Product Characteristics
SPS	Summary of Pharmacovigilance Systems
SOP	Standard operating procedure
SUSAR	Suspected unexpected serious adverse reaction
THR	Traditional herbal registration
WHO	World Health Organization

1

Qualified Person Responsible for Pharmacovigilance in the European Economic Area

Editor's note	European Union (EU) legislation states that the Qualified Person for Pharmacovigilance (QPPV) has specific legal responsibilities in the European Economic Area (EEA) and has primary responsibility for ensuring that the Marketing Authorisation Holder's (MAH) pharmacovigilance system is compliant with EU requirements.[1] It is expected that the MAH will adequately support the QPPV in this important role.

The responsibilities of the QPPV can be addressed using a variety of models, and the MAH is responsible for implementing an appropriate model for the company. The appropriateness of the processes and procedures implemented by the company will be assessed during inspections conducted by the Competent Authorities.

The requirements relating to the obligations of the EEA QPPV are contained in Regulation 726/2004 and Directive 2001/83/EC (as amended). Detailed guidance on the roles and responsibilities of the QPPV can be found in Volume 9A, Part 1, Section 1.2. The requirements and legal responsibilities relating to the QPPV, which are described in this chapter, also apply to companies that register traditional herbal medicinal products in the Community under Directive 2004/24/EC.

1.1 Appointment of the Qualified Person for Pharmacovigilance

It is the responsibility of the company, that is, Applicant/MAH or group of MAHs using a common pharmacovigilance system, to appoint a QPPV. The appointment of the QPPV should be documented in an appropriate way, for example in a job description or written agreement. A signed

---

[1] Iceland, Liechtenstein and Norway have through the Agreement of the European Economic Area (EEA) adopted the complete Community acquis (that is the legislation at EU level, guidelines and judgments) on medicinal products. As such, reference to the EU throughout this guide will include these countries.

QPPV statement is also required as part of the company's detailed description of the pharmacovigilance system (DDPS) in EU marketing authorisation applications. A QPPV should not be appointed to this role without their knowledge and agreement.

Volume 9A reinforces the requirement for there to be one EEA QPPV per MAH pharmacovigilance system. More than one EEA QPPV per system is not considered to be acceptable as an individual is required to take responsibility for the overall functioning of the system. A QPPV can, however, be employed by more than one MAH, provided the QPPV is able to fulfil their obligations for all of the MAHs where they are employed. Back-up arrangements should be in place for when the EEA QPPV is unavailable, such as another appropriately qualified individual who can assume the role and responsibilities of the EEA QPPV in their absence (while the role itself cannot be distributed among a number of personnel, tasks may be delegated to a variety of individuals).

National regulations in some Member States require a nominated individual in that country who has specific legal obligations in respect of pharmacovigilance at a national level. One such individual may also act as the QPPV for the whole EEA. Alternatively, the QPPV for the EEA may be a separate person.

Applicants who are applying for their first EU marketing authorisation must have the services of an EEA QPPV in place when they submit their application.

It is acknowledged that small companies may not have sufficient resource available in-house to address the requirements for an EEA QPPV and appropriate back-up arrangements. Volume 9A indicates that a MAH may transfer any or all pharmacovigilance tasks and functions, including the role of the QPPV, to another person(s) or organisation. The ultimate responsibility for the fulfilment of pharmacovigilance requirements always resides with the MAH, but a contract QPPV also assumes specific legal responsibilities. When a contract QPPV is employed:

(i)   The MAH is responsible for ensuring that there is a contract in place between the company and the contractor, which adequately describes the responsibilities of each party and the tasks to be allocated to the contractor, prior to the contractor commencing work with the MAH. Details of the contractual arrangements for pharmacovigilance activities have to be notified to the appropriate Competent Authorities, for example within the DDPS that is included as part of a marketing authorisation application. The contract should be appropriately amended or updated when changes to contractual arrangements occur.

(ii) The MAH, or persons(s) appointed by the MAH for this task, should assess the contract QPPV (or back-up QPPV) in order to ensure that he/she is appropriately qualified, has knowledge of the applicable regulatory requirements and has the ability to fulfil the tasks that have been assigned to him/her by the MAH, for example adequate arrangements for 24-hour availability. This assessment should be documented.

(iii) The contract QPPV would be expected to perform an assessment of the MAH's pharmacovigilance system.

(iv) The MAH should ensure that the contract QPPV has sufficient authority to instigate changes to the MAH's pharmacovigilance system in order to promote, maintain and improve compliance with regulatory requirements.

(v) The contract QPPV should implement appropriate quality assurance (QA) and quality control (QC) procedures in relation to the tasks that they have agreed to undertake on behalf of the MAH.

1.2 Notification of details of the Qualified Person for Pharmacovigilance

The DDPS that must be included in applications for marketing authorisations in the EU should contain information relating to the QPPV (Volume 9A, Part I, Section 2.2).

1.2.1 Checklist for the detailed description of the pharmacovigilance system

- A signed statement from the QPPV that the applicant has their services available as QPPV.
- The name of the EEA QPPV and their business address including contact details. For example, companies might provide a 24-hour telephone number through which the QPPV or their back-up can be reached. It is the expectation of Competent Authorities that contact arrangements should be periodically tested and records of these tests should be retained.
- A summary curriculum vitae (CV) of the QPPV with the key information relevant to their role (main qualifications, training and experience). A summary CV and not a complete CV is requested to avoid the need for Competent Authorities to be notified every time the CV is updated.
- A summary job description for the QPPV. A summary job description is requested and not a complete job description to avoid the need for Competent Authorities to be notified every time the job description is amended. Major changes to the role of the QPPV may require notification to the Competent Authorities and the European Medicines Agency (EMEA), as appropriate.

- A description of the back-up procedure in the absence of the QPPV, for example the name and contact details for the individual who will assume the role and responsibilities of the QPPV in his or her absence.
- Organisational charts that clearly show the position of the EEA QPPV within the organisation.
- An indication of whether there are written procedures in place that describe the activities of the QPPV and that describe the back-up procedure to apply in their absence. It is the expectation of Competent Authorities that the MAH will have such written procedures and that appropriate personnel will receive training in relation to the procedures. Appropriate personnel within the company should have an awareness of the details, role and responsibilities of the EEA QPPV. Contractors, distributors and co-licensing partners may also need to be provided with EEA QPPV's details, depending on the contractual agreements that are in place.
- A copy of the registration of the QPPV with the EudraVigilance system. However, the QPPV is not required personally to submit reports via the EudraVigilance system.
- An indication of whether the role and responsibilities of the EEA QPPV have been contracted out and, if so, an outline of the contractual arrangements.

Failure to submit these details in a marketing application may lead to delays in the processing of the application. Inadequate details may provide grounds for rejection of the application. EU inspectors will check the consistency of the pharmacovigilance system with the DDPS submitted by the MAH (and any subsequent variations) during pharmacovigilance inspections. If the MAH changes its QPPV, the same information as that listed above must be provided for the new QPPV. The MAH should have a mechanism in place for notification of QPPV changes to the Competent Authorities and EMEA, as appropriate, for example a process for DDPS variations.

Even if a MAH with products authorised in the EU has not submitted a DDPS, the MAH should provide concerned Competent Authorities in the Member States and, for centrally authorised products, the EMEA, with current 24-hour contact details of their QPPV and details of the back-up arrangements.

If a MAH holds EU marketing authorisations but does not currently market any of these medicinal products, the company is still required to have an EEA QPPV in place as pharmacovigilance requirements, for example expedited reporting, Periodic Safety Update Report (PSUR) production and literature searching, still apply.

Competent Authorities will maintain a list of QPPVs within the EEA. This list will include business address and contact details (including out-of-business hours contact details). Where applicable, this will include national contact points in the Member State concerned.

1.3 Who can be a Qualified Person for Pharmacovigilance?

The EEA QPPV should reside and perform their functions as QPPV in the EEA. It is not acceptable for the QPPV to provide an address in the EEA but perform their activities as QPPV outside the EEA. An appropriately qualified person who assumes the role and responsibilities of the QPPV when the QPPV is absent should also reside in the Community when they act as QPPV.

What sort of pharmacovigilance experience should the QPPV have? Detailed guidance is not currently included in Volume 9A. However, the expectation is that the EEA QPPV should be able to demonstrate (e.g. through qualifications, work experience and formal training) that he/she has knowledge of applicable EU pharmacovigilance legislation and guidance, international standards for pharmacovigilance (e.g. International Conference on Harmonisation (ICH) and Council for International Organizations of Medical Sciences (CIOMS) guidance) and of key pharmacovigilance activities performed as part of the MAH's pharmacovigilance system. Ideally, the QPPV will have a relevant biological sciences/pharmacy/medical degree or degrees and will have worked for some years in the field of pharmacovigilance.

Medically qualified persons who provide pharmacovigilance support to the QPPV should also have training and experience appropriate to their role and responsibilities. The MAH should ensure that the QPPV has access to a medically qualified person if the QPPV is not medically qualified. The process that the QPPV would use to obtain medical advice if he/she is not medically qualified, including outside of normal working hours, should be clearly documented in a written procedure or agreement.

It is recognised that this important role of the QPPV may impose extensive tasks on the QPPV, depending on the size and complexity of the pharmacovigilance system and the number and type of products for which the company holds authorisations. The QPPV may, therefore, delegate specific tasks, under supervision, to appropriately qualified and trained individuals (e.g. acting as safety experts for specific products), provided that the QPPV maintains oversight of the system and an overview of the tasks that have been delegated. Methods by which this oversight can be obtained are described below.

1.4 What are the responsibilities of the Qualified Person for Pharmacovigilance?

In EU legislation, the EEA QPPV is responsible for addressing specific requirements (as listed below). Tasks may be delegated to other personnel in order for the requirements to be met, but the QPPV retains legal responsibility for compliance with these specific requirements. In accordance with applicable legislation in each Member State, enforcement action may be taken directly against the QPPV, and against other responsible persons within the MAH, for non-compliance with these specific legal requirements (Annex 3). In addition, the Commission may take infringement action in accordance with EU Commission Regulation 658/2007. In order to meet the requirements, it is essential that the MAH ensures that the QPPV has sufficient authority to implement changes to the pharmacovigilance system in order to promote, maintain and improve compliance. The processes used to address these requirements may vary between MAHs. General guidance that may assist compliance is included below.

1.4.1 Overview of the pharmacovigilance system

> **QPPV RESPONSIBILITY 1:**
>
> The QPPV shall be responsible for establishing and managing/maintaining a system which ensures that information concerning all suspected adverse reactions that are reported to the personnel of the company and to medical representatives is collected, evaluated and collated so that it may be accessed at least at one point within the Community.

What mechanisms can a QPPV use to obtain an overview of the functioning and adequacy of the MAH's pharmacovigilance system? Volume 9A states that the QPPV's oversight should cover the functioning of the MAH's pharmacovigilance system in all relevant aspects, including QC and QA procedures, standard operating procedures (SOPs), database operations, contractual arrangements, compliance data (e.g. in relation to the quality, completeness and timeliness for expedited reporting and submission of PSURs), audit reports and training of personnel in relation to pharmacovigilance. In practice, what does this mean? Expectations with respect to QPPV oversight are as follows.

(I) STANDARD OPERATING PROCEDURES

The QPPV should have an awareness of the MAH's procedures for key pharmacovigilance activities. As appropriate, the QPPV may have input into or approve key written procedures in order to assure compliance with the requirements. If the company has global and local written procedures for key pharmacovigilance activities, the QPPV may need to have an awareness of both types of procedure in order to ensure consistency and compliance across the organisation.

(II)   DATABASES

The QPPV should be aware of the system that is used to collect, evaluate and collate information concerning all suspected adverse reactions at least at one point within the Community. A computer database is often an essential part of such a system. However, alternatives to a computer database may be acceptable provided that the MAH is able to comply with the requirements to send electronic reports to the EudraVigilance database. If a computer database is used for collection and collation of adverse reaction information, the QPPV should be aware of the validation status of the database, including any failures that occurred during validation and the corrective actions that have been taken to address the failures.

The QPPV is not required to be an expert in the use of the database or in the extraction of information from the database. In addition, the QPPV does not have to be located at the point where adverse reaction reports are collated. However, the MAH should implement a procedure to ensure that the QPPV is able to obtain information from the database at any time, for example to respond to requests for information from Competent Authorities. If this procedure requires the involvement of other personnel (e.g. information technology (IT) programmers), then this should be taken into account in the arrangements made by the MAH for supporting the QPPV outside of normal working hours. It may be appropriate for the QPPV to be notified if significant changes to the pharmacovigilance database are planned, such as being provided with the impact assessment report.

Pharmacovigilance data may be stored on a computer server located outside the EU provided that the data can be accessed at least at one point within the Community at any time. When EU data are stored outside the EU, the MAH should consider and address relevant data protection requirements.

(III)   QUALITY CONTROL AND QUALITY ASSURANCE PROCEDURES

The QPPV should have an awareness of the QC procedures that are used for key pharmacovigilance activities, for example for case processing and PSUR production. These procedures should be adequately documented. The MAH should implement a periodic QA audit programme for pharmacovigilance of a type appropriate to the MAH's system.

Audits should cover all departments that may receive adverse reaction reports or that are involved in pharmacovigilance activities (including drug safety, clinical research, product quality, medical information, regulatory affairs, sales and marketing, the legal department) plus affiliate, contractor, co-licensing and co-distribution companies, as appropriate (see Section 9.3). Audit and inspection report findings relating to pharmacovigilance should be made available to appropriate MAH personnel, in particular, the QPPV. The QPPV should also be made aware of the corrective actions that are taken to address significant audit findings and compliance issues.

(IV)   COMPLIANCE DATA

The QPPV has specific legal responsibilities with respect to the preparation for Competent Authorities of serious adverse reaction reports, PSURs and Post-authorisation Safety Study (PASS) reports. While the QPPV is not required to be involved in the preparation of every individual report that is to be expedited to the Competent Authorities, the QPPV should receive compliance information on a periodic basis to enable him/her to assess the quality, completeness and timeliness of submission of these reports. The type of compliance information and the frequency with which it is produced will depend on a variety of factors. What is appropriate for companies with many products on the EU market and that receive a large volume of adverse event (AE) reports every year may not be appropriate for companies that receive very few reports.

(V)   CONTRACTUAL ARRANGEMENTS

Where pharmacovigilance tasks have been transferred to another person or organisation, detailed and clearly documented contractual arrangements are required that adequately describe the responsibilities of each party and the information to be exchanged between the parties. The QPPV should have an awareness of those agreements that include pharmacovigilance tasks and safety data exchange in order to ensure that the agreements facilitate compliance with EU pharmacovigilance requirements. The MAH should implement mechanisms to facilitate this.

When a MAH intends to expand its product portfolio, for example by acquisition of another MAH or by purchasing individual products from another MAH, it is advisable that the QPPV is notified at an early stage of the due diligence process in order that the potential impact on the pharmacovigilance system can be assessed. The QPPV may also have a role to play in determining what pharmacovigilance data should be requested from the other MAH either pre- or post-acquisition. In this situation, it is advisable for the QPPV to be made aware of the sections of the contractual agreements that relate to responsibilities for pharmacovigilance activities and safety data exchange.

(VI) TRAINING

The QPPV is expected to have received appropriate training in relation to the MAH's pharmacovigilance system and this training should be documented. The QPPV should also have an awareness of the system for, and type of, pharmacovigilance training provided to other MAH personnel. MAH personnel should be made aware of the identity, contact details and responsibilities of the QPPV, as appropriate. Ways in which a MAH can raise the profile of the QPPV within an organisation include posting details of the QPPV on the company's intranet, highlighting the role of the QPPV in company newsletters or visits by the QPPV to affiliate offices.

The expectations listed above also apply to any person who assumes the role of the QPPV, when the QPPV is unavailable.

Should the QPPV have management responsibility for pharmacovigilance personnel? While this is a model that is adopted by some MAHs, it is not a requirement. MAHs can implement procedures and a structure for the QPPV to be provided with sufficient authority to instigate changes to the pharmacovigilance system without assigning management responsibility to the QPPV. In order to facilitate this, it is expected that the QPPV will receive adequate support from senior management within the MAH to enable him/her to address his/her responsibilities. Indeed, Volume 9A (Part I, Section 1.2.2) states that the MAH should adequately support the QPPV and ensure that there are appropriate processes, resources, communication mechanisms and access to all sources of relevant information in place for the fulfilment of the QPPV's responsibilities and tasks.

1.4.2 Preparation of reports

> **QPPV RESPONSIBILITY 2:**
>
> The QPPV shall be responsible for the preparation for the Competent Authorities of suspected serious adverse reaction reports and periodic safety update reports, in accordance with applicable legislative requirements and guidance.

It should be stressed that the QPPV is not required personally to prepare the above reports (although that is a model adopted by some MAHs). However, the QPPV should have an adequate and appropriate overview of the quality, completeness and timeliness of adverse reaction reports and PSURs submitted to Competent Authorities, and, where appropriate, to the EMEA, for all products for which the MAH holds a marketing authorisation in the EU. The QPPV should have sufficient authority to make changes to the pharmacovigilance system, where appropriate on an international basis, to ensure compliance with reporting obligations.

Possible mechanisms by which the QPPV can obtain an overview of compliance include, but are not limited to:

- awareness and input into the processes and procedures established by the MAH for the preparation and submission of adverse reaction reports and PSURs;
- awareness and input into the training of key personnel involved in these activities;
- periodic receipt and review of compliance data relating to preparation and submission of adverse reaction reports and PSURs;
- receipt and review of appropriate QC data and QA audit reports.

In relation to PSURs for centrally authorised products, guidance from the EMEA (available at the time of this Guide going to press) is that the QPPV must prepare and sign the PSUR in accordance with Article 23(b) of Regulation (EC) 726/2004. The responsible QPPV may delegate the preparation of the PSUR to an appropriately qualified and trained individual. That individual may also sign the PSUR provided that there is a letter of delegation signed by the QPPV and attached to the PSUR cover letter. Such a letter may cover more than one medicinal product and/or more than one PSUR.

1.4.3   Requests from Competent Authorities

QPPV RESPONSIBILITY 3:

The QPPV shall be responsible for ensuring that any request from the Competent Authorities for the provision of additional information necessary for the evaluation of the benefits and risks afforded by a medicinal product is answered fully and promptly, including the provision of information about the volume of sales or prescriptions of the medicinal product concerned.

A process should be established to ensure that requests to the MAH from Competent Authorities for the provision of information necessary for the evaluation of benefits and risks are promptly communicated to the QPPV. This process should include affiliate offices, contractors, co-distribution and co-marketing partners, as appropriate. The requests may be received and managed by regulatory affairs personnel, but if the request relates to the provision of information necessary for the evaluation of benefits and risks, the QPPV should be made aware of the request and the response (see Section 10.4).

The QPPV should have adequate and appropriate access to safety information, sales data and product expertise to enable the QPPV to respond fully and promptly to requests for information from Competent

Authorities. Although the task of responding to requests may be delegated to other personnel, the QPPV is legally responsible for the completeness, accuracy and promptness of responses to requests from Competent Authorities for information necessary for the evaluation of benefits and risks. It is recommended that the QPPV should have awareness of the process for producing the response, should receive a copy of the response and, where appropriate, should review and approve the response.

The QPPV should assess whether the response provided to one Competent Authority, following a request for information necessary for the evaluation of benefits and risks, should also be provided to other Competent Authorities. This assessment should be documented. Although not a legal requirement, the MAH/QPPV should consider implementing a system to capture and track requests for information from Competent Authorities, and the information provided in response to such requests. The documentation associated with a Competent Authority request and with the MAH's response to the request should be retained. The system implemented may also be used to track specific Competent Authority requests for presentation and discussion of data in PSURs.

1.4.4   Ongoing safety monitoring

> **QPPV RESPONSIBILITY 4:**
>
> The QPPV shall be responsible for the provision to the Competent Authorities of any other information relevant to the evaluation of the benefits and risks afforded by a medicinal product, including appropriate information on post-authorisation safety studies.

Volume 9A states that the QPPV should have oversight, either directly or through supervision, of the conduct of continuous overall pharmacovigilance evaluation during the post-authorisation period. For this purpose, the QPPV should have an overview of the safety profiles and any emerging safety concerns relating to the medicinal products for which the MAH holds authorisations in the EU.

This does not mean that the QPPV has to be a product safety expert for all products, but the QPPV is expected to have access to appropriate product-specific expertise when required.

The MAH is expected to implement mechanisms by which the QPPV can be kept informed of emerging safety concerns and any other information relating to the evaluation of the risk–benefit balance. This should include information from ongoing or completed clinical trials and other studies of which the MAH is aware and which may be relevant to the safety of the medicinal product, as well as information from other sources, for example from those with whom the MAH has contractual arrangements.

Some questions that the QPPV/MAH may want to consider in relation to this point are given below.

(i)   What mechanisms have been implemented to keep the QPPV informed of emerging safety concerns and any other information relating to the evaluation of benefits and risks? This should include relevant information from clinical trials (e.g. recommendations from clinical trial safety-monitoring boards that may have implications for the use of the product in authorised indications) and, where relevant to the evaluation of benefits and risks, clinical trial Annual Safety Reports (ASRs) and study reports for products authorised in the EU. How would the communication of relevant information be documented?

(ii) Is the QPPV involved in or aware of safety committee meetings, where applicable? If not, does he/she receive information or minutes from relevant meetings in order to be informed of emerging safety issues and the actions that have been taken to address these issues?

(iii) Is the same information on emerging safety concerns provided to the person who would act as a back-up when the QPPV is absent?

(iv) Volume 9A, Part I, Section 7.3 states that QPPV at EEA level and/or, where applicable, the nominated person responsible for pharmacovigilance at national level should be involved in the review of protocols for all PASS sponsored by the MAH (involving products authorised in the EU), in order to ensure compliance with pharmacovigilance requirements. How would PASS protocols be made available to the QPPV and how would the QPPV's review be documented?

(v)   When a PASS is conducted in the EU, the QPPV is responsible for providing Competent Authorities with appropriate information relating to these studies. How would the QPPV be made aware of the status of the studies and be provided with copies of study reports (interim and final)? How would the QPPV be made aware that protocols and reports had been submitted to Competent Authorities to ensure compliance with the legislation and Volume 9A? Are these mechanisms described in MAH procedures?

The QPPV should be involved in decisions to provide EU Competent Authorities and the EMEA, as appropriate, with new information relevant to the evaluation of the benefits and risks, for products authorised in the EU. The QPPV should approve the submissions that are made.

The QPPV should be informed of the findings and have access to the reports from PASS for products authorised in the EU and sponsored by the MAH (within and outside the EU). A safety concern may unexpectedly be identified during a study on a medicinal product authorised in the EU but in a study or clinical trial that is not classified as a PASS. In this case, the MAH and specifically the QPPV are expected to inform the relevant Competent Authorities immediately and to provide a brief report on progress at intervals and at study end as requested by the Authorities.

The QPPV should be made aware of commitments made at the time of authorisation (including in Risk Management Plans (RMPs)) to Member State Competent Authorities or the Committee for Medicinal Products for Human Use (CHMP) for provision of additional information relevant to the evaluation of the benefits and risks, and the QPPV should ensure that these commitments are adequately addressed. The tasks may be delegated to other personnel, but the QPPV should have an overview of how the commitments are addressed.

Volume 9A, Part II, Section 1.6 states that liaison between Competent Authorities and the MAH on pharmacovigilance-related issues should take place via the QPPV.

1.5 What Other Tasks Might the Qualified Person for Pharmacovigilance Perform?

Volume 9A, Part I, Section 1.2.1 states that the QPPV should also act as the MAH's contact point for pharmacovigilance inspections or should be made aware by the MAH of any inspection that may impact the pharmacovigilance system, in order to be available as necessary.

MAH procedures should describe the communication process to be followed when an inspection notification is received. The QPPV should be kept informed concerning the inspection arrangements. For EU inspections requested by the CHMP, the Competent Authority for inspection of the MAH's pharmacovigilance system will usually be the Competent Authority of the Member State in whose territory the MAH's QPPV is located. For EU inspections, the QPPV will routinely be interviewed as part of the inspection process.

Where appropriate, the MAH should ensure that the QPPV is informed about inspections performed by non-EU regulatory inspectors within and outside the EU. Findings from these inspections may be relevant to the responsibilities of the QPPV. The MAH should ensure that the QPPV is notified of inspection findings relevant to the role and responsibilities of the QPPV.

The MAH should ensure that the QPPV has sufficient authority to provide input into RMPs and into the preparation of regulatory action in response to emerging safety concerns, for example variations, urgent safety restrictions and, as appropriate, communication to patients and healthcare professionals (HCPs).

1.5.1   Points to consider

(i)   Is the mechanism for input or review of RMPs by the QPPV described in written procedures?

(ii)   How are final, approved versions of RMPs made available to the QPPV?

(iii) How is the QPPV kept informed of the progress of RMP commitments? How is this documented?

(iv)   How is the QPPV involved in decisions to take action in response to emerging safety concerns or notified of such actions? Is this described in written procedures (e.g. the procedures for signal generation, safety committee meetings, changes to labelling, safety-related batch/product recalls, communication with authorities, urgent safety restrictions) and how is this documented?

Volume 9A, Part I, Section 8.2 states that the MAH should immediately inform the Competent Authorities in all Member States where the product is authorised and additionally, for centrally authorised products, the EMEA, of any prohibition or restriction imposed by the Competent/Regulatory Authorities of any country in the world in which the medicinal product is marketed and of any other new information that might influence the evaluation of the benefits and risks of the medicinal product. It is recommended that the QPPV be notified promptly of any prohibitions or restrictions imposed by Competent/Regulatory Authorities for products authorised in the EU.

1.6   Examples of Inspection Findings

In the first three years of the MHRA pharmacovigilance inspection programme, approximately 20% of critical inspection findings related to the roles and responsibilities of the QPPV. Examples of areas of concern that have been identified during inspections are provided below. This is not an exhaustive list but serves to summarise some of the key points from this chapter and highlights areas that can be problematic. It is anticipated that examples will prove useful to help MAHs to address such issues.

(i)   The QPPV has little or no knowledge/understanding of EU pharmacovigilance legislative requirements and guidance documents. Since the publication of Volume 9A and following the increasing number of pharmacovigilance inspections performed by EU Competent Authorities, this finding has become less common.

(ii) The QPPV has inadequate oversight of the MAH's pharmacovigilance system. If the system is generally compliant but the mechanisms used to provide the QPPV with oversight are inadequate, the impact may be less than if the system is seriously non-compliant and the QPPV is unaware of this.

(iii) The QPPV lacks the authority to make the necessary changes to the MAH's pharmacovigilance system. It has been observed that the QPPV is aware of serious deficiencies in the pharmacovigilance system, but he/she has not received adequate MAH support to address these deficiencies. This may be more common when a contract QPPV is employed or when the global headquarter for pharmacovigilance is based outside the EU.

(iv) There are inadequate procedures for QPPV contact outside of normal working hours and/or inadequate back-up arrangements.

(v) The QPPV is unaware of safety issues relating to the company's products.

(vi) The QPPV who is not medically qualified has inadequate access to medically qualified personnel.

Current metrics relating to MHRA pharmacovigilance inspection findings can be found on our website. The exact nature of findings will vary from company to company, and findings are graded on a case-by-case basis, taking into account the evidence relating to the issue and the impact of the finding on, for example, public safety or other areas of the pharmacovigilance system.

Management of Pharmacovigilance Data

> **Editor's note** Pharmacovigilance is based upon the information that a MAH receives concerning adverse experiences to a medicinal product. MAHs must have the necessary personnel, processes and procedures in place in order to manage these data in such a way as to meet the legislative requirements contained in Regulation 726/2004 and Directive 2001/83/EC (as amended). This chapter introduces the principles of management of pharmacovigilance information, including definitions of the terms used to describe the data and the expectations around handling of the data, such as information on the use of computer systems.
>
> It should be noted that the legislation requires a MAH to have a system in place to collect and collate pharmacovigilance information, but it does not dictate the form this system should take. It is, therefore, up to individual MAHs to assess their own needs and establish a system that best meets the legislative requirements, such as through a purely paper-based system, through use of a bespoke or commercial safety database or through a hybrid system. This chapter is applicable for all sources of information except that which originates from interventional clinical trials, although some of the principles described may still apply to such trials.

2.1 Terminology

PHARMACOVIGILANCE DATUM

Information provided to a MAH is regarded as a *pharmacovigilance datum* when it details that a person has:

- had an untoward medical occurrence;
- used a medicinal product during pregnancy;
- experienced lack of efficacy;
- had a suspected transmission of an infectious agent by a medicinal product;
- had an overdose;
- experienced a drug interaction;

- abused/misused/made unapproved (off-label) use of a medicinal product;
- had a medication error (or near miss).

This is defined as the set that contains all relevant notifications to a MAH, including those that are AEs, special circumstances, adverse reactions or duplicates (Fig. 2.1, area A).

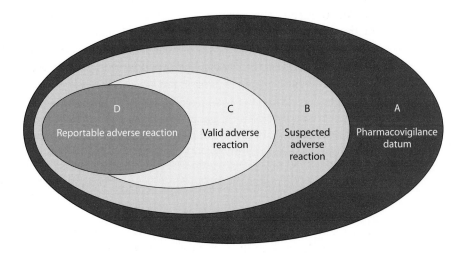

Figure 2.1 Venn diagram illustrating sets of pharmacovigilance data relating to adverse events (AEs).

SUSPECTED ADVERSE DRUG REACTIONS

A subset of the pharmacovigilance data is the *suspected adverse reaction* set (Fig. 2.1, area B). A suspected adverse reaction is a report suggesting that a person has received a MAH's medicinal product and there is a possible causal relationship between the event (or special circumstance) and the product. This set contains all notifications with a possible causal relationship including cases that require follow-up and consumer reports (Fig. 2.1, area B). This set is the basis for all pharmacovigilance analysis activities.

VALID ADVERSE DRUG REACTIONS

A subset of the suspected adverse drug reaction group is the *valid adverse reaction* set (Fig. 2.1, area C). A valid adverse reaction is defined in Volume 9A as a suspected adverse reaction report that contains an identifiable HCP reporter, identifiable patient and identified drug. An adverse drug reaction is not considered as valid if it is missing one or more of the above pieces of information. If information is provided that enables identification of the item but not the exact details, for example a drug name but not the formulation or strength, this is sufficient for the report to be considered valid.

MAHs often have different processes in place for case reports that do not have an identifiable patient, reporter, drug or reaction, such as not forwarding these from local affiliates to central processing centres for inclusion in the pharmacovigilance system. If reports are received that provide details of a drug and reaction term but not an identifiable patient and/or reporter, they may still provide valuable information in terms of the ongoing monitoring of the safety of that product. MAHs should, therefore, consider carefully the best way to capture such data so that they are available for consideration when performing signal generation activities, including when re-evaluating risk–benefit at the time of PSUR production.

REPORTABLE ADVERSE DRUG REACTIONS

A further subset of the suspected adverse reactions is the *reportable adverse reaction* set (Fig. 2.1, area D). A reportable adverse reaction is defined as a report that contains all the elements required for a suspected adverse reaction and also meets the legislative requirements for reporting to a Competent Authority. Of the reportable adverse reactions in set D, some are also valid adverse reactions (set C, see above), but some would be classified as not valid; for example, consumer reports may be reported in a PSUR but are not classified as valid as they do not contain an identifiable HCP reporter. Owing to the large degree of intersection between the reportable and valid sets, they have been presented in the figure as merging into one another. Within this category, there are subsets for expedited and periodic reports and the sets required for different authorities; however, these are not represented in Figure 2.1.

Pharmacovigilance data may move between these sets or definitions as detail is collected over time, or during assessment. For example, follow-up information that a patient was hospitalised for a *valid adverse reaction* previously regarded as non-serious could mean that the case now meets the requirements for regulatory reporting and is reclassified as a *reportable adverse reaction*. Alternatively, confirmation that the event occurred before the product was administered would reclassify the *valid adverse reaction* as a *pharmacovigilance datum*.

SYSTEM

A system is the combination of people, processes, procedures and technology used to accomplish a set of functions. The technology used, be it paper, computer, a hybrid of paper and computer or other, is not a defining factor.

A computer system is the combination of people, processes, procedures, computer network, hardware and software used to accomplish a set of functions. As such, computer systems are a subset of all systems.

2.2 Information Collection and Collation

There must be a system in place that ensures that information about all suspected adverse reactions associated with an active ingredient in a product with marketing authorisation in the EU is collected and collated by the MAH and accessible within the EU. It should be stressed that this system should allow for the collation of suspected adverse reactions on a global basis, where applicable. It is acceptable for there to be systems in place that are used to record information on a local basis. However, there should also be a global system in place that includes data from all markets should the product be marketed by the MAH in countries other than the UK. This system should be designed such that all notifications that contain pharmacovigilance data are recorded appropriately and transferred from the person receiving them (e.g. from a medical representative) to the personnel undertaking pharmacovigilance. This transfer must happen in a timely manner so that reportable adverse reactions are notified to Competent Authorities in the correct timeframe (Section 3.5). When transferring a pharmacovigilance datum report, it is considered good practice to include the source data, or an image of the source data. Examples of source data include letters, emails or records of telephone calls to the company from HCPs or consumers that include details of an event. Compliance with applicable data protection requirements must be ensured when transferring data. Personnel within the pharmacovigilance function must maintain adequate records of all pharmacovigilance data received.

2.2.1 Reconciliation

When transfer of pharmacovigilance data occurs, the mechanism should be such that there is confidence that all notifications are received, in that a confirmation and/or reconciliation process is undertaken. This is appropriate for both internal transfers, such as that between the medical information and the pharmacovigilance departments, and external transfers, such as that with licence partners. In order for reconciliation to occur, both the originator and the recipient should use unique identifiers to track every transaction.

Confirmation of receipt can be done on a case-by-case basis or periodically. The latter may be more appropriate when larger numbers of cases are involved. If confirmation of receipt is provided periodically, the periodicity of the activity needs to be carefully considered so that the ability to meet regulatory timeframes for expedited reporting is not compromised (Section 3.5). Caution should be exercised when using automatic reply systems such as email delivery notifications. Just because an email has been delivered does not mean that someone has read it and dealt with it appropriately.

In addition to the above, the term reconciliation is used to refer to the concept of ensuring that all appropriate information has been correctly identified and transferred: for example a check that all pharmacovigilance data from product technical complaints or medical information enquiries have been appropriately recorded in the pharmacovigilance system. This can be achieved by undertaking periodic checks of information, including correspondence files, line listings or database reviews. The MAH should define the periodicity of such checks. Where samples are used rather than a review of a complete set, the sample size should be justified. If a sample check is performed, it is considered good practice to include some level of randomness in the review: that is, do not always perform the check on the same day(s) of the week/month.

When undertaking a review of, for example, product technical complaints to ensure that all pharmacovigilance data have been identified, do not only check those complaints that have already been categorised as such, as this will not include notifications that have been incorrectly classified in the first place. Such a review would fail to identify these data and ensure they are reported to the pharmacovigilance system.

If no notifications have been received during the review period, it is good practice to document this fact. This provides evidence that reconciliation activities are being performed.

If problems are noted during reconciliation activities, for example pharmacovigilance data that have not been identified and transferred to the pharmacovigilance system or transfers that have not been successfully received, some form of root-cause analysis should be performed to identify the reason for the failure and to identify the corrective actions that need to be put in place to prevent recurrence of the error. This may necessitate a retrospective review of all available notifications to identify any other pharmacovigilance data that have either not been identified or not been transferred correctly. This will allow an MAH to establish whether the failure was a random error or a systematic error that requires corrective action. Corrective action could take the form of additional training for staff to remind them of what information needs to be transferred and the process for doing so.

2.2.2 Duplicate reports

There should be an appropriate mechanism in place for identifying pharmacovigilance data reported to the MAH's personnel more than once: duplicate reports. Common causes of duplicate reports are:

- a consumer and HCP reporting the same event occurrence;
- multiple HCPs treating the same patient reporting the same event occurrence;
- an event occurrence being reported by the original reporter to both the MAH and the Competent Authorities;
- literature and spontaneous reporting of the same event occurrence;
- an event being reported to multiple MAHs.

A MAH should consider the potential mechanisms for duplicate generation and the appropriate points in their system to detect them. If duplicates are identified, analysis of the root cause should be performed and corrective action taken, if appropriate.

When duplicates are detected, one of the cases becomes the master case and retains its classification (e.g. "valid adverse reaction" (as in Fig. 2.1), while the duplicate case(s) is/are reclassified as "pharmacovigilance datum (data)"). Additional details contained within the duplicate reports should be integrated into the master case, and the master case should then be used for all subsequent pharmacovigilance activities, such as expedited and periodic reporting. The source data for all of the cases should be retained and there should be adequate cross-referencing between case files and/or database entries. Case reference numbers previously assigned to cases that subsequently merged with a master case should not be reused. When duplicate cases have been identified, it is useful to include a comment in the case narrative to that effect (Section 3.3.5).

2.3 Access to Pharmacovigilance Data

Information about suspected adverse reactions associated with an active ingredient in a product with marketing authorisation in the EU that is reported to the MAH's personnel, anywhere in the world, must be accessible within the European Community. Immediate access, for example less than one hour, should be possible for a summary of information including, at a minimum, the unique case number, suspected product, event term and narrative. Full details of a case including source data should be quickly available, for example in less than three days.

The need for cases to be accessible may be driven by the experience of a single case or a potential signal of multiple cases. As such, the MAH's system should include a mechanism for identifying appropriate cases as well as making them accessible.

2.4   Preparation of Reports

MAHs should have a system in place that gives them the capacity to prepare Individual Case Safety Reports (ICSRs) and PSURs.

In terms of individual case reports, appropriate follow-up should be performed on all initially received pharmacovigilance data to gather sufficient information to classify them correctly to one of the more specific sets (Section 3.3). It may not be possible to obtain follow-up on all cases, and a MAH's procedure should reflect this. For example, reports received from the UK Medicines and Healthcare products Regulatory Agency (MHRA) are in an anonymised format with no reporter details given. Routinely, follow-up should not be requested for reports provided by the MHRA. However, the MHRA will automatically send follow-up information if volunteered by the initial reporter.

All attempts to perform follow-up should be recorded within the case file irrespective of whether a response was obtained or not. The dates when follow-up was requested or received should also be recorded appropriately.

Both expedited individual cases and periodic reports submitted to Competent Authorities must be an accurate representation of the data received and its evaluation. If systematic changes are made to data, for example coding, de-coding or translations, the details of how the changes are made must be maintained by the MAH.

2.5   Requests from Competent Authorities

MAHs should ensure that any request from the Competent Authorities for the provision of additional information necessary for the evaluation of the benefits and risks afforded by a medicinal product is answered fully and in a timely manner. The active set for providing information to requests for information is the suspected adverse reactions set.

A reliable and reproducible method must be established for the accurate and timely (depending on the urgency of the enquiry) retrieval and output of stored data or records from the pharmacovigilance system.

2.6   Use of Computer Systems

All computer systems used to fulfil pharmacovigilance obligations must be fit for purpose. The MAH should analyse the pharmacovigilance system and document what computer systems are used. Systems that fall within the scope of this analysis would be used to:

- capture source data;
- transfer electronic versions of the source data from a capture to collation system;
- collate suspected adverse reactions;
- make reportability decisions or provide reference data for this purpose;
- produce expedited or periodic reports for submission to Competent Authorities;
- perform the exchange of data with Competent Authorities;
- extract, transfer and load data from a collation to analysis system;
- perform analysis of pharmacovigilance data.

The MAH must ensure and document that the computerised system(s) identified above conform to their established requirements for data completeness, data accuracy, system reliability and consistent intended performance. The method used for documenting the requirements and ensuring conformance will depend on the criticality and complexity of the particular computer systems.

2.6.1   Checklist of requirements for computer systems

The following is a list of requirements for computer systems.

- All computer systems should have in place a security system that prevents unauthorised access and changes to the data.
- Applicable laws concerning data privacy and consequent requirements should be documented.
- The MAH must maintain a list of individuals who are authorised to access the system and make data changes.
- The MAH must maintain adequate back-up of the data.
- The MAH must ensure that pharmacovigilance activities can be undertaken within the required timeframe if there is disruption to the system, for example by having a business continuity plan.
- The MAH must ensure that there are adequate measures in place in case of major service disruption, for example by having a disaster recovery plan.
- The MAH must provide sufficient training to ensure staff competence in using the computer system and data processing for pharmacovigilance activities.
- The MAH must maintain procedures for using the systems.
- The MAH must ensure that data migration is undertaken in a controlled manner.
- The MAH must provide training in the interpretation of migrated or other legacy data if these differ from current data.

● The MAH must update the system in a controlled manner that ensures continuing fitness for purpose throughout the life-cycle of the system.

Additional requirements for systems that collate or store data for transfer to Competent Authorities are that the system permits data changes in such a way that these changes are chronologically traceable to the individual undertaking the change and that there is a record of previously entered data: that is the inclusion of an audit trail.

Additional requirements for systems that determine reportability or perform analyses on pharmacovigilance data are that the system keeps a record of why a reportability or analysis decision was taken.

For hybrid systems that combine paper and electronic records, the requirements must include both the paper and electronic sections of the system, including confirmation that the whole system is fit for purpose.

A pharmacovigilance system using standard office software such as email should be shown to be fit for purpose if it falls within the scope of the types of system listed above. However, it is assumed that the standard functionality of the software works. For example, if a dedicated mailbox is set up for pharmacovigilance datum reporting, proof needs to exist that the correct people can access the mailbox, and there is a method of undertaking the pharmacovigilance activity if there is a failure, but not that it works as a mailbox.

When changes are made to a system with existing data, analysis should be performed to ascertain the impact on the legacy data as well as on the new data. This is sometimes referred to as impact assessment. If functionality changes are made, an assessment should be made as to whether any unintended changes have been made. This is sometimes referred to as a regression test.

2.7 Use of Paper-based Systems

As previously highlighted, the type of system a MAH uses to collect and collate safety information is not mandated within EU pharmacovigilance legislation or guidance documents. It is, therefore, up to individual MAHs to assess their own needs and establish a system that best meets the legislative requirements, such as through a purely paper-based system, through use of a bespoke or commercial safety database or through a hybrid system. Factors that might have an impact on this decision include the MAH's product portfolio, the number of countries in which the MAH holds authorisations and the average number of reports the MAH receives during a week, month or year.

If a MAH chooses to use either a purely paper-based system or a hybrid system (such as paper files supplemented by an electronic spreadsheet), the principles highlighted in this chapter still apply. Some additional points should also be considered.

- Is it possible to check for duplicate reports within the system?
- How can cumulative data be analysed within the system?
- How are data extracted from the system to generate regulatory reports, such as ICSRs or PSURs?
- How can MAHs meet the requirement for electronic reporting of ICSRs?
- Can the appropriate personnel access the data in a timely manner if the MAH were to receive an urgent request from a Competent Authority?

2.8 Examples of Inspection Findings

Examples of areas of concern that have been identified during inspections are provided below. This is not an exhaustive list but serves to summarise some of the key points from this chapter and highlights areas that can be problematic. It is anticipated that examples will prove useful to help MAHs to address such issues.

(i)   Not all suspected adverse reactions received by the company are collected and collated within the pharmacovigilance system. This deficiency has been seen when a company does not have a policy in place for assessment of pharmacovigilance data or exchange of suspected adverse reactions between all parts of the organisation, such as between affiliate offices and the department(s) responsible for processing of ICSRs.

(ii) The reconciliation activity between pharmacovigilance and either internal departments or external partners is inadequate or absent. For example, the MAH only checks medical information enquiries that have already been classified as suspected adverse reactions rather than assessing if all pharmacovigilance data have been correctly identified.

(iii) The MAH is not able to undertake expedited reporting in an electronic format that is acceptable to EU Competent Authorities.

(iv) Not all computer systems used for pharmacovigilance activities have had an assessment of their regulatory status and need for validation.

(v)   Changes to the pharmacovigilance system have not been implemented in a controlled manner. For example, a change to the PSUR production tool used to extract data from a company safety database could result in incomplete/inaccurate data being presented within the PSUR if the change is not handled correctly.

Current metrics relating to MHRA pharmacovigilance inspection findings can be found on our website. The exact nature of findings will vary from company to company and findings are graded on a case-by-case basis, taking into account the evidence relating to the issue and the impact of the finding on, for example, public safety or other areas of the pharmacovigilance system.

3

Spontaneous Case Processing

Editor's note In order to ensure that a MAH fulfils the legislative requirements in terms of expedited and periodic reporting of ICSRs, it is important that all relevant information reaches the pharmacovigilance system. There are many aspects to processing of ICSRs, including collection, collation, coding, categorisation, assessment and reporting to Competent Authorities, and these are discussed below. It is also important to consider how the data are going to be used, such as for expedited reporting, for inclusion in periodic reports or for the purpose of signal detection and risk management.

Chapter 2 discussed the type of information relevant to pharmacovigilance, including descriptions of the terminology and details on how systems can be used to handle data in order to facilitate compliance with legislative requirements. The purpose of this chapter is to discuss considerations in the day-to-day handling of ICSRs and other special situations that may qualify for expedited reporting.

The requirements relate to the obligations contained in Regulation 726/2004 and Directive 2001/83/EC (as amended), unless otherwise stated.

3.1 Sources of Suspected Adverse Reactions

It is important that MAHs are alert to the different routes by which AEs and other pharmacovigilance data may reach the organisation as there are a number of potential sources of ICSRs, and a variety of factors that can influence the most likely source of ICSRs for individual MAHs. Under-reporting of adverse reactions is a well-known problem associated with spontaneous reporting and, therefore, MAHs should be proactive about the process of collecting adverse reactions. If only a low volume of cases is received by an MAH, are they looking in the right places for them?

There are a number of potential sources of ICSRs.

3.1.1   Medical information enquiries

A medical information department can be the source of valuable information, for consumers, HCPs and personnel of the organisation. When an enquirer contacts a MAH regarding one of their products, they often want information. From the MAH's point of view, it is important to understand the reason for the request, as a general enquiry may have been raised because an individual patient has experienced an AE.

A pharmacist may ask whether or not two drugs are known to interact. This may be a proactive enquiry as a patient is about to commence therapy with a particular combination of drugs. It may also be a retrospective enquiry, the patient having taken the combination of products and subsequently experienced an AE or a reduction in efficacy. In such situations, it is important for medical information staff to ask questions proactively to ascertain if there is a patient involved. Documenting that such questioning has taken place is also important so that an MAH can demonstrate due diligence in attempting to collect and collate pharmacovigilance data. This can be as simple as having a tick-box on a form or recording the questions that were asked.

For those enquiries that relate to pharmacovigilance data, the MAHs should ensure there is a mechanism in place to transfer details of such cases to the pharmacovigilance system. Reconciliation activities between the two departments should also be undertaken (Section 2.2.1).

3.1.2   "Contact us" emails and website enquiry forms

The wealth of information available on the internet and its widespread accessibility means it is an increasingly popular way to seek and share information. "Contact Us" pages now frequently display generic company email addresses or website enquiry forms. The MAH must consider the mechanism by which incoming information is monitored to allow the identification and transfer of pharmacovigilance data to the correct person in an appropriate timeframe to meet regulatory reporting requirements.

3.1.3   Product technical complaints

When something goes wrong, people often want to complain. It is not uncommon for a product technical complaint to be associated with an AE or for an AE to be reported via the product technical complaint route, in some instances with very serious consequences.

The information contained within product technical complaints can be viewed from different perspectives; someone with a manufacturing background will likely have a very different focus to someone with a pharmacovigilance background: the former looking at efficacy-related issues or problems with the manufacturing process, while the latter focusing more on aspects of drug safety. It is expected that someone with appropriate knowledge and understanding of pharmacovigilance requirements will review product technical complaints to identify those relevant to pharmacovigilance (Section 2.2.1). This should be done on an ongoing basis to ensure that any reports that fulfil the requirements for expedited reporting can be submitted within the regulatory timeframes. In particular, reports of lack of efficacy may be subject to expedited reporting if the product is used for the treatment of a life-threatening disease, or is a vaccine or a contraceptive. Medically relevant reports of lack of efficacy should also be discussed in the relevant PSUR.

Similarly, it is important that all product technical complaints that are received as part of an AE report or medical information enquiry are forwarded to the product quality department so that they can be recorded and investigated in accordance with good manufacturing practice requirements.

3.1.4 Medical representatives

As the public face of the MAH, medical representatives can be in a position where they receive information about the use of the products, both positive and negative. The types of customer they interact with, such as prescribers, dispensers or wholesalers, will influence the likelihood of a company representative being told about an AE or other safety-related issue. However, all representatives should be alert to the possibility. They need to know what sort of information they should be listening for and what to do with the information, that is, how to record the information, who to send it to, how to send the information and when to do so. If a medical representative makes notes of an AE or other safety-related issue during the course of a conversation with a HCP, for example on a notepad or in a diary, these are considered source documents and should be retained. It is not necessary for medical representatives to make an assessment of seriousness, as all reports of AEs should be forwarded to the pharmacovigilance system. For those staff who do not frequently deal with pharmacovigilance data, it may be useful to provide them with a simple aide-memoire to cover the essentials of safety reporting within the organisation (including information on the types of case that should be reported, for example lack of efficacy, misuse, overdose, abuse and pregnancy reports, in addition to AEs) and a standard form to capture basic information.

3.1.5   Published literature

Information in published literature is discussed in more detail in Chapter 4.

3.1.6   Reports from Competent Authorities

Expedited reporting of ICSRs applies not only to MAHs but also to EU Competent Authorities. EU Competent Authorities are required by legislation to provide reports within 15 days of receipt of all serious reportable adverse reactions occurring within their country to MAHs for the suspected medicinal product and to the EMEA. This ensures that serious adverse reaction reports sent directly from HCPs to EU Competent Authorities are also made available to MAHs for the concerned active substance(s).

The MHRA and the Commission on Human Medicines run the UK's spontaneous adverse reaction reporting scheme, called the Yellow Card Scheme. This receives reports of suspected AEs from HCPs and patients. Notifications received via this scheme of ICSRs from HCPs and patient reports that are medically validated are sent out by the MHRA in the form of Anonymised Single Patient Reports (ASPRs). The MHRA only sends reports that have been assessed as serious, either by the reporter or the MHRA. Currently, ASPRs are either sent out in hard copy or can be downloaded by the MAH from the MHRA portal.

MAHs must assess the Competent Authority reports they receive to see if they describe a reaction associated with their brand. Where only the active substance or generic name is available and the brand name is not provided, MAHs should take a conservative approach and consider these cases as potentially related to their product. For either of these situations, these reports may qualify for expedited reporting in other countries (Section 3.5) and also for periodic reporting. Where the brand name of the suspected medicine is specified, those MAHs who receive the report, but who are not the brand-owner, should still consider the information within the report in the context of assessment of the risks and benefits of the active substance.

3.1.7   Contractual partners

Many different types of contractual partnership exist within the pharmaceutical industry, for example for co-marketing, co-promotion, in-licensing, out-licensing and distribution. As with any contract between multiple parties, the responsibilities of each party must be clearly defined (see Chapter 11). Contractual partners are a potential source of ICSRs and mechanisms should be in place for the exchange of these reports in an appropriate timeframe to meet regulatory requirements.

The above are examples of unsolicited sources of ICSRs. Pharmacovigilance data can also be obtained from solicited sources (see Chapter 12).

3.2   Recording Individual Case Safety Report information

3.2.1   Date of receipt

In the context of both expedited and periodic reports, it is essential to record the date of receipt for each case; this applies to both initial notification and any follow-up communication regarding a case. This should be the date that anyone within the MAH, or working on behalf of the MAH, such as contractors, receives the information, regardless of whether they are qualified to identify an ICSR as a reportable case.

Letters and written records of verbal communications can easily be date-stamped. Email and fax headers usually record the date of receipt of the communication.

3.2.2   Methods of recording information

There are various ways in which ICSR information can be recorded. In most circumstances, the method used will depend on the complexity of the organisation and the amount of data received. The methods of recording data can include simple paper-based systems, electronic spreadsheets or specialised databases.

Requirements for the receipt, transfer and storage of ICSR information are discussed in more detail in Chapter 2.

3.2.3   Coding

For the purposes of regulatory reporting (expedited and periodic), MAHs are required to code reports using the *Medical Dictionary for Regulatory Activities* (MedDRA) terminology. Coding of reports also facilitates the organisation of safety data to enable systematic review for the purposes of signal detection and risk–benefit assessment.

For further information on coding of AEs, please refer to the "MedDRA Term Selection: Points to Consider" document, which is available from the Maintenance and Support Services Organization (MSSO) website (www.msso.org).

3.3 Follow-up of Adverse Events

There are different scenarios in which it is necessary to obtain follow-up information. These are described below.

3.3.1 Information to validate a case

The criteria for a valid case are:

- an identifiable patient;
- a suspect drug;
- a suspect reaction;
- an identifiable HCP reporter.

When one or more of these criteria are missing, it is expected that the MAH attempts to follow the case up in order to validate the report. The MAH should also consider the way in which these cases are collected and collated; for example, if the MAH uses a computerised database for recording pharmacovigilance data, should this type of case also be entered?

With regard to consumer reports, it is expected that the MAH seeks the consumer's consent to contact their HCP so that medical confirmation of the suspect reaction can be obtained. This applies to reports from all territories, for example US affiliates may not routinely follow up consumer reports for medical confirmation as the US Food and Drug Administration accepts reports from patients. Attempts at follow-up should not just be directed at the patient's doctor, as there may be many situations in which the patient did not need to consult their doctor but spoke with a pharmacist, nurse or other HCP about the reaction. It should be noted that review of a report by a HCP employed by the MAH does not constitute medical confirmation of the suspected reaction. There are circumstances whereby HCP confirmation of a report could be supplied by a consumer, for example in medical notes relating to the event and the specific patient.

In the context of expedited reporting, day zero should be considered the day on which the minimum criteria for a reportable adverse reaction report becomes available to the MAH. In order to be in receipt of the minimum criteria for a case in the shortest timeframe, personnel should have a clear understanding of what makes a case valid (as detailed above). This would then provide an opportunity to attempt to obtain this information on first notification. Personnel should, however, not delay reporting a non-valid case to the pharmacovigilance department if the minimum criteria are not initially available.

3.3.2   Information relevant for case evaluation

When a report of an AE is made, the information made available may be minimal and insufficient to form an accurate opinion of whether there is a suspected causal relationship between the drug and the event. The MAH is expected to make attempts to obtain additional information relevant to the evaluation of the case. The information requested may be general in nature (e.g. past medical history, concomitant medications) or more specific to the event being reported. The type of information required to understand an event adequately could be a diagnosis (when only signs and symptoms are reported), a cause of death (postmortem results), an outcome or dechallenge/rechallenge information. For example, a report of neutropenia would warrant a request for details of blood test results.

For ICSRs published in the worldwide literature, it is expected that the MAH attempts to obtain follow-up information if it would provide information relevant to the assessment of the case. For example, in a publication listing multiple medications it may be unclear whether all of the medications are considered to be causally related to the reaction. It may, therefore, be useful to attempt to obtain follow-up information to clarify which of the drugs was specifically thought to be causally related. Publications often provide the contact details of the author(s) for correspondence, such as an email address.

The need to request follow-up information should not affect expedited reporting activities: an initial report should be made as soon as the minimum criteria for a reportable adverse reaction report become available. Any follow-up information received should be reported within 15 days of receipt if it adds to or changes the case information.

3.3.3   Reports of drug exposure during pregnancy

Volume 9A states that the MAH should follow up all reports relating to pregnancies where the fetus may have been exposed to one of its medicinal products; this can be the result of either maternal exposure or transmission of a medicinal product via semen following paternal exposure. The MAH should gather information relating to both normal and abnormal outcomes. Consequently, a mechanism is required to ensure that reports of use of a drug during pregnancy are followed up at suitable intervals, for example following the initial report and also around/after the expected delivery date.

3.3.4   Reports of overdose, abuse and misuse

Volume 9A discusses the need to follow up reports of overdose, abuse and misuse to obtain details of any associated clinical effects. Reports of overdose, abuse and misuse that are associated with serious adverse reactions (SARs) qualify for expedited reporting (Section 3.5) and so information received in response to a request for follow-up will contribute to the assessment of whether or not the case requires expedited reporting.

Reports of overdose, abuse and misuse that are not associated with SARs should be recorded in the pharmacovigilance system as they provide useful information relevant to the risk–benefit assessment of a product. These issues should be considered in PSURs and RMPs.

In terms of overdose, a HCP may submit a report of an adverse reaction where the patient has received a larger than approved dose, but not explicitly use the term "overdose". The MAH should consider how to record such an event in the pharmacovigilance database to aid retrieval of such cases. This is particularly important for products that have a narrow therapeutic margin. For example, if such an event is not coded as overdose in the MAH's database, will it still be retrieved when running a query to identify all cases where patients have received a larger than approved dose?

3.3.5   Additional considerations regarding follow-up attempts

Consideration should be given to the types of report that should be followed up (serious versus non-serious, expected versus unexpected), the number of attempts to obtain follow-up information per report, the frequency of requests and the method of obtaining the information. These details should be recorded in procedural documents.

This is discussed in ICH E2D: "In any scheme to optimize the value of follow-up, the first consideration should be prioritization of case reports by importance. The priority for follow-up should be as follows: cases that are 1) serious and unexpected, 2) serious and expected, and 3) non-serious and unexpected. In addition to seriousness and expectedness as criteria, cases "of special interest" also deserve extra attention as a high priority (e.g. adverse reactions under active surveillance at the request of the regulators), as well as any cases that might lead to a labelling change decision."

All attempts at follow-up should be documented: for example, if a letter was sent, a copy should be retained; if an attempt was made to follow up via telephone, a record of the call should be made. In this way the MAH can demonstrate due diligence in attempting to obtain follow-up information. The availability of reporter contact details (telephone or fax number, postal or email address) will to a great extent determine the method used to obtain follow-up information. When urgent information is required, it may be more appropriate to attempt to follow up by telephone rather than sending a letter.

For routine follow-up requests, use of standard forms may facilitate collection of standard data elements. Including a reference number on the form will make it easier to link the original report to the follow-up information when it is returned. The success rate for obtaining follow-up is often quite low, and time constraints may affect whether or not a HCP fulfils a request for follow-up information. Therefore, consideration should be given to pre-populating some data fields to make completion of the form less burdensome. This is also useful when a case was initially reported by a consumer, thus enabling the HCP to provide further information about the report.

Even when standard follow-up questions or reporting forms are used, there should always be consideration of additional follow-up requirements and questions on a case-by-case basis.

3.4 Case Assessment

The requirements for expedited reporting depend upon several criteria, including:

- seriousness of the reaction;
- causality;
- expectedness of the reaction (in terms of the local Summary of Product Characteristics (SPC) for the product);
- country of origin of the report;
- method of marketing authorisation.

In addition, Competent Authorities may lay down expedited reporting requirements over and above the standard requirements for specific issues, either at the time of licensing or at any point during the life-cycle of the product when there is cause for concern.

The company's assessments of seriousness, expectedness and causality should be documented. If additional information relevant to these assessments becomes available, the MAH should:

- reassess the case;
- document the reassessment and the reason for any changes from the original assessment;

- consider the impact of any changed assessments on the case classifications, including expedited reporting requirements.

3.4.1 Seriousness assessment

For each ICSR received by the MAH, an assessment of seriousness should be made. Volume 9A defines seriousness as follows.

> *Serious adverse reaction means an adverse reaction that results in death, is life-threatening, requires in-patient hospitalisation or prolongation of existing hospitalisation, results in persistent or significant disability or incapacity, or is a congenital anomaly/birth defect.*

> *Life threatening in this context refers to a reaction in which the patient was at risk of death at the time of the reaction; it does not refer to a reaction that hypothetically might have caused death if more severe.*

> *Medical and scientific judgement should be exercised in deciding whether other situations should be considered serious reactions, such as important medical events that might not be immediately life-threatening or result in death or hospitalisation but might jeopardise the patient or might require intervention to prevent one of the other outcomes listed above. Examples of such events are intensive treatment in an emergency room or at home for allergic bronchospasm, blood dyscrasias or convulsions that do not result in hospitalisation or development of dependency or abuse.*

> *Any suspected transmission via a medicinal product of an infectious agent is also considered a serious adverse reaction.*

In some scenarios, it is easy to judge if the ICSR was serious, for example if the patient was hospitalised owing to a reaction. In some instances, the reporter may provide an assessment of seriousness to the MAH. In the presence or absence of a seriousness assessment from the reporter, the MAH should assess each event for seriousness. When there is more than one reported event within a report, the MAH should consider seriousness at both the event and case level. It would be expected that a MAH takes a conservative approach in this scenario; that is, when an ICSR describes more than one event term, if any of the individual terms are assessed as serious, the case-level seriousness should be considered as serious.

Where there are differences in opinion between the reporter and the MAH regarding a seriousness assessment, a conservative approach should again be taken; that is, if either the reporter or the MAH considers the event or report to be serious, it should be treated as such. It is inappropriate for the MAH to downgrade an assessment to non-serious if the reporter considers it to be serious.

Some MAHs choose to make use of lists of reaction terms that are always considered to be serious. This may provide useful guidance for staff when assessing cases. However, a common pitfall associated with such lists relates to a lack of control and maintenance of the document. There is also the possibility that individuals assessing seriousness become too reliant on the list and, therefore, do not accurately assess the information contained within each individual report. This may result in non-reporting or inappropriate reporting of cases.

3.4.2 Causality assessment

Information about an AE that is reported to an MAH spontaneously should be treated as causally related unless the reporter explicitly states otherwise. It is considered that there is an implied level of causality if an individual has taken the time to contact the MAH regarding an AE. If a reporter does state that the event is not related to the product, then the MAH should make their own assessment of causality, as those events that the MAH considers related, but that the reporter does not, are still subject to expedited reporting.

If a MAH makes its own assessment of causality, where there are both reporter and MAH assessments, the most conservative assessment should take precedence when considering whether the report qualifies for expedited reporting.

There are various factors to consider when assessing causality, but some common ones include:

- biological or pharmacological plausibility;
- temporal relationship;
- dechallenge/rechallenge information;
- confounding factors or alternative aetiology.

3.4.3 Expectedness assessment

For the purposes of expedited reporting, an assessment of expectedness should be made against the relevant SPC. Volume 9A describes that, "For products authorised nationally, the relevant SPC is that approved by the Competent Authority in the Member State to whom the reaction is being reported. For centrally authorised products, the relevant SPC is the SPC authorised by the European Commission." So, for example, if a UK affiliate received a serious adverse reaction report from the company's office in the USA (for a product that held a marketing authorisation within the UK), there would have to be an assessment of whether that report was considered to be unexpected against the local UK SPC, if it were a nationally authorised product.

The concept of expectedness relates to whether or not a reported reaction has been previously observed, rather than what might be anticipated from the pharmacological properties of the active substance. The patient's pre-existing illness should not be considered as a factor when assessing expectedness of a reaction. For authorised products, an expected adverse reaction is one which the nature, severity or outcome is consistent with the SPC.

Consideration should be given to the nature and severity of the reaction, for example if the SPC describes an event that would not normally result in death, reports of a fatality in relation to that particular reaction would be unexpected. In addition, the specificity of the reported reaction(s) should be taken into consideration. For example, a report of hepatitis would not be considered expected if "raised liver enzymes" was the term described in the SPC.

The MAH should assess each adverse reaction term reported for expectedness against the SPC for each of the company's suspect drugs. As with seriousness, it would normally be expected that a MAH makes both an event-level and case-level assessment of expectedness. To determine whether a case should be expedited, for those instances where expectedness is relevant, it must contain at least one event classified as being both serious and unexpected or be assessed as unexpected at a case level (it is possible to have an unexpected case where the individual reaction(s) reported are considered to be expected).

When an assessment of "listedness" is made against the Company Core Safety Information (CCSI), an additional assessment of expectedness against the relevant SPC should also be made to determine the reportability of the case in each EU Member State.

3.4.4 Upgrading and downgrading of cases

There may be circumstances when the MAH considers it appropriate to re-evaluate the case assessments, for example when follow-up information relating to the case is received. In some circumstances, additional information may result in changes to the original assessment of seriousness, expectedness or causality. For example, a case may have initially been assessed as non-serious, but follow-up information indicating the patient was hospitalised results in the case fulfilling one of the criteria for a serious report. When a case is upgraded, it is vital to reconsider the need for submitting an expedited report. Day zero for expedited reporting should be taken as the day that the information used to upgrade the case was received, and not just the date that the decision to upgrade the case was made.

Conversely, follow-up information may result in downgrading of a case, for example an alternative explanation for the reaction may have been identified and the reporter no longer considers the reaction to be causally related to the use of the drug. In relation to causality, only when the reporter explicitly states there is no longer a causal relationship and the MAH agrees should a case be downgraded.

In either situation, the reason for upgrading or downgrading the case should be documented. During regulatory inspections, inspectors expect to see evidence of review of this type of activity to identify any problems, such as issues identified from QC checks. If a case was initially submitted as an expedited report and upon receipt of follow-up information was downgraded, this should be notified to the Competent Authorities who received the initial report, on an expedited basis.

3.4.5 Deletion/deactivation of cases

Some electronic systems may include the ability to delete or deactivate cases. This may be applicable when, for example, duplicates of a case exist within the system (Section 2.2.2). There should be clearly documented procedures describing the scenarios when cases may be deleted and the process for doing so. A record of why a case has been deleted should also be retained. If a case is deleted/deactivated having previously been submitted electronically to Competent Authorities or the EMEA, then a nullification case report will need to be submitted. Table III.6.A of Volume 9A discusses different scenarios for which case nullifications should and should not be sent.

Consideration should be given as to which members of staff have the authority to approve deletion of cases and which members carry out the actual deletion process to ensure that the two processes are independent.

3.5 Expedited Reporting

3.5.1 What to expedite

Establishing which suspected adverse reaction reports need to be expedited to Competent Authorities and the EMEA is based upon the assessments of seriousness, expectedness and causality, but it also requires knowledge of the country of origin of the report, the authorisation procedure for the product concerned (national, mutual recognition, centralised, decentralised), source of reporter, whether the event reported is one requiring special reporting and the source of the report (spontaneous, clinical trial, post-authorisation study, etc.).

This chapter addresses expedited reporting requirements for spontaneous reports, those originating from the worldwide scientific literature and non-interventional post-authorisation studies. Expedited reporting requirements for interventional studies are provided in Chapter 12.

In general, expedited reporting applies to the following types of report:

- all valid SARs occurring within the EU;
- all valid unexpected SARs occurring in the territory of a non-EU country.

Expedited reporting requirements for the EU are provided in Part I, Chapter 4 of Volume 9A, with additional details of specific requirements for Member States provided in Annex 6. In the UK, additional reporting requirements are in place relating to products that are subject to intensive monitoring, also known as "black triangle" products. For such products, MAHs are expected to report to the MHRA all serious reactions that originate from within the EU and are reported or confirmed by an HCP.

In some electronic systems, it is possible to make use of decision trees or algorithms to decide which cases to report. In other situations, a case-by-case assessment of reportability may be appropriate. When using algorithms built into databases, it is important that both business users and technical personnel are involved in identifying the criteria and implementing the reporting rules. Assurance should be obtained that the algorithm is selecting appropriate cases for expediting. It is also necessary to have a review mechanism in place to ensure that algorithms are updated when reporting requirements change or when the MAH acquires a new marketing authorisation.

An example of a reportability decision tree is provided in figure 3.1. In some instances a Competent Authority may request additional reporting requirements, for example non-serious reports of a particular event of concern. It is important that appropriate mechanisms are in place to ensure that these additional reporting requirements are communicated to all staff involved in processing and reporting of ICSRs. The example decision tree does not include all scenarios, in particular those referred to in Section 6.2. An example of the use of a decision tree in reporting decisions is given in the box on p.44.

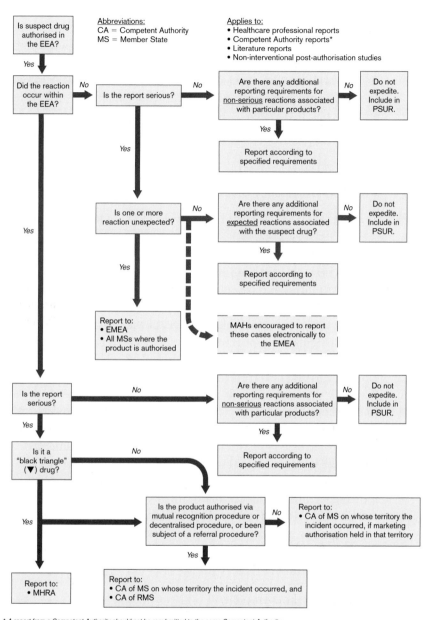

Figure 3.1 Decision tree for expedited reporting of spontaneous reports. Applies to Healthcare Professional reports, Competent Authority reports (a report from a Competent Authority should not be resubmitted to the same Competent Authority), literature reports and non-interventional post-authorisation studies. CA, Competent Authority; EEA, European Economic Area; EMEA, European Medicines Agency; MAH, Marketing Authorisation Holder; MS, Member State; PSUR, Periodic Safety Update Report; RMS, Reference Member State.

Example of reporting based on the decision tree

Product X is authorised via the mutual recognition procedure, with France acting as the Reference Member State. In the UK, the product is designated as a "black triangle" product (i.e. is subject to intensive monitoring). A serious report associated with this product originating from a healthcare professional in Sweden is received by the MAH. Following the decision tree, this report would qualify for expedited reporting to the following Competent Authorities:

- Sweden: the report originated from this country;
- France: this country is acting as Reference Member State;
- UK: the product is subject to "black triangle" reporting requirements.

Other information, if deemed a significant safety issue, should be submitted on an expedited basis.

The MAH and in particular the QPPV need to have assurance that the correct reports are expedited to Competent Authorities. It is expected that reporting decisions are subject to QC checks to provide such assurance. This is particularly important when less-experienced staff are responsible for making the decision whether or not to report a case. Depending on the volume of cases that are processed, it may not be practical to perform a QC check on every case. If a sample of cases is checked, the size of the sample should be carefully considered to ensure that results of the check provide meaningful and reliable data. It is important that appropriateness of the sample size is justified and the rationale is documented.

It could be argued that there is no need to perform QC checks on reporting decisions for those systems that use algorithms or automated reporting facilities and are maintained in a validated state. However, in most situations observed by the MHRA Pharmacovigilance Inspectorate, there is always an element of human intervention in the decision-making process, which could potentially result in an error in the reporting decision. For example, in a global organisation, algorithms are used to identify cases that need to be distributed to affiliates, but then personnel at the affiliate are required to assess whether or not those cases distributed to them fulfil the local requirements for expedited reporting. It is at the second step that there is the potential for error, and so this should be subject to QC checks.

3.5.2   Additional information to expedite

Volume 9A discusses in detail the requirements for expedited reporting of ICSRs. Attention is drawn to some specific scenarios below.

- Any suspected transmission via a medicinal product of an infectious agent is considered a SAR and should be reported in an expedited manner.
- Use of a medicinal product during pregnancy that results in an abnormal outcome in the fetus/child.
- Adverse reactions suspected in infants following exposure from breast milk.
- Lack of efficacy for certain types of product, and products used for life-threatening conditions.
- Cases of overdose, abuse and misuse that lead to SARs.
- Medication errors associated with SARs.

It is important that all who receive training on adverse reaction reporting are made aware of the additional types of information to report, to ensure that this type of information is communicated to the pharmacovigilance department.

3.5.3 What not to report

Non-serious adverse reactions and non-HCP confirmed (consumer) reports should not usually be reported in an expedited manner. Exceptions are on request of a Competent Authority, or when an important change in the risk–benefit profile of a product is identified.

Over-reporting, that is, expedited reporting of inappropriate cases, may have as negative an impact on the assessment of risks and benefits as under-reporting of appropriate cases.

3.5.4 When to expedite

Volume 9A states, "The Marketing Authorisation Holder should transmit all ICSRs requiring expedited reporting promptly and no later than 15 calendar days from receipt. This applies to initial and follow up information."

For the purposes of expedited reporting, day zero is considered the day that the minimum information required for a reportable adverse reaction report is received by any personnel of the MAH, or anyone working on behalf of the MAH, for example contractual partners. It is not the date on which pharmacovigilance staff assess an ICSR as a reportable case. The MHRA requires that expedited ICSRs are received by day 15. Therefore, it is essential that the MAH keeps accurate records of the date of initial receipt of any adverse reaction information.

In cases where additional information is received regarding the case, the same timelines apply: that is, follow-up information that affects the assessment of the case is also subject to expedited reporting within 15 days.

If follow-up information is received for an initial case report prior to an expedited report being submitted, the clock for expedited reporting of the case is not reset.

3.5.5 How to expedite

Article 104 of Directive 2001/83/EC and Article 24 of Regulation (EC) 726/2004 state that suspected adverse reaction reports should be communicated electronically in the form of a report in accordance with the guidelines referred to in Article 106(1), save in exceptional circumstances. This requirement became mandatory from 20 November 2005.

It is expected that MAHs are capable of reporting electronically. For further information regarding electronic reporting, please refer to Volume 9A, Part III.

3.6 Compliance Monitoring

The QPPV has the responsibility to ensure that expedited reports are prepared for the Competent Authorities of Member States and the EMEA; this can be achieved through delegation. However, it is important that the MAH and the QPPV have oversight of compliance of submissions in terms of accuracy of information, timeliness of submissions and appropriateness of reporting (Section 1.4.2). There should be assurance that reports containing an accurate representation of the source data are being submitted within 15 days and also that the correct types of report are being submitted.

Therefore, there is an expectation placed on MAHs to have in place a mechanism of monitoring compliance of expedited submissions. This procedure should be documented, and there should be evidence that compliance information is reviewed by appropriate personnel, for example the QPPV.

3.7 UK Requirements for "Specials"

The information provided within this chapter relates to products for which marketing authorisations have been granted. However, issues relating to safety are also applicable to unlicensed relevant medicinal products for human use, commonly known as "specials". Information about the manufacture and importation of unlicensed medicines for human use is provided in the "Rules and Guidance for Pharmaceutical Manufacturers and Distributors 2007" (The Orange Guide). The pharmacovigilance requirements placed upon the sellers and suppliers of specials in terms of recording and reporting AEs are described in MHRA Guidance Note 14 "The Supply of Unlicensed Relevant Medicinal Products for Individual Patients".

A special is defined within Statutory Instrument 1994/3144, as, "a relevant medicinal product supplied in response to a bona fide unsolicited order, formulated in accordance with the specification of a doctor or dentist and for use by his individual patients on his direct personal responsibility in order to fulfil the special needs of those patients. . ."

The requirements relating to suspected adverse reactions are that:

6. *Any person who sells or supplies a relevant medicinal product in accordance with any of paragraphs 1 to 4 shall maintain, and keep for a period of at least 5 years, a record showing (e) details of any suspected adverse reaction to the product so sold or supplied of which he is aware.*

7. *A person required to maintain the records mentioned in paragraph 6 shall. . .*

   (a) *notify the licensing authority of any suspected adverse reaction such as is mentioned in head (e) of that paragraph which is a serious adverse reaction; and*

   (b) *make available for inspection at all reasonable times by the licensing authority the records mentioned in that paragraph.*

3.8 Examples of Inspection Findings

Examples of areas of concern that have been identified during inspections are provided below. This is not an exhaustive list but serves to summarise some of the key points from this chapter and highlights areas that can be problematic. It is anticipated that examples will prove useful to help MAHs to address such issues.

(i)   There is a lack of documentation within the medical information enquiry files to demonstrate that appropriate questions have been asked to determine whether an enquiry relates to a specific patient with an adverse reaction.

(ii) There are inadequate or no mechanisms in place to ensure that all adverse reactions have been appropriately identified and transferred to the pharmacovigilance department from other internal departments, for example medical information, or from external partners.

(iii) The process to validate adverse reactions, particularly consumer reports, is inadequate.

(iv)   There is no mechanism in place to track the expected date of delivery of pregnant women, resulting in no follow-up attempt to obtain the outcome.

(v)   There is evidence of incorrect assessments of expectedness, for example a reported event of hepatitis is assessed as expected where the product SPC contains "elevated transaminase levels" in the Undesirable effects section.

(vi)   There is a lack of timely assessment of cases to determine seriousness, resulting in a backlog of cases that may require expedited reporting.

(vii)   There is a lack of QC of data entry onto the safety database.

(viii)   There is no routine QC check of cases that may require expedited reporting to Competent Authorities to confirm that the correct reporting decision has been made. In addition, where cases are not submitted, the decision-making process is not clearly documented. This can result in incorrect expedited reporting decisions being made, for example SARs originating from within the EU not being reported to the Reference Member State, if they occurred in another territory.

(ix)   Compliance with expedited reporting is unacceptable as a high percentage of cases are reported late to Competent Authorities. Processes are not in place to ensure that regulatory reporting timeframes are met.

Current metrics relating to MHRA pharmacovigilance inspection findings can be found on our website. The exact nature of findings will vary from company to company and findings are graded on a case-by-case basis, taking into account the evidence relating to the issue and the impact of the finding on, for example, public safety or other areas of the pharmacovigilance system.

4

Literature Searching

> **Editor's note** This chapter explores the obligations in relation to the screening of published literature as contained in Regulation 726/2004 and Directive 2001/83/EC (as amended). Detailed guidance on literature searching can be found in Volume 9A, Part I, Sections 4, 6 and 8. Deficiencies in searching that could result in the lack of retrieval of relevant published literature are viewed in the context of a failure to report published safety articles as required by the legislation. In order to meet their obligations, a MAH may need to use several different types of search, a variety of relevant databases and reference to locally published literature.

4.1 Identification of Individual Case Safety Reports

Volume 9A confirms that adverse reactions which appear in the published literature are included in the requirements for reporting ICSRs. Volume 9A, Part I, Section 4.3.2 states that ICSRs from the worldwide literature are considered to be reports of which the MAH can be reasonably expected to be aware and have knowledge.

The MAH is expected to maintain awareness of possible publications by accessing a widely used systematic literature review and reference database (for example Medline, Excerpta Medica or Embase) no less frequently than once a week. It is the MAH's responsibility to ensure the adequacy of the resources they are using to undertake searches, such as the coverage of the database.

In addition, local company offices are required to be aware of publications in their local journals and to bring them to the attention of the QPPV as appropriate. Local publications may not be included in worldwide literature databases. In particular, publications that may be taken by company personnel for purposes other than pharmacovigilance are less likely to be available in worldwide literature databases but may be a source of relevant safety information. The requirement to report ICSRs identified in local literature is consistent with obligations for reporting of ICSRs received by any personnel of the MAH.

Cases of suspected adverse reactions from the scientific and medical literature, including relevant published abstracts from meetings and draft manuscripts, should be reviewed to identify individual cases that might qualify for expedited reporting. In the context of local literature, where the MAH sponsors local or national scientific meetings, the requirement is to review publications and communications so that ICSRs can be reported to Competent Authorities in advance of publication, whenever possible.

4.2   Requirements Relating to Periodic Safety Update Reports

Volume 9A, Part I, Section 6.3.7 states that MAHs "should monitor stand-ard, recognised medical and scientific journals for safety information rele-vant to their products and/or make use of one or more literature search/summary services for that purpose". This text relates to the pres-entation of individual case histories within the PSUR. It is likely that most ICSRs will already have been identified through the MAH's weekly literature screening service for expediting reporting purposes. The frequency of searching for the purposes of PSURs and the use of particu-lar databases is not specified in Volume 9A. The selection of a source of information for the purposes of inclusion in PSURs must be relevant to the product and could be a defined set of journals.

Information on published studies should also be discussed as part of the PSUR (Volume 9A, Part 1, Section 6.3.8.c). MAHs are expected to summarise reports containing important positive or negative findings that have been published, including those from relevant published abstracts from meetings. The publication reference should also be provided. This requirement widens the search from ICSRs, as studies reporting safety outcomes in a group of subjects should also be described.

The special types of safety information that should be included, but which may not found by a search constructed specifically to identify ICSRs, include:

- pregnancy outcomes (including termination) with no adverse outcomes;
- use in the paediatric population;
- compassionate supply, named patient use;
- lack of efficacy;
- asymptomatic overdose, abuse or misuse;
- medication error where no AEs occurred, or "near misses";
- important non-clinical safety results.

4.3   Risk–benefit Assessment

Data published in the worldwide scientific literature or presented as abstracts, posters or communications are an important source of information for MAHs in terms of ongoing safety evaluation of medicinal products.

The scope of risk covers not only AEs, but also includes *in vitro* and *in vivo* laboratory experiments, the potential for overdose, misuse, off-label use and medication errors and reduction in benefit (lack of efficacy). Special populations of particular interest for risk assessment are the very young, elderly, pregnant or organ-impaired and additionally those otherwise-healthy individuals who may receive a medicinal product (as with some vaccines) or even if there are issues with disposal of a medicine. Class effects for groups of pharmacologically similar products could also be important to the assessment of risk. A search constructed to find reportable ICSRs may not satisfy all the requirements for identifying publications relevant to risk–benefit assessment.

4.4   When to Start and Stop

Volume 9A specifies that, in addition to routine expedited and periodic reporting requirements, the MAH has an obligation to report the worldwide experience with the medicinal product in specific situations: in the period between the submission of the marketing authorisation application and the granting of the marketing authorisation, and following suspension or withdrawal of the marketing authorisation for safety or commercial reasons.

The worldwide experience would include published literature. For the period between submission and granting of a marketing authorisation, literature searching should be conducted to identify published articles that provide information that could impact on the risk–benefit assessment of the product under assessment.

It should be noted that the requirement for literature searching is not dependent on a product being marketed. Literature searches should be conducted for all products with a marketing authorisation, irrespective of commercial status. Following suspension or withdrawal, the focus of reporting is on delayed-onset adverse reactions and retrospectively notified cases. It would, therefore, be expected that literature searching would start on submission of a marketing authorisation application, and continue while the authorisation is active, and for a period following withdrawal to account for stock available for use and delays to publication of safety-related articles.

4.5   Where to Look

Articles relevant to the safety of medicinal products are usually published in well-recognised scientific journals, although new and important information may be first presented at international symposia or in local journals. Although the most well-known databases (e.g. Medline) cover the majority of scientific journals, the most relevant publications may be collated elsewhere in very specialised medical fields, for certain types of product (e.g. herbal medicinal products) or where safety concerns are subject to non-clinical research. The MAH should establish the most relevant source of published literature for each product.

Volume 9A gives examples of Medline, Embase and Excerpta Medica for the purposes of finding ICSRs. These databases have broad medical subject coverage. The database providers can advise on the sources of records, the currency of the data, and the nature of database inclusions. The MAH is expected to have selected one or more databases appropriate to the product. For example, in risk–benefit assessment, safety issues arising during non-clinical safety studies may necessitate regular review of a database that has a less clinical focus and includes more laboratory-based publications.

The requirement to utilise data found in abstracts, posters or communications from scientific meetings is specified in the risk–benefit assessment section of Volume 9A. The section for PSURs specifies that relevant published abstracts from meetings should be included, and that meeting abstracts and draft manuscripts should be reviewed for reportable ICSRs.

Although it is not a requirement for MAHs to attend all such meetings, if there are company personnel at such a meeting, or it is sponsored by a MAH, it is expected that articles of relevance would be available to the MAH's pharmacovigilance system. In addition, literature that is produced or sponsored by the MAH should be reviewed, so that any reportable ICSRs can be reported to Competent Authorities as required in advance of publication.

If ICSRs are brought to the attention of the MAH from this source, they should be processed in the same way as ICSRs found on searching a database or reviewing a journal. Abstracts from major scientific meetings are indexed and available in some databases, but posters and communications are rarely available from this source.

4.6   Database Searches

A search is more than a collection of terms used to interrogate a database. Decisions about the database selection, approach to records retrieval, term or text selection and the application of limits need to be relevant to the purpose of the search. For searches in pharmacovigilance, some of the considerations for database searching are described below.

4.6.1   Precision and recall

Medical and scientific databases are a collection of records relating to a set of publications. For any given record, each database has a structure that facilitates the organisation of records and searching by various means, from simple text to complex indexing terms with associated subheadings. Search terms (text or indexed) can be linked using Boolean operators and proximity codes to combine concepts, increasing or decreasing the specificity of a search. In addition, limits to the output can be set. When searching, the application of search terms means that the output is less than the entire database of the records held. The success of a search can be measured according to precision and recall (also called sensitivity). Recall is the proportion of records retrieved ("hits") when considering the total number of relevant records that are present in the database. Precision is the proportion of "hits" that are relevant when considering the number of records that were retrieved. In general, the higher recall searches would result in low precision.

4.6.2   Search construction

Databases vary in structure, lag time in indexing and indexing policy for new terms. While some database providers give information about the history of a particular indexing term or the application of synonyms, other databases are less sophisticated. In addition, author abstracts are not always consistent in the choice of words relating to pharmacovigilance concepts or drug names.

When constructing a search for pharmacovigilance, the highest recall for a search would be to enter the drug name (in all its variants) only. In practice, additional indexing terms and text are added to increase precision and to reduce the search result to return records that are of relevance to pharmacovigilance. There is a balance to be achieved. It is, therefore, expected that complicated searches are accompanied by initial testing to check that relevant records are not omitted; however, there is no defined acceptable loss of recall when searching for pharmacovigilance purposes. Term selection must be relevant to the database used and the subject of the search.

4.6.3   Selection of product terms

Searches should be performed to find records for active ingredients and not for brand names only. This can include excipients that may have a pharmacological effect. When choosing search terms for drugs, there are a number of considerations.

- Is the active ingredient an indexed term?
- What spellings might be used by authors (particularly if the active ingredient is not indexed)?
- What alternative names might apply (numbers or codes used for products newly developed, chemical names, brand names, active metabolites)?
- Is it medically relevant to search only for a particular salt or specific compound for an active ingredient?

During searches for ICSRs, it may be possible to construct a search that excludes records for formulations or routes of administration different to that of the subject product; however, restrictions must allow for the inclusion of articles where this is not specified. Search construction should also allow for the retrieval of misadministration, medication error or misuse information, which could be poorly indexed. Searches should also not routinely exclude records of unbranded products or records for other company brands (Section 4.7).

4.6.4 Selection of search terms

As described previously, there is no acceptable loss of recall when searching published literature for pharmacovigilance. The use of search terms (free text or use of indexing) to construct more precise searches may assist in managing the output. Deficiencies that have been found frequently during Competent Authority inspections include:

- the omission of outcome terms; for example "death" as an outcome may be the only indexed term in a case of unexplained death;
- the omission of terms to include special types of report (for example asymptomatic overdose);
- the omission of pregnancy terms:
  - to find uneventful pregnancy reports for PSUR and risk–benefit purposes,
  - to find adverse outcomes in pregnancy for ICSR reporting.

4.6.5 "Limits"

Some databases apply indexing that allows the application of limits to a search, for example by subject age, sex, publication type. The limits applied to a search are not always shown in the "search strategy" or search string.

If limits are applied, they must be relevant to the purpose of the search. When searching a worldwide literature database, titles and abstracts are usually in English language. The use of limits that reduce the search result to only those published in English language is generally not acceptable (Section 4.7.6). Limits applied to patient types, or other aspects of an article, for example human, would need to be justified in the context of the purpose of a search.

Limits can be applied to produce results for date ranges; for example, weekly searches can be obtained by specifying the start and end date for the records to be retrieved. Care should be taken to ensure that the search is inclusive for an entire time period; for example, records that may have been added later in the day for the day of the search should be covered in the next search period. The search should also retrieve all records added in that period, and not just those initially entered or published during the specified period (so that records that have been updated or retrospectively added are retrieved). This should be checked with the database provider if it is not clear.

Although one of the purposes of searching is to identify ICSRs for reporting, the use of publication type limits is not robust. ICSRs may be presented within review or study publications, and such records may not be indexed as "case-reports", resulting in their omission from search results limited by publication type.

4.7 Handling Search Results

4.7.1 Record keeping

There is no absolute requirement for retaining records of literature searches. However, the MAH may be asked to demonstrate due diligence in searching for published literature, and this would be difficult to do without reference to the search strategy used. In addition, there is an expectation that record keeping for decisions over whether or not to report a particular ICSR would include retention of information about the search output. It is always good practice to retain a record of the search construction, the database used and the date the search was run. In addition, it may be useful to retain results of the search for an appropriate period of time, particularly in the event of zero results. If decision making is documented on the results, it is particularly important to retain this information. This information is routinely requested during pharmacovigilance inspections conducted by EU Competent Authorities.

4.7.2 Outputs

Databases can show search results in different ways, for example titles only or title and abstract with or without indexing terms. Some publications are of obvious relevance at first glance, whereas others may be more difficult to identify. Consistent with the requirement to provide the full citation for an article and to identify relevant publications, the title, citation and abstract (if available) should always be retrieved and reviewed.

4.7.3 Review and selection of articles

It is recognised that literature search results are a surrogate for the actual article. Therefore, it is expected that the person reviewing the results of a search is qualified to identify the articles of relevance. This may be an information professional trained in pharmacovigilance or a pharmacovigilance professional with knowledge of the database used. Recorded confirmation that the search results have been reviewed will assist the MAH in demonstrating that there is a systematic approach to collecting information about suspected adverse reactions from literature sources.

A common deficiency found during Competent Authority inspections is that review of search outputs reflects the purposes of identification of ICSRs only. Where the review is also used as the basis for collating articles for PSUR production, relevant studies with no ICSRs must be identified, as well as those ICSRs that do not qualify for expedited reporting.

Outputs from searches may contain enough information to be a valid ICSR, in which case the article should be ordered (Section 4.7.5). All articles for search results that are likely to be relevant to pharmacovigilance requirements should be obtained, as there is a requirement to provide a reportable publication in full. The urgency with which this occurs should be appropriate to the content and requirement for action by the MAH.

Articles can be excluded from reporting by the MAH if another company's branded product is the suspect product. Volume 9A states that, in the absence of a specified product source and/or invented name, ownership of the product should be assumed for articles about an active substance. Alternative reasons for exclusion of a published article are a specified formulation or a route of administration that is not consistent with the MAH's product presentation. The caveat is that articles may describe the misuse of a product, or the preparation of an extemporaneous product (for example making solutions from solid dose forms), and could, therefore, be reportable.

Volume 9A describes the selection of reportable published literature based on a causality assessment. If multiple medicinal products are mentioned in a publication, a report should be submitted only for the product that is identified by the publication's author as having at least a possible causal relationship with the reaction. Consistent with guidance for all ICSRs, the published article should not be reported if the author has made an explicit statement that a causal relationship between the product and the event(s) is excluded. If the author describes other causes for the reaction that do not include the product, the product could be regarded as a co-medication and not suspect. These types of report can be upgraded by the MAH, if the company believes there to be a possible relationship between the product and the event(s), and reported accordingly.

4.7.4   Follow-up

The requirements for follow up of ICSRs apply to published reports (Section 3.3).

4.7.5   Day zero

As described in Volume 9A, day zero is the date on which the MAH becomes aware of a publication containing the minimum information for a reportable adverse reaction. Awareness of a publication includes any personnel of the MAH, or third parties with contractual arrangements with the MAH (Section 4.8). It is sometimes possible to identify the date on which a record was available on a database, although with weekly literature searching, day zero for a reportable adverse reaction present in an abstract is taken to be the date on which the search was conducted. For articles that have been ordered as a result of literature search results, the date when the minimum information for a valid case was available is day zero. The MAH should take appropriate measures to obtain articles promptly in order to confirm the validity of a case.

4.7.6   Translations

Published articles reported to the Competent Authority must be provided in English. Abstracts in English may be reported, followed by the translated article.

4.7.7   Reporting

Articles citing multiple individual identifiable patients should be reported as separate ICSRs if they meet the requirements for expedited reporting. Part III of Volume 9A gives specific guidance on electronic reporting of adverse reaction reports published in the worldwide literature. For either electronic or paper reporting, the full citation should be included, in the style of the Vancouver Convention. Initial reports made from published abstracts should be followed up with a report from the full article, if the article is not available to allow initial reporting within the 15-day reporting deadline.

4.7.8   Duplicates

Consistent with the requirements for reporting ICSRs, literature cases should be checked to prevent reporting of duplicates, and previously reported cases should be identified as such when reported. It is, therefore, expected that Competent Authority reports (ASPRs in the UK) are checked to identify literature articles that have already been reported (Section 2.2.2). MAHs should agree with the Competent Authority whether it is necessary to provide the full article if a report is made for a case and the MAH knows that it had already been received by the authority (that is the MAH is in receipt of an ASPR for the literature case).

4.8   Contracting out Literature Search Services

The MAH may use the services of another party to conduct searches of the published literature. In this event, the MAH retains responsibility for the performance of the search and subsequent reporting to Competent Authorities. As described in Volume 9A, the transfer of a pharmacovigilance task or function must be detailed in a contract between the MAH and the service provider (Chapter 11). The nature of third party arrangements for literature searching can range from access to a particular database interface only (access to a technology) to full literature searching, review and reporting (using the professional pharmacovigilance services of another organisation).

It is recognised that more than one MAH may share services of a third party to conduct searches for generic active ingredients. In this instance, each MAH must satisfy itself that the search and service is appropriate to their needs. The MHRA's "Better Regulation of Medicines Initiative" is currently looking at ways of reducing the duplication of effort in the area of literature searching, particularly in relation to generic medicines, potentially including the use of a shared third party contractor (Annex 5).

Where the MAH is dependent on a particular service provider for literature searching, it is expected that an assessment of the service(s) is undertaken to determine whether it meets the needs of the MAH. In any case, the arrangement should be clearly documented.

The clock start for expedited reporting of ICSRs begins with awareness of the minimum information by either the MAH or the contractual partner (whichever is the earliest). This must be borne in mind where a third party provides a review or collated report of the published literature, in order to ensure that published literature cases are reported as required within the legislated timeframes. That is, day zero is the date the search was run if the minimum criteria are available in the abstract and not the date the information was supplied to the MAH.

4.9 Examples of Inspection Findings

Examples of areas of concern that have been identified during inspections are provided below. This is not an exhaustive list but serves to summarise some of the key points from this chapter and highlights areas that can be problematic. It is anticipated that examples will prove useful to help MAHs to address such issues.

(i)   The MAH is not conducting literature searches for products that are not currently marketed.

(ii) There is no mechanism in place to ensure that the literature search strategy is updated when new Market Authorisations are obtained and when regulatory reporting requirements change.

(iii) The MAH does not take a conservative approach regarding literature articles that describe an adverse reaction but where the brand name of the product is not specified. If the MAH cannot exclude ownership of the product described in an article on the basis of the active substance(s), formulation or route of administration, the MAH should assume that it is one of their products.

(iv) Literature articles describing adverse reactions that are both non-serious and expected are not captured and collated. Although such reports would not necessarily qualify for expedited or periodic reporting, they may contribute to the identification of changes in frequency of expected reactions.

(v)   The literature-search strategy is designed to identify ICSRs and does not identify all literature articles that are relevant for discussion in the PSUR.

Current metrics relating to MHRA pharmacovigilance inspection findings can be found on our website. The exact nature of findings will vary from company to company and findings are graded on a case-by-case basis, taking into account the evidence relating to the issue and the impact of the finding on, for example, public safety or other areas of the pharmacovigilance system.

5

Periodic Safety Update Reports

<table>
<tr>
<td>

Editor's
note

</td>
<td>

Detailed guidance is provided on the requirements for PSURs in Part I, Section 6 of Volume 9A, and so this section of the Guide will deal with commonly encountered deficiencies and misunderstandings concerning PSURs observed during pharmacovigilance inspections.

PSURs are important pharmacovigilance documents intended to provide an update of the worldwide safety experience of a medicinal product to Competent Authorities at defined time points post-authorisation. They provide an opportunity for MAHs to review the safety profile of their products and ensure that SPCs and patient information leaflets (PILs) are up to date. Since they also provide Competent Authorities with valuable pharmacovigilance data, great importance is placed on compliance with periodic reporting requirements.

Within PSURs, MAHs are expected to provide succinct summary information together with a critical evaluation of the risk–benefit balance of the product in the light of new or changing information. This evaluation should ascertain whether further investigations need to be carried out and whether changes should be made to the marketing authorisation and product information.

A number of areas in pharmacovigilance have an impact on the ability of MAHs to produce compliant PSURs, for example processing of spontaneous and clinical study adverse reactions, literature searching, signal detection, medical and scientific assessment and the maintenance of product safety information. The quality of PSURs, therefore, provides a good indication of the overall state of a MAH's pharmacovigilance system.

</td>
</tr>
</table>

5.1 Who is Responsible for Producing Periodic Safety Update Reports?

As per the legislation, it is the QPPV's responsibility to ensure PSURs are of sufficient quality and are prepared and submitted in a timely fashion (Section 1.4.2). In order to discharge this responsibility, they should have adequate oversight of the PSUR production process and be involved in the review of the reports themselves. Where this is not practical, such as in large organisations with many products, formal documented procedures should be in place to delegate these responsibilities to other suitably qualified staff.

In relation to PSURs for centrally authorised products, guidance from the EMEA (available at the time of this Guide going to press) is that the QPPV must prepare and sign the PSUR. Preparation of the PSUR may be delegated to an appropriately qualified and trained individual. That individual may also sign the PSUR provided that there is a letter of delegation signed by the QPPV and attached to the PSUR cover letter. Such a letter may cover more than one medicinal product and/or more than one PSUR.

5.2 When Should Periodic Safety Update Reports be Submitted?

Current EU PSUR submission requirements are:

- after authorisation but before initial placement on the EU market:
  - immediately upon request from a Competent Authority or the Agency, and
  - at least every 6 months after authorisation (see Section 10.4.6 for the impact of the Sunset Clause);
- after initial placement on the EU market:
  - six-monthly PSUR submissions should be continued until two full years of marketing experience in the EU has been gained,
  - yearly PSURs for the following two years, and
  - thereafter PSURs submitted at three-yearly intervals, or
  - immediately upon request from a Competent Authority.

It should be noted that initial launch dates within the EU, as well as approval dates, need to be taken into consideration when scheduling PSUR production. For details of PSURs and renewals please refer to Section 5.4.

Most generic products can be placed straight on to the same cycle as the innovator. In most cases, this will be straight to a three-yearly schedule, but only if the MAH requested this in the marketing authorisation application and it was accepted by the Competent Authority. However, the standard PSUR schedule will still apply for biosimilars and some generic products with safety issues (e.g. isotretinoin and clozapine), and for novel formulations, routes of administration or indications. If an organisation is taking over a marketing authorisation under a change of ownership, it is important that the organisation ascertains the agreed PSUR schedule.

Under the auspices of the EU Heads of Medicines Agencies, a PSUR synchronisation initiative has been undertaken to ensure that medicinal products with the same active substance follow the same PSUR submission scheme in all EU Member States. To this end, a consolidated list of adopted EU harmonised "virtual" birth dates (HBDs) and accompanying data lock points (DLPs) for the forthcoming PSURs has been produced and published on the agency's website (http://www.hma.eu). The list will be periodically updated and should be taken into account by MAHs when scheduling PSUR production for products containing active substances on the list. However, the existence of a HBD for an active substance does not override a MAH's obligations to produce PSURs at the required frequency. Six-monthly PSURs will still be required for products that contain active substances with a HBD if these products have a novel formulation, route of administration, indication, etc.

In the UK, products registered under the traditional herbal registration scheme will often go straight to a three-yearly PSUR cycle, with the exception of substances for which there are known safety issues, such as black cohosh. Details of the international birth date for herbal substances can be found on the MHRA website.

5.3 Submission Dates for Periodic Safety Update Reports

Each PSUR should cover the period of time since the last PSUR DLP and should be submitted within 60 days of its DLP. If a MAH is unable to meet the 60-day submission deadline, then it may, under exceptional circumstances, make a request to the appropriate EU Competent Authority (such as the RMS or rapporteur, where applicable) for a 30 calendar day extension, ideally before the DLP of the PSUR. The reasons why an extension is being requested should always be specified and may include circumstances such as:

- a large number of case reports for the reporting period, provided that there is no new significant safety concern;
- safety concerns raised by Competent Authorities in the previous PSUR for which the MAH is preparing additional or further analysis in the next PSUR; and/or
- safety concerns identified by the MAH that might require additional or further analysis.

Such requests will only apply to the specific PSUR in question and not to subsequent PSURs, which will be expected to be submitted on the appropriate date in line with their original periodicity.

5.4 Renewals and Periodic Safety Update Reports

For all marketing authorisations not renewed before 30 October 2005, a renewal application should be submitted six months prior to expiry and this should be supported by four years and four months of PSUR data. There is no need to resubmit PSURs that have been submitted previously, but where more than one PSUR covers the period from grant to renewal a summary bridging report should be submitted.

For UK national marketing authorisations that have already been subject to a renewal before 30 October 2005, subsequent renewals are being replaced by three-yearly PSURs and no further renewal application is required. For all other marketing authorisations (mutual recognition, centralised) renewed before 30 October 2005, at least one further renewal is required, which must be submitted six months prior to expiry of the marketing authorisations.

Renewal applications can be submitted earlier than six months before the expiry date of the marketing authorisation in order to synchronise the PSUR submission with the EU HBD. The minimum time between marketing authorisation granting and renewal is one year and eight months: that is, the renewal application must be supported by at least a 12-month PSUR.

Although marketing authorisation renewals require the submission of a PSUR, with a DLP of four years, four months after the date of the first marketing authorisation approval, the PSUR and renewal schedules remain independent of each other. Therefore, MAHs must continue to submit PSURs in line with their required periodicity, no matter what stage the renewal process is at.

5.5 Data Selection and Inclusion

Adverse reaction data from the following sources are potentially available to the MAH and so would be expected to be included in the PSUR if they exist.

- Direct reports to the MAH. This includes reports such as those spontaneously notified by HCPs, from MAH-sponsored studies, from named-patient or compassionate use schemes and from patients or consumers.
- Adverse reaction reports from the literature.
- Adverse reaction reports received from regulatory authorities worldwide. This may include non-medically confirmed patient or consumer reports.
- Reports from other sources such as those from other companies, from registries, from poison control centres or epidemiological databases.

Data on individual case reports should be presented in PSURs in the form of line listings and/or summary tabulations. Table 5.1 sets out which type of reports should be included in line listings and summary tabulations. Attempts should be made to avoid duplicate reporting of cases from literature and regulatory sources.

Table 5.1 Types of adverse reaction report to be included in line listings and summary tabulations of the Periodic Safety Update Report

Source of report	Type	Line listings		Summary tabulations
		Main report	Annex	
Spontaneous from HCPs	All serious Non-serious unlisted	Yes		Yes
Post-authorisation safety studies	All serious	Yes		Yes
Clinical studies	All serious considered related by sponsor or investigator	Yes		Yes
Named patient/ compassionate use	All serious	Yes		Yes
Literature	All serious Non-serious unlisted	Yes		Yes
Regulatory authorities	All serious	Yes		Yes
Spontaneous from HCP	Non-serious listed		Yes	Yes
Patients/consumers or other non-HCPs	All serious All non-serious		Yes	No[a]
Registries	All serious	No	No	Yes
Poison control centres	All serious	No	No	Yes
Epidemiological databases	All serious	No	No	Yes
Contractual partners[b]	All serious	No	No	Yes

HCP, healthcare professionals; MAH, Marketing Authorisation Holder.
[a]The MAH should include data from non-HCP reports in summary tabulations if it provides useful/significant information (e.g. if the product is available without a prescription or if non-HCP reports add information relevant to a potential safety concern or other area of interest). However, these should be presented in separate tables or columns.
[b]In this instance, the term contractual partners does not refer to persons and organisations to whom the MAH has transferred pharmacovigilance tasks and functions (these are considered to be equivalent to reports sent directly to the MAH), but to partners who market related products (e.g. same active substance but with a different indication and/or route of administration) and for which they produce their own Periodic Safety Update Report.

MAHs should have formal procedures and processes in place to ensure that all pertinent cases are included in PSURs. This will involve the use of validated search and extraction utilities used to retrieve information from safety databases.

Relevant cases from clinical trials, that is, "suspected unexpected serious adverse reactions" (SUSARs) and suspected SARs, occurring during the reporting period should be considered for inclusion in PSURs. For blinded studies, all relevant cases reported to the MAH in the period that have been unblinded (that is, SUSARs for the purposes of expedited reporting) should be included in the PSUR.

Cases involving SARs, where the identity of the study medication remains blinded, should be reviewed by the MAH to identify any potential safety signals. The unblinded SUSAR reports should be used to help to place data from the blinded SAR reports into context. If this review indicates a potential new safety signal, then the MAH should include both blinded SARs and unblinded SUSARs in the PSUR. These data should be presented in the form of line listings and summary tabulations, with the blinded data being clearly identified as such.

If the MAH considers that the blinded SAR data provide no new safety information, then these may, temporarily, be excluded from inclusion in PSURs. However, the MAH should explicitly state that this is occurring in the main text of the PSUR and provide information on the number of clinical trial reports excluded because the identity of the study medication was blinded.

Once a study has been completed and unblinded, then all SARs from the study that concern the relevant suspect drug should be included in the next PSUR, even if they occurred prior to the reporting period of this PSUR. If there are cases that have been reported in a blinded fashion in a previous PSUR, then these should be reported again in an unblinded fashion, together with a statement detailing in which previous PSUR(s) they had initially been included.

All safety information concerning the product that arises from any study (non-clinical, clinical and epidemiological) during the period covered by the PSUR should be discussed if it alters the product's risk–benefit profile in any way. This includes lack of efficacy data, such as studies that fail to meet their end point(s). The status of targeted safety studies and studies that are part of the RMP should always be discussed even if they have not yet been completed/reported and are still in the planning or execution phase.

For products that have a RMP, the current status of all associated activities and commitments should be reported in the PSUR, cross-referring to information contained in other sections of the PSUR or other documents/reports as required.

5.6 Combination Products and Differing Formulations of the Same Active Substance

Generally an MAH should prepare a single PSUR containing information on all indications, dosage forms, routes of administration and regimens for a given active substance contained in any of the medicinal products authorised to the MAH. When relevant, data relating to a particular indication, dosage form, route of administration or dosing regimen should be presented in separate sections of the PSUR.

However, in some circumstances, it may be appropriate to produce separate PSURs for the same active substance or fixed-dose combination products containing the same active substance or substances (if the MAH separately markets more than one of the active compounds contained in the fixed-dose combination product). This should only be done if the safety profiles of the products differ significantly (e.g. chloramphenicol eye drops compared with systemic chloramphenicol). Such differences may be demonstrated by comparing the system organ classes of the AEs reported for the products to see if they are significantly different.

The agreement of the relevant Competent Authorities should be sought before an MAH prepares separate PSURs for the same active substance. When such separate reports are produced by an MAH, the PSURs should cross-refer to each other so that any reviewer will be aware that additional safety data concerning the active substance can be found in other PSURs. A justification for the production of separate PSURs should also be included in the reports.

5.7 Special Patient Populations

The CHMP Guideline on Conduct of Pharmacovigilance for Medicines Used by the Paediatric Population (EMEA/CHMP/PhVWP/235910/2005) includes a requirement for a discussion of the use of a medicinal product in the paediatric population to be included in a separate section of the PSUR if there is "evidence of significant "off-label" use or if there are adverse reactions reported in the paediatric population".

A combination of ethical difficulties and clinical trial exclusion criteria result in paediatric and geriatric patients either being excluded or under-represented in the clinical trials that are conducted for the purpose of obtaining a marketing authorisation. Paradoxically, these populations, particularly the elderly, are more likely to require treatment with medicinal products than the general adult population. PSURs, therefore, provide an essential opportunity to assess the safety of medicinal products in these populations. In terms of the paediatric population, the legislation requires that any new safety issues are addressed in the PSUR, whether it applies to the whole population or to a specific age group or indication. Data from completed or ongoing studies should be presented separately from spontaneous reports.

Many PSURs contain adverse reaction reports involving children (< 18 years) and nearly all contain reports involving the elderly (≥ 65 years). Therefore, adverse reactions involving these two populations should always be discussed in PSURs. If there are no, or very few, reports involving children and/or the elderly, then statements to this effect should be included in the PSUR. The actual number of these reports, and what proportion they form of the total number of reports received in the period, should always be quoted.

Strategies used to analyse adverse reactions in special patient populations usually revolve around comparing these populations with the standard adult population (18–64 years). Methods may include:

- comparing adverse reactions in the two populations by system organ class; and/or
- comparing the most frequently reported AEs in the two populations.

Consideration should be given to displaying these data either in a tabular or graphical format (such as bar graphs).

The standard age groups that should be used to stratify analyses of paediatric data are those defined in ICH E11. They are defined in completed days, months or years:

- preterm newborn infants;
- term newborn infants (0 to 27 days);
- infants and toddlers (28 days to 23 months);
- children (2 to 11 years);
- adolescents (lower limit of 12 to 16 years and upper of 18 years, dependent on region).

In the EU, adolescents are defined as being 12 to 18 years.

MAHs may use other developmentally meaningful groups but should provide a justification for doing so.

The addition of a paediatric indication to an existing EU marketing authorisation will reset the clock for submissions of PSURs to a six-monthly frequency for the following two years. These reports should pay particular attention to paediatric use. Thereafter the periodicity of the PSUR submission should be phased in with the PSUR submission schedule already in place.

In addition to the above considerations for PSURs, EU Regulations (EC) 1901/2006 and (EC) 1902/2006 on medicinal products for paediatric use have recently been introduced to provide a binding EU-wide framework to enhance the development of medicinal products for use in the paediatric population. These require applicants for marketing authorisations to submit a paediatric investigation plan in the early stages of clinical development, unless a waiver or deferral has been granted.

In addition to analysing special patient populations, consideration should always be given to routine description of the demographics of all patients (age and gender, where reported) who experienced the AEs reported during the period covered by the PSUR.

5.8 Reference Safety Information

Guidance on Reference Safety Information (RSI) within PSURs can be found in Part I, Section 6.2.5 and Section 6.3.5 of Volume 9A.

A MAH may use either the CCSI or an approved EU SPC as the RSI in order to determine which adverse reactions in the report are considered to be listed or unlisted (Chapter 8). In both cases, the following requirements apply:

- all RSIs should be dated and version controlled;
- the version of the RSI used in the PSUR should be included as an appendix to the report;
- the correct version of the RSI should be used: for six-monthly or yearly PSURs, the version current at the beginning of the period covered by the PSUR should be used and for three-yearly PSURs the version current at the end of the reporting period should be used (see Section 6.2.5 of Volume 9A);
- all changes to the RSI occurring during the reporting period should be discussed in the main text of the PSUR, and so superseded copies of RSI must be available to the PSUR author;
- meaningful differences between the RSI used in the PSUR and the current EU or national SPC should be described in the covering letter that accompanies the submission of the PSUR to the Competent Authorities.

Significant safety-related changes made to a product's approved prescribing information anywhere in the world should be described in the PSUR section "Update of Regulatory Authority or Marketing Authorisation Holder Actions taken for Safety Reasons" (see Section 6.3.4 of Volume 9A).

5.9 Review of Cumulative Data

In addition to presenting information in the form of line listings, information should also be presented in the PSUR in the form of summary tabulations. These tabulations should be based on the reports included in the line listings, as well as reports from other sources, such as reports and epidemiological databases (Table 5.1).

The summary tabulation for serious unlisted adverse reactions should contain cumulative data; that is, data derived from all cases received to date. This table should only contain events that are unlisted according to the RSI used to compile the PSUR (Section 5.8). Summary tabulations for serious listed, non-serious unlisted and non-serious listed adverse reactions should only contain data received during the period of the report. If the number of cases for inclusion in a particular summary tabulation is very small, or there are no cases for inclusion, then a narrative description or a statement that there are no cases rather than a table is considered acceptable.

Reviews of specific areas of concern should be cumulative rather than just focusing on data received during the period. This applies particularly to reviews requested by Competent Authorities in assessment reports of previous PSURs. If the area of concern has been reviewed in previous PSURs, then reference can be made to those PSURs. However, in these situations, a summary of the cumulative data should still be included.

5.10 Quality Control

Since the QPPV is responsible for the production of PSURs, he or she should ensure that there are formal processes and procedures in place to check the accuracy and completeness of the data presented in these reports (Section 1.4.2). This may be achieved by a combination of in-process checks (e.g. does the number of cases add up to the total expected), peer review and physician review. A MAH may want to consider documenting QC checks through the use of a QC checklist, for example.

5.11 Examples of Inspection Findings

Examples of areas of concern that have been identified during inspections are provided below. This is not an exhaustive list but serves to summarise some of the key points from this chapter and highlights areas that can be problematic. It is anticipated that examples will prove useful to help MAHs to address such issues.

(i)   PSURs are not being submitted at the required frequency and/or are being submitted late.

(ii)   The conclusion of the PSUR does not adequately reflect the data presented within the PSUR. For example, significant changes to the safety sections of the SPC are recommended throughout the PSUR, but the conclusion section states that there were no significant issues relating to changes in the risk–benefit profile of the product.

(iii)   PSURs do not contain all relevant individual case histories. The criteria used to select individual case histories for inclusion in a particular PSUR should always be clear. It is often simpler, and more transparent, to specify the criteria used to exclude cases from a particular PSUR.

(iv)   There is no system to ensure that PSURs contain cases received prior to the current reporting period, but for which significant follow-up information has been received within the current reporting period. Cases where follow-up information is not considered to have any impact on the overall assessment of the case, and has not led to relevant coding changes for the case, do not need to be discussed in the body of the PSUR.

(v)   There is no mechanism in place to ensure that Competent Authority requests made at the time of assessment of a PSUR are addressed in subsequent PSURs.

(vi)   The summary tabulation for serious unlisted adverse reactions only contains data from the period covered by the PSUR rather than cumulative data.

(vii)   When a PSUR concludes that a product's CCSI or SPC requires amending, no variation or timetable for its submission is submitted along with the PSUR.

(viii)   The meaningful differences between the RSI used to prepare the PSUR and the EU or national SPC for the product(s) are not described in the PSUR submission letter.

Current metrics relating to MHRA pharmacovigilance inspection findings can be found on our website. The exact nature of findings will vary from company to company and findings are graded on a case-by-case basis, taking into account the evidence relating to the issue and the impact of the finding on, for example, public safety or other areas of the pharmacovigilance system.

6

Evaluation of Safety Data

> **Editor's note** At the time a new medicine is approved for marketing, the experience of its safety is limited to its use in clinical trials, where generally a relatively small number of carefully selected patients are treated for a limited period of time. Even with large-scale clinical trials, some suspected adverse reactions may not be seen until significantly more people have received the medicine.
>
> During the post-authorisation period, larger and more diverse populations than those studied during the development of the product will be exposed to the drug, and possibly for longer periods that those studied. New information on the benefits and risks of the product will be generated, and evaluation of this information and any safety concerns should be an ongoing process, both by the MAH and by the Competent Authorities.
>
> Guidance on evaluation of pharmacovigilance data during the post-authorisation period can be found in Volume 9A, Part 1, Section 8.

6.1   General Considerations for Signal Detection

It is vital that the safety of all medicines is monitored throughout their marketed life. In order to do so, both the MAH and the Competent Authorities must have systems in place in order to fulfil the following responsibilities:

- ensuring that all sources of information are screened regularly to identify any potential signals;
- ensuring that appropriate action is taken in response to new evidence that impacts on the known risk–benefit balance;
- keeping the Competent Authorities, HCPs and patients informed of changes in the risk–benefit balance.

There are various sources of information and methods available to enable MAHs to perform signal detection activities. The methods used should be determined by the product portfolio and the number of reports of suspected adverse reactions received. However, all MAHs are expected to have in place systems and procedures for systematic signal detection.

All MAHs should have formal written procedural documents in place, such as SOPs, that adequately describe the way in which the MAH performs signal detection. These documents should provide detail about the roles and responsibilities of all personnel involved, the sources of information included in the analysis and the methods used for signal detection. In the DDPS included in EU marketing authorisation applications, the applicant is required to indicate whether their written procedures cover signal generation and review.

In addition, formal written procedural documents should describe what actions MAHs intend to take based on the outcomes generated from signal detection activities. This could include escalation procedures following identification of a potential signal, such as further analysis that will be undertaken or referral to a company committee.

The MAH is expected to document adequately its signal detection activities, including any outcomes or decisions taken during the course of these activities.

The MAH may have committed to particular signal detection activities as part of a RMP for a specific product. As such, the MAH will be expected to be carrying out the activities as described. The assessment of potential risks included in the RMP should guide the signal detection activities post-authorisation (Section 7.1)

6.2 Methods of Signal Detection

6.2.1 Individual case review

Individual case reports, from any source, can constitute an early warning of a potential signal, particularly a new unexpected adverse reaction. It would, therefore, be expected that the MAH has a system in place whereby individual reports are reviewed by an appropriately qualified person(s) to make the assessment of whether the individual report constitutes a potential signal. The quality of such reports and the amount of information provided will, of course, impact on the ability of the MAH to make such an assessment, and so it would be expected that the MAH has an appropriate system in place to follow up such reports (Section 3.3).

If a report that constitutes a potential signal were to originate from a consumer/patient, it would not be considered appropriate to disregard this report just because it is not medically confirmed. Again, it would be expected that appropriate follow-up procedures are in place for such reports in order to try to obtain confirmation of the report by a HCP. Even if the report is not medically confirmed, the MAH should still consider whether to initiate further investigations, taking into account such things as the quality of the report and the concerns raised by the reaction described within the report.

A single report of a suspected adverse reaction can only rarely be considered as a signal in itself. New reports should be routinely and systematically reviewed in the context of the existing cumulative data to see if they represent a potential new signal.

6.2.2   Systematic review of multiple case reports

The periodicity of systematic review of cumulative data for the purpose of signal detection is something the MAH should consider carefully, based on the amount of safety data received during a period, the type of products for which it holds marketing authorisations and the specific commitments made to Competent Authorities. Reporting rates can of course fluctuate (for example a media report can lead to a large increase in reports received by the MAH) and so the MAH should identify the way in which an increase in reporting rates for a particular product can be evaluated for its impact.

The legislation requires all MAHs to monitor the safety of their products. Systematic review of cumulative data is just as important a component of a pharmacovigilance system for a generics manufacturer as for an innovative pharmaceutical company. In some cases, generics manufacturers receive a smaller number of direct reports, in comparison to the innovator company, for example when generic products first enter the market. However, this situation may change, such as when the innovator product ceases to be actively marketed. In addition, new safety issues may be identified with generic products, such as reactions that only become apparent after many years or decades of use, interactions with other products or types of product that have recently been placed on the market, or as a result of changes in the way that the product is used. Counterfeiting of marketed products could potentially be detected from reviews of AEs, product technical complaints or lack of efficacy reports.

As can be seen from Figure 6.1, there are various methods for review of data as part of signal detection, ranging from manual review of individual cases to the use of computer algorithms for interrogation of drug-safety databases, sometimes known as "data mining". Every method has its pros and cons. Individual case review enables a person to evaluate fully every aspect of the case, but it can be resource intensive. Simple counts of the number of suspected adverse reactions or a frequency analysis can highlight the appearance of a new reaction or an increase in the occurrence of a known reaction. The MAH needs to consider at what point an increase in the number or frequency of a suspected adverse reaction becomes significant. Could it be because of other factors, such as an increase in sales (a surrogate measure for exposure)?

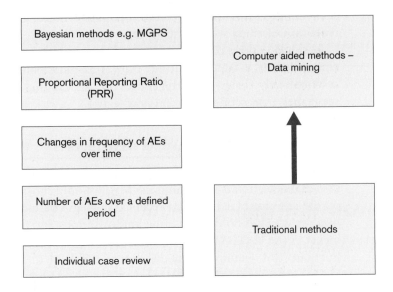

Figure 6.1 Methods of signal detection. MGPS, multi-item gamma Poisson shrinker.

Automated statistical methods used in the analysis of safety data include the proportional reporting ratio (PRR): the proportion of reports for a specific suspected adverse reaction for a medicinal product compared with the proportion for the same suspected adverse reaction for all other drugs. This method was used by the MHRA for signal detection purposes for a number of years. It does, however, require a large data set, and exceptionally high reporting of suspected adverse reactions of one type or in one system organ class can sometime suppress the detection of other signals for that drug or the same reaction with other drugs. A number of MAHs and Competent Authorities (including the MHRA) now employ empirical Bayesian methods, such as the multi-item gamma Poisson shrinker, for the purposes of signal detection. This is a disproportionality method that essentially works the same way as PRR, but unlike PRR it is more stable with small numbers as shrinkage is applied to avoid false positives. As for PRR, a large volume of data is required, although MAHs with smaller in-house data sets can pay to access large external databases such as the Adverse Event Reporting System of the US Food and Drug Administration or the Vigibase database of the World Health Organization (WHO), to supplement their data set. Use of automated tools for signal detection can help to save time when dealing with large data sets and may detect possible drug-safety issues earlier.

Whichever method is employed by MAHs for signal detection, certain criteria should apply, namely:

- the method used is appropriate for the MAH's data set; for example, the use of complex statistical tools may not be appropriate for MAHs with a small data set;
- that data from all appropriate sources are considered;
- MAHs have systems in place to assure the quality of their signal detection processes;
- that any outputs from cumulative data review are assessed by an appropriately qualified person in a timely manner;
- that the MAH takes timely and appropriate actions and decisions based on the outputs from cumulative data review;
- that the MAH adequately documents signal detection and evaluation.

Whichever cumulative data review method is used, it should enable the MAH to review data reported for a product during a specific period in the context of that previously reported, so that new unexpected reactions can be identified as well as changes in severity, characteristics or frequency of expected reactions. When considering how best to identify changes in the known adverse reaction profile, a MAH should carefully consider their search strategy. For example, how can a change in severity be identified from the MAH's data set? If a known reaction to a product is thrombocytopenia, will reports of "a drop in platelets" be included when assessing any change in frequency?

As with individual case review, inclusion of consumer reports in cumulative data reviews can yield important new safety information. If a potential signal arises from a review of consumer reports for which medical confirmation has not been received, then it would be expected that the MAH would initiate further investigations as appropriate.

6.2.3   Periodic Safety Update Reports

PSURs provide an opportunity for MAHs to review formally data that have been received in the period of the report, in addition to a cumulative review of certain data, such as SUSARs, and are, therefore, an important component of any MAH's signal detection system.

As with other sources of information, it is important that appropriate personnel review PSURs so that any potential signals can be identified and appropriate actions taken as necessary.

Further information on PSURs is provided in Chapter 5 of this Guide.

6.2.4   Other sources of information

In addition to the above sources, a MAH may have access to other sources of safety information that should be considered for inclusion in the signal detection process: for example information from new non-clinical research, post-authorisation studies, clinical trials or from initiatives such as registries and surveys. A company might also be alerted to a potential safety issue for investigation from either medical information enquiries or product technical complaint data. The MAH should, therefore, have systems and mechanisms in place so that such information is notified to the correct personnel and included in any signal detection activities.

Of note, the MAH should ensure that there are systems in place so that safety information is being notified to the pharmacovigilance department not only from research and development departments but also from other departments such as sales and marketing, who may run studies or other post-marketing initiatives where safety data are collected. In addition, studies or other initiatives undertaken in unauthorised indications may provide safety information that is relevant in the context of the authorised use. This should be clearly communicated to all departments (both research and development and others) involved in such activities.

Data published in the worldwide scientific literature or presented as abstracts, posters or communications form another potential source of information relevant to the evaluation of benefit and risk (Section 4.3).

The value of safety information from a range of sources for use in signal detection activities can be seen from Table 6.1, which gives examples of safety signals that have been detected by the MHRA as part of their routine signal detection process.

Table 6.1 Examples of signals identified by the MHRA that have led to a change in product information

Drug	Reaction	Source
Trazodone	Hyponatraemia	Yellow card
Nicorandil	Colovaginal fistula	Yellow card
Imatinib	Lichenoid keratosis	Yellow card (black triangle)
Ethinylestradiol and norelgestromin	Venous thrombosis	Published literature (post-marketing studies)
Domperidone	Electrocardiogram QT prolongation	Clinical trial
Co-trimoxazole	Rhabdomyolysis	Other regulatory authority; spontaneous reports

6.3 Investigation of Potential Signals

Potential signals will generally require further investigation to allow the MAH to come to a decision about whether their product caused the reaction in question. It is recommended that the MAH performs a review of the case(s) that prompted the initial signal alert in addition to performing a search for any additional cases and other information relevant to the issue. When performing such searches in spontaneous reporting databases, the MAH should carefully consider the search terms to be included to ensure that all relevant cases are retrieved. Standardised MedDRA queries should be used where available.

Investigation of signals is an iterative process and at each stage there should be consideration of the need for communication with regulatory authorities and/or implementation of risk-minimisation measures. It is strongly recommended that if risk-minimisation measures are being considered, the MAH contacts the appropriate Competent Authorities for discussion prior to their implementation. These decisions should be made on the basis of the strength of the evidence in support of a safety concern and the potential public health impact of the signal, if confirmed. Signals arising from case reports on suspected transmission of an infectious agent should be investigated as for other adverse reactions.

Whatever investigation method is chosen, it should be clear who will be involved in review of these additional data and ultimately who, whether it be an individual or committee, takes final responsibility for making the decision as to whether the data support a confirmed signal. As outlined in Chapter I.1 Section 2 of Volume 9A, the QPPV is responsible for the conduct of continuous overall pharmacovigilance evaluation during the post-authorisation period and so should routinely be kept up to date with all emerging safety concerns and be involved in any decision-making process (Section 1.4.4).

6.4 Follow-up of Potential Signals

When a new signal is identified, it is important not only to consider the potential increased risk but also to re-evaluate the benefit of the product to determine whether there is a change in its risk–benefit profile. Benefit is usually considered in terms of positive results for an individual or population, such as response rate or quality of life, and the probability of achieving such results. At the time of authorisation, such efficacy information would generally be available from pivotal company trials. Post-authorisation, additional information may be available from sources such as additional company-sponsored studies, published studies in the literature, or registries. Other points to consider in terms of benefit may be the level of patient compliance with treatment in naturalistic setting (as opposed to study conditions) and any information on misuse of the product.

When considering the risk–benefit profile, it is important to take into consideration the disease under treatment. For example, if the medicinal product is used to treat a condition associated with a high mortality, a high risk of SARs may be acceptable providing the benefits of the treatment are greater. Conversely, where a product provides symptom relief for a minor illness, acceptable risk levels would be low. Special considerations might apply when assessing acceptable risk for otherwise healthy recipients of medicines such as contraceptives or vaccines. Consideration should also be given to the availability of alternative therapies or interventions, where possible.

It is the responsibility of the MAH, and in particular the QPPV, to provide Competent Authorities with any information relevant to the risk–benefit profile of a medicinal product, including information on post-authorisation studies (Section 1.4). In the event of any such information becoming available, the MAH should immediately inform all the Competent Authorities in the countries where the product is authorised, and the EMEA as well in the case of centrally authorised products. If a MAH is unsure whether or not a potential signal is an issue of concern, early dialogue and consultation with the Competent Authority is strongly recommended.

PASS may be a useful way of validating signals identified from other sources. These may be requested by Competent Authorities or performed on the initiative of the MAH. As described in Volume 9A, PASS range in objectives and designs, but some examples include prescription-event monitoring, registries, cohort studies and case–control studies.

Information regarding RMPs is provided in Chapter 7. However, it is important to note that specific follow-up commitments made in RMPs do not obviate the need for routine signal detection activities.

6.5 Communication of Potential Signals

As highlighted above, it is the responsibility of the MAH, and in particular the QPPV, to notify the regulatory authorities immediately of any change in the balance of risks and benefits of their products. As part of this process, it would normally be expected that at some point the MAH would provide a data package relating to the potential signal. This should provide a comprehensive discussion of the issue in the context of the benefits of the product. As part of this document, data should be presented clearly and in an appropriate format. Analysis of the data undertaken by the MAH should be summarised to include any conclusions reached by the MAH.

Upon confirmation of a new signal for a product, the following actions may be initiated either by the MAH or by the Competent Authority:

- variation of the SPC or PIL (Chapter 8);
- provision of safety information directly to HCPs and/or patients or the public, for example through letters or the company's website.

It should be noted that the legislation requires that MAHs must not communicate information relating to safety issues to HCPs, patients or the public without first or simultaneously notifying the Competent Authorities. The content of such communications and the timeframe for their distribution should, in general, be agreed with the relevant Competent Authorities prior to distribution.

6.5.1 Direct Healthcare Professional Communications

Detailed guidance on Direct Healthcare Professional Communications (DHPCs) is contained in Part IV of Volume 9A. Scenarios in which a DHPC is usually required include suspension, withdrawal or revocation of a marketing authorisation with the recall of the product for safety reasons or important changes to the SPC in relation to safety. Other situations where a DHPC should be considered include confirmation that a product is not as efficacious as previously thought; encouragement of close monitoring of patients for a suspected, but not yet confirmed, safety issue; or provision of information in relation to an issue that has been subject to significant media coverage.

A DHPC is a key tool in providing prescribers with up-to-date information on the safety of a product. As such it should:

- be clear, concise and to the point;
- be objective and not include statements that might constitute advertising;
- provide an explanation as to why the letter is being circulated at a particular time;
- provide recommendations on how to minimise the risk (if known);
- place the safety concern in the context of the overall benefit of the treatment;
- provide contact information to allow HCPs to contact the company for further information, such as for the company's medical information department.

A template for DHPCs is available in Section 5.4.1 of Part IV of Volume 9A. Internal distribution of DHPCs is discussed in Chapter 10.

Letters that have been sent to HCPs are available on the MHRA website at www.mhra.gov.uk/mhra/HealthcareProfessionalLetters. This includes letters that originate from MAHs and also letters issued by the MHRA.

6.6 Counterfeit Medicines

One of the wider issues relevant to patient safety is counterfeit medicines. There are no requirements placed upon MAHs within the pharmacovigilance legislation regarding counterfeit medicines. Indeed, in the strictest sense, a counterfeit product does not "belong" to the MAH; however, it is in the interest of public safety for the MAH to work closely with the MHRA in handling such situations, although they are not responsible for the manufacture of such products. Information on pharmaceutical quality is very relevant for the assessment of risks.

The supply of counterfeit medicines and medical devices is a growing problem worldwide. The WHO estimates that up to 1% of medicines available in the developed world are likely to be counterfeit. This figure rises to 10% globally, although in some developing countries they estimate one-third of medicines are counterfeit.

Counterfeit medicine available in the UK originally focused upon "lifestyle" medicines, including erectile dysfunction and weight-loss medicines. Worryingly, counterfeiters are now also focusing on "life-saving medicines", including cancer and heart medicines. All counterfeit medicines are dangerous. They may have little, none or too much of the required quantity of the active ingredient. All of these scenarios could present significant risk of harm to the patient.

In the UK since 2004, there have been nine recalls of counterfeit medicines that had reached pharmacy and patient levels. A further five cases were discovered during the same period at the wholesaler level before they reached the market.

From a patient safety point of view, MAHs should consider how information relating to counterfeiting of their products is handled.

- How is the QPPV notified of counterfeiting issues?
- Who is responsible for reporting suspicions to the MHRA?
- How is information communicated to other areas of the organisation, such as the medical information department, in order to respond appropriately to any enquiries?
- Would knowledge about a counterfeit prompt a review of any safety data, for example ICSRs associated with a given batch number?
- Does the MAH have processes and procedures in place to facilitate the detection of counterfeits and subsequent incident handling?
- Is there an awareness within the MAH of potential counterfeit issues relating to products that the MAH markets, and what mechanisms are used to address this?

The MHRA has made it easier to report potential counterfeit incidents by setting up a 24-hour dedicated reporting hotline that can be accessed by email on counterfeit@mhra.gsi.gov.uk, through the website (www.mhra.gov.uk) or by phone on 020 7084 2701.

6.7 Examples of Inspection Findings

Examples of areas of concern that have been identified during inspections are provided below. This is not an exhaustive list, but serves to summarise some of the key points from this chapter and highlights areas that can be problematic. It is anticipated that examples will prove useful to help MAHs to address such issues.

(i)   The MAH has not implemented a formal and routine procedure for signal generation/trend analysis, except for that performed at the time of PSUR production. As highlighted in this chapter, the requirements for ongoing safety evaluation of medicinal products apply to all MAHs, irrespective of product portfolio, although the logistics of how signal detection activities are performed may vary. If a MAH is only analysing its safety data at the time of PSUR production, which could be only once every three years for older products, then they must have a strong rationale for this approach, which will need to be justified at the time of a Competent Authority inspection.

(ii) The MAH does not have adequate procedures/documentation in place relating to its safety detection activities. Examples have been seen during inspection where MAHs are performing adequate signal detection activities, but these activities are either not well described in company procedures or poorly documented. As with all pharmacovigilance activities, it is important that a MAH adheres to good documentation practices. This is especially important when key decisions have been made on the basis of signal detection activities, such as an update to a CCSI or SPC.

Current metrics relating to MHRA pharmacovigilance inspection findings can be found on our website. The exact nature of findings will vary from company to company and findings are graded on a case-by-case basis, taking into account the evidence relating to the issue and the impact of the finding on, for example, public safety or other areas of the pharmacovigilance system.

CHAPTER

7

Risk Management Plans

Editor's note A risk management system can be defined as a set of pharmacovigilance activities and interventions designed to identify, characterise, prevent or minimise risks relating to medicinal products, and the assessment of the effectiveness of those interventions. A RMP is a mechanism by which such a risk management system can be presented to Competent Authorities

The format of RMPs was developed through the ICH. The relevant guideline, ICH E2E was adopted in November 2004 and implemented in the EU in late 2005. Guidance issued by the CHMP may be found on the EMEA website (http://www.emea.europa.eu). In summary, RMPs are required with marketing authorisation applications for:

- all new active substances;
- significant changes to marketing authorisations (e.g. new indication, new formulation) unless the Competent Authority agrees it is unnecessary;
- when an unexpected new hazard is identified (this may be requested by the national Competent Authority).

It is important to note that there are differences between the EU RMP, and the US RiskMAP. The US RiskMAP most closely reflects the purpose of the risk-minimisation section of the EU RMP by concentrating on the measures proposed to minimise the identified risks.

7.1 Purpose

All medicinal products are associated with some risks, and the broad purpose of RMPs is to ensure that these are actively managed in order, as far as possible, to minimise SARs in users. The specific objectives of RMPs are threefold:

(i)   to specify what is and is not known about *safety* at the time of authorisation;

(ii) to make a plan with milestones indicating how safety knowledge will be extended post-authorisation;

(iii) where necessary, to define the necessary measures to minimise known risks and monitor the success of these measures.

A template for the creation of EU RMPs is available from the EMEA website and applicants are strongly encouraged to provide the RMP in this format as far as is practical.

7.2   Content of the European Union Risk Management Plan

The EU RMP is in two parts. Part 1 contains the safety specification and pharmacovigilance plan; Part 2 contains the risk-minimisation plan.

7.2.1   Safety specification

The safety specification is a summary of the known safety profile of the product and includes exposure data from clinical trials and post-authorisation use. Any identified safety issues are discussed in this section as are potential safety issues and various aspects related to the use of the product, such as the potential for misuse, abuse or off-label use. An important aspect of the safety specification is the epidemiology section, which should present information on the population likely to be exposed to the product (target population) and the relevant co-morbidities in this population.

7.2.2   Pharmacovigilance plan

The pharmacovigilance plan is primarily designed to document product-specific pharmacovigilance measures that relate to the identified/potential risks discussed in the safety specification, and to extending the safety knowledge of the product. There should not be a lengthy presentation of the routine pharmacovigilance activities (e.g. signal detection), which would be covered in the DDPS.

The pharmacovigilance plan should document for each identified or potential risk what specific measures will be used to monitor the risk and gather further information, in addition to any studies planned to extend safety knowledge on the product. This can include routine pharmacovigilance but may also include pharmacoepidemiology studies or (pre)clinical studies.

7.2.3   Risk minimisation

The risk-minimisation part of the RMP should provide a description of the measures that will be required to minimise the risk for each identified and potential risk mentioned in the safety specification. Specific risk-minimisation measures are not necessarily required for each product; however, if no specific risk-minimisation measures are intended, justification must be provided that routine measures (such as the SPC and PIL) will adequately address any identified or potential risks.

When RMPs are updated, reference to this should be included in PSURs. If there has been no update to the RMP during the period of the PSUR, a statement to this effect should also be included.

7.3 Key Assessment Issues

It is important to note that not all products will have RMPs. The RMPs are designed to be relatively short stand-alone documents that are assessed and agreed with the company prior to authorisation and at various milestones. Updates to RMPs are generally provided with the PSUR but should also be provided when milestones, such as the end of planned studies, are reached. This is particularly relevant after the product has moved from six-monthly PSURs, or in the event of a RMP being requested for an older product with a new safety issue. If there have been no updates to the RMP at the time of PSUR preparation, a clear statement to this effect should generally be included.

Prior to a Competent Authority inspection, a MAH may be asked to provide a list of their products that have associated active RMPs together with a list of associated ongoing studies, milestones, etc., for each RMP.

During an inspection, any identified RMPs could be inspected for the following documentation: safety specification, pharmacovigilance plan, risk minimisation and any other relevant information.

7.3.1 Safety specification

This should contain the following information, within the specified sections of the RMP.

- Initial RMP (or for a change in indication, etc.) should contain projected usage patterns, projected population exposure and projected market position in Section 1.4.1.
- Updates to the EU RMP should contain actual post-authorisation usage data in Section 1.4.2.
- Any regulatory action taken (worldwide) should be clearly documented in Section 1.4.3.
- Any new safety issues arising since the last RMP update should be clearly documented in Section 1.5.1.

The activities surrounding the collection and analysis of the information in this section may be examined during inspection; for example, whether all relevant sources have been identified and utilised when assessing unlicensed use, or whether safety signals that have been identified since the approval of the RMP are used to inform RMP update decisions.

7.3.2 Pharmacovigilance plan

Completed studies: summaries of the studies completed since the last RMP update should be in the safety specification, and the pharmacovigilance plan should be updated to reflect the fact that the study is completed.

Ongoing studies should show that:

- relevant protocols, protocol amendments are in place;
- relevant contract(s) with external organisations are in place;
- relevant interim reports have been provided to the relevant national Competent Authority;
- correct procedures for notification of adverse reactions are in place.

Progress on these activities could be reviewed at the time of an inspection to ascertain whether the MAH is undertaking what has been presented, and that appropriate pharmacovigilance processes are being applied and adhered to.

7.3.3 Risk minimisation

Criteria for verifying the success of proposed risk-minimisation measures and a proposed review period of the measures should be included in Section 4 of the RMP. Relevant reports within the inspection timelines should be available on request.

7.3.4 Other information

- Date for next review should be included on the plan.
- Contact points should be current.

7.4 Examples of Issues

By the end of 2007, the MHRA had assessed approximately 100 RMPs. This experience has shown that there are very few "all good" or "all bad" RMPs, but in order to provide guidance to MAHs some examples of problems identified during the assessment of RMPs are provided below.

(i) RMPs tend to focus on what is already known rather than identifying the areas in which information is lacking.

(ii) Information is poorly presented, with long and complicated tables. This does not facilitate the assessment process.

(iii) The relevance of the epidemiology of the disease to the target indication is not sufficiently considered. For example, the proposed new indication for a given drug is for a specific complication of poorly controlled type 2 diabetes mellitus. Several pages of information are provided describing the epidemiology of type 2 diabetes, without any reference to the target indication.

(iv) The pharmacovigilance plan emphasises routine pharmacovigilance rather than concentrating on product-specific measures.

(v) Insufficient time is allowed to develop study protocols.

(vi) Milestones are not well defined in the pharmacovigilance plan.

(vii) Justification is often not provided by the MAH when it is considered that extra measures are not required in the risk-minimisation section.

(viii) Promotional activities are not separated from risk-minimisation activities; for example educational materials are not necessarily risk-minimisation tools and should not be routinely included in the RMP.

(ix) Plans for monitoring the success of risk-minimisation activities are often lacking.

(x) Discrepancies exist between the DDPS and the pharmacovigilance plan, because of a failure of communication between the different groups within organisations responsible for writing the different documents or sections within the documents.

RMPs can be used to support existing pharmacovigilance activities to understand more fully the safety profile of a product. In essence, the RMP is a means by which the MAH can assure itself, Competent Authorities and the public of how the safety of the medicine will be specifically monitored and the risk to public health minimised.

Reference Safety Information

Editor's note RSI has various functions within the area of pharmacovigilance. This section of the guide looks at the types and uses of RSI, considers some of the issues relating to control and maintenance of these documents, and also highlights some of the common inspection findings in this area. RSI is of primary importance to prescribers and patients, who rely on information provided by MAHs to make decisions relating to the safe and effective use of medicinal products.

8.1 Types of Reference Safety Information

There are various types of document that are used as RSI. Some examples are:

- Developmental Core Safety Information (DCSI)/Developmental Core Data Sheet (DCDS)
- investigator brochures (IBs)
- Company Core Safety Information (CCSI)/Company Core Data Sheet (CCDS)
- Summaries of Product Characteristics (SPC)
- patient information leaflets (PILs)
- product monographs.

8.2 Uses of Reference Safety Information

The above documents play a key role in pharmacovigilance in that they act as a primary information source on the safety of a product for HCPs and patients. RSI also has important roles to play within companies. In the context of expedited and periodic reporting, RSI documents are used to assess the expectedness of ICSRs or serious adverse events (SAEs) from clinical trials and the listedness of adverse reactions reported within PSURs. RSI can also be used as the basis for the production of promotional materials.

8.3   Availability of Reference Safety Information

It is important that each type of RSI is available to all relevant members of staff (Chapter 10). Members of the medical information department need to have access to up-to-date SPCs, as do medical representatives. Staff involved in the processing of ICSRs should have access to RSI (SPCs, IBs, CCSIs and/or DCSIs) appropriate to their role. For clinical trials, concerned investigators, ethics committees and Competent Authorities must be provided with up-to-date copies of the IB. Access to RSI may be provided via paper copies or electronic documents. Within the company, the latter may be accessible via internal or external websites or via shared areas on a company server. To ensure that accidental changes cannot be made to these documents, they should be made available in a read-only format.

8.4   Consistency Between Different Types of Reference Safety Information

Given the different types of RSI available and the various uses of such documents, it is possible that they may contain different information. However, it is important that companies are alert to these differences, have a sound scientific/medical rationale for them, assess their impact on pharmacovigilance processes and, where possible, aim to harmonise these documents.

Use of CCSI is one way to facilitate this, as this contains the minimum information that should be present in all documents relating to the safety of a given product.

When a change is made to one document in the RSI, there should be a mechanism in place to evaluate the impact of the change on other documents in the RSI and on other company documents that may be based on the RSI. For example, when a change is made to a SPC, an assessment should be made as to whether equivalent changes should be made to other SPCs for related products and to the CCSI/CCDS, PIL, abbreviated prescribing information, any associated promotional materials, IBs (where applicable), etc. Such assessments and any subsequent decisions and actions should be documented.

8.5 Updates to Reference Safety Information

8.5.1 Triggers for updates

Regardless of its use, it is vital that RSI is kept up to date. There are several reasons that may trigger an update to RSI, such as newly identified AEs, changes in the frequency of a known reaction, new information about drug interactions, additional warnings, precautions or contraindications. Changes may either be requested by a Competent Authority or proposed by the MAH as a result of:

- analysis of data in the PSUR;
- analysis of data from clinical trials;
- ongoing safety-monitoring activities;
- review of competitor/reference product RSI.

8.5.2 Labelling committees

Depending on the size of the organisation and its product portfolio, some MAHs utilise labelling committees to review and approve proposed changes to RSI.

If this is the case, it is expected that procedural documentation is in place that describes the activities of these meetings, for example defining the frequency of meetings, the mandate of the committee, required/optional attendees, the types of information considered by the committee, the method for documenting decisions made and any escalation process.

Regardless of whether a labelling committee is involved in the decision-making process, it is expected that a MAH will document and maintain records of decisions on whether or not to update product information, and the rationale for doing so. During Competent Authority inspections, the appropriateness of decisions taken as to whether or not to update a SPC may be examined.

Where it is assessed that there is insufficient evidence to warrant a change to RSI, but alternative action is proposed (e.g. monitoring of individual case reports of a particular event), there needs to be a mechanism in place to ensure that this alternative action is undertaken.

8.5.3 Points to consider

It is vital that when changes are made to RSI, all relevant parties are notified and that approvals are obtained where required. Notification is not limited to company personnel but may extend to external partners, contract service providers, clinical trial investigators, Competent Authorities, ethics committees and external reference sources such as the electronic Medicines Compendium (eMC) website (http://emc.medicines.org.uk/). MAHs should, therefore, implement mechanisms to identify these parties and provide assurance that they have the most up-to-date version of a RSI document. For example, notification of an approved, updated SPC or IB could be accompanied by an acknowledgement form (electronic or paper based) that the recipient would be required to complete and return to confirm receipt. Such completed acknowledgement forms would then be collated and reviewed to ensure that all recipients had responded. Failure to return an acknowledgement form would trigger the sender to follow up with the recipient.

It is also important to remove out-of-date copies of documents from circulation. It may be sufficient to inform staff to destroy old copies; alternatively, it may be more appropriate to request staff to return their old copies for destruction. At least one master copy of superseded RSI documents needs to be retained and archived by the MAH. In addition, for the purposes of PSUR production, staff may need access to CCSIs and SPCs that were current at the beginning of a PSUR period. Therefore, the MAH needs to ensure that appropriate staff will have access to superseded copies if required.

To allow individuals and organisations to identify whether or not they have the most up-to-date copy of a RSI document, such documents should be date and version controlled.

In addition to procedures concerning the maintenance and implementation of RSI and product labelling, MAHs should have additional procedures covering the processing and implementation of urgent safety restrictions (Section 10.4.1).

8.6 Timelines

8.6.1 Timelines for periodic review

It is good practice to review the RSI periodically to ensure that it is up to date and accurately reflects the knowledge currently available about the product. IBs should be reviewed at least annually and revised as necessary. The requirements for updating SPCs are less well defined, although Directive 2001/83/EC requires that the information should be updated on a "regular basis".

8.6.2 Timelines for updates

Once a decision has been made that an update to a RSI document is required, it is important that the change is managed in a timely fashion. The overall process comprises several steps, such as the review of evidence for the proposed change, agreeing wording, compiling the variation documentation (where required), awaiting approval by the Competent Authority (where required), notifying relevant parties of approved updates and implementing changes into product packaging and other materials within an appropriate timeframe.

Although it is not possible to define a timeline for the whole process (e.g. approval by the Competent Authority is out of the control of the MAH), it is expected that the MAH will identify and keep track of key milestones. The MAH should ensure that updates to SPCs and PILs are performed without undue delay, as they provide vital information to patients and prescribers that will impact upon patient safety.

In some circumstances, a Competent Authority may define timelines for the implementation of a change to a RSI. In any case, it is expected that MAHs will have defined timelines relating to:

- circulating updated RSI to appropriate parties (including company personnel, partners and contractors) following Competent Authority approval;
- implementing changes to SPCs in associated product information, such as PILs;
- updating external reference sources such as the eMC website, *British National Formulary*, *Monthly Index of Medical Specialties*, etc.

8.7 Introduction of New Labels and Patient Information Leaflets Following Approval of Changes

The regulations require that a product should comply with any changes from the actual date on which the change was approved. However, in common with other changes to marketing authorisations, companies are expected to implement new approved labelling within three to six months of its approval, subject to production schedules. In circumstances where a safety issue is involved, the expedited implementation of new product information may be necessary and is something the Competent Authorities may insist on. For example, the MHRA may require the quarantining and repackaging of existing stock.

Where a MAH is unable to adhere to the three to six month timescale, they should contact the MHRA for advice on how to proceed.

8.8 Considerations for Herbal Products

Many herbal medicines on the UK market are older products. In some cases, the product information may not have been reviewed for some years and may, therefore, not fully reflect current knowledge and philosophy. Alongside this historic position, the current view on information relevant to the safe usage of a growing number of specific herbal medicinal products is becoming available through two related developments following introduction of Directive 2004/24/EC on traditional herbal medicinal products. First, products are progressively being registered under the UK's traditional herbal registration scheme. These products have been assessed by the MHRA and reflect the agency's current view on the appropriate information required for the safe usage of the herbal medicine in question. Second, the EMEA is publishing a growing number of EC herbal product monographs drawn up by the Committee on Herbal Medicinal Products. These monographs include detailed information on the safe usage of the product. Member States are required to take account of these monographs, but they are not binding. On the basis of early experience in the operation of Directive 2004/24/EC, it is likely that the MHRA will often be in agreement with all or most of the information on safe usage contained in the monographs of the Committee on Herbal Medicinal Products, but there are likely to be some cases where the MHRA has a divergent view on one or more specific elements.

Updating product information for older herbal products will need careful management as this is a complex issue. The MHRA will discuss proposals with industry and issue further guidance as necessary.

In the meantime, companies should await any specific instructions from the MHRA, which may be given on a case by case basis:

- as to whether their product information for herbal products with marketing authorisations or traditional herbal registrations should be updated to reflect new or revised monographs published by the EMEA;
- as to whether product information for herbal products with an existing marketing authorisation should be updated in the light of product information for related products that have subsequently been approved via the traditional herbal registration scheme.

8.9   Examples of Inspection Findings

Examples of areas of concern that have been identified during inspections are provided below. This is not an exhaustive list but serves to summarise some of the key points from this chapter and highlights areas that can be problematic. It is anticipated that examples will prove useful to help MAHs to address such issues.

(i)   The MAH does not have an effective mechanism for controlling RSI, such as SPCs/PILs, and ensuring that employees have access to the most current version. Using out-of-date RSI may result in provision of inaccurate information to prescribers or members of the public, and in inaccurate assessments of ICSRs.

(ii) The eMC website does not display the most up-to-date version of the SPCs. The eMC website is widely used by HCPs as a source of product information and it is vital that the information displayed is accurate and up to date. MAHs should have processes and procedures in place to ensure that this is addressed.

(iii) The most recent version of the product SPC does not display the black triangle symbol, which indicates to HCPs that the product is subject to intensive monitoring. Although it is not a statutory requirement to display the black triangle symbol, it is a common industry practice to do so. The Commission on Human Medicines and the MHRA wish to receive all reports of suspected adverse reactions associated with black triangle products from HCPs, in order to confirm the risk–benefit profile of the drug, to increase understanding of the safety profile of new medicines and to ensure that previously unrecognised adverse reactions are identified as quickly as possible. By removing the black triangle symbol from product information such as the SPC, HCPs would be led to believe that the product is no longer subject to intensive monitoring and they would no longer continue to submit reports of non-serious adverse reaction to the company and/or the Yellow Card Scheme. MAHs should ensure that all SPCs for black triangle status products have the symbol to enable prescribers to identify the additional reporting requirements for these products.

(iv) The date being used for Section 10 of the SPC (date of revision of text) is not consistent with SPC guidelines. The MAH uses the date that the SPC was approved internally, which was prior to the submission to the Competent Authorities, rather than the date of approval by the Competent Authority. The date of revision of the text provides an easy way to identify or verify that the version of the SPC to which a member of staff is referring is the most up-to-date.

(v) No minutes of meetings of the labelling committee are produced. Therefore, the rationale for decisions made at these meetings is not transparent.

(vi) Once a new safety issue has been identified, there are unacceptable delays in submitting variations for changes to SPCs. Company procedures should facilitate timely submission of variations to ensure there is no undue delay in updating documents (such as SPCs and PILs) relied upon by prescribers and patients to make decisions relating to the safe and effective use of medicinal products.

(vii) Differences between RSI documents, such as the SPC and the IB, may impact on expedited reporting decisions. If a reaction is listed in the IB but not in the SPC, a report of that term originating from a spontaneous source would be considered unexpected and would qualify for expedited reporting, but a report of the same term originating from an interventional trial would be considered expected and would not qualify for expedited reporting. Consequently, this affects the effectiveness of review of the data on an ongoing basis by Competent Authorities. This is discussed further in Section 12.3.3.

Current metrics relating to MHRA pharmacovigilance inspection findings can be found on our website. The exact nature of findings will vary from company to company and findings are graded on a case-by-case basis, taking into account the evidence relating to the issue and the impact of the findings on, for example, public safety or other areas of the pharmacovigilance system.

9

Quality Management System

| Editor's note | The MAH must have a quality management system in place to support the pharmacovigilance activities that have been implemented to meet pharmacovigilance legislation and guidelines. Essential features of the quality management system include clearly documented procedures, adequate training of staff, QC and QA procedures and sound record retention policies. |

9.1 Written Procedures

An essential element of any pharmacovigilance system is that there are clear written procedures in place to ensure that the system functions properly, that the roles and responsibilities and required tasks are clear to all parties involved and that there is provision for proper control and, when needed, change of the system.

Written procedures may take the form of SOPs, policy documents, working practices, guidelines, work instructions, etc. All types of procedure that have been implemented to meet the pharmacovigilance legislation and guidelines must be:

(i) reflective of the requirements in pharmacovigilance legislation and guidance;

(ii) written and reviewed by adequately trained personnel;

(iii) approved by personnel within the MAH who have appropriate authority;

(iv) distributed to and immediately available to all appropriate members of the MAH (and any other parties performing work on behalf of the MAH) once the procedures are effective; a period of time between approval of the procedure and the procedure becoming effective should be considered to allow for the training of relevant personnel;

(v) reviewed on a periodic basis to ensure that they accurately reflect current practice.

Any significant deviations from procedures relating to pharmacovigilance activities should be documented.

Where activities have been contracted out to third parties by the MAH, relevant procedures may be written and controlled by the contractor, but the MAH should review these procedures to ensure that they are adequate and compliant with applicable requirements. Copies of these procedures should be retained, by either the contractor or the MAH or both.

Figure 9.1 indicates topics that should usually be covered by written procedures. This is not an exclusive list and some topics may not be relevant to all MAHs. A procedure may cover one or more of the topics, or one topic may have one or more procedures depending on its complexity and the organisation of the company. For further details, please refer to Part 1, Section 2.2.2 (c) of Volume 9A.

Case processing
Collection and processing
of ICSRs from different sources
Follow-up procedures
Duplicate case detection
Expedited reporting
Electronic reporting

Activities of the QPPV

Ongoing safety evaluation
Signal detection and review
Risk management and
minimisation systems

Periodic reporting
PSURs
ASRs

Regulatory
Response to requests for
information from Competent
Authorities
Handling urgent safety restrictions
Handling safety variations and
labelling changes
Meeting commitments to
Competent Authorities

Clinical trial activities
Investigator notifications
Updates to Investigator
Brochures
Safety monitoring boards
SAE processing and expedited
reporting

General
Creation and control of procedural documents
Training
Archiving
QA activities
Management and use of databases

Figure 9.1 Suggested topics to be covered by written procedures. ASR, Annual Safety Report; ICSR, Individual Case Safety Report; PSUR, Periodic Safety Update Report; QA, quality assurance; QPPV, Qualified Person for Pharmacovigilance; SAE, serious adverse event.

If the MAH employs both global and local procedures for pharmacovigilance activities, for example at headquarter and affiliate offices, adequate processes should be implemented to ensure that the procedures correctly reflect applicable requirements and are consistent with each other.

It is important that MAHs control their procedural documents to ensure that staff are working to the current approved procedure. Ways in which this can be achieved include version and date control of procedures, controlled distribution of procedures and controlled access to procedural documents for updating purposes. It is considered good practice for MAHs to have in place a procedural document that sets out how SOPs and other procedural documents are to be controlled. It is recommended that this includes such things as the maximum period of review for different types of procedural document, the update and approval process, the distribution of and training on new or updated procedural documents and the policy for storage of both current and superseded procedures.

9.2 Training

Staff should be appropriately trained for performing pharmacovigilance-related activities. Refresher training should be provided as appropriate. Personnel working in the drug-safety function should receive training in applicable pharmacovigilance legislation and guidelines in addition to specific training in process activities for which they are responsible and/or undertake. Personnel working in other departments who receive or process safety reports, such as sales personnel, medical information officers, clinical research staff and, in some companies, legal personnel, should also be adequately trained.

In terms of other staff members, all personnel in the MAH, including those working on a contract or temporary basis, could potentially be made aware of an AE or other pharmacovigilance information relating to one of the MAH's products, for example pregnancy, lack of efficacy, overdose. Therefore, all personnel should receive an appropriate level of training that would allow them to identify such situations and process the information appropriately. Other personnel working for the MAH or working on behalf of the MAH may require training to meet specific requirements for the management of safety information, for example the management of safety information in clinical trials by clinical trial staff at investigator sites.

The following is a checklist of what a basic training package for use in training all staff should generally include:

- WHAT is an AE;
- WHAT other safety information needs to be collected, such as pregnancies, reports of lack of effect, etc.;
- WHAT type of information to try to collect if a person becomes aware of the above, such as contact details for reporter or source of report (literature, lay press, website), information on the patient, information on the event and information on the product;
- WHO to report the information to, including contact details of where to send the report, such as an email address or telephone/fax number;
- HOW to report the information, such as the format and method of reporting;
- WHEN the information needs to be reported, such as within 24 hours or as soon as possible.

It must be stressed that if a person becomes aware of a potential AE or other safety concern, then they should notify the appropriate person(s) even if only minimal information is available.

A company may also consider including an outline of the basic principles of pharmacovigilance and why pharmacovigilance is important as part of their training package. However, the training should be kept as simple and as clear as possible so that all staff members are able to understand what they are required to do. A mechanism for ensuring understanding of what is required by each employee may also be appropriate following the training, such as a short quiz. (See also Chapter 10 for refresher training.)

With regards to the training system, it is recommended to include formal training plans tailored to the individual needs of pharmacovigilance personnel (to ensure they are, and remain, appropriately trained for their role). The formal training plan should cover key training required to perform the function. This may include safety database training, MedDRA coding, ICSR assessments as well as mandatory SOP training. A system for recording self-learning, for example reading of legislation and guidance documentation, may be appropriate. This is perhaps particularly relevant to the trainers themselves, who have to keep abreast of changes in pharmacovigilance requirements and may not necessarily receive formal training.

Training records, CVs and job descriptions are required to provide evidence of the experience, responsibilities and training of personnel.

In addition to formal training activities, MAHs could consider making use of other methods of information sharing, such as:

- posters in coffee points;
- company newsletters or bulletins;

- webpage about adverse drug reaction reporting and the responsibilities of individuals;
- credit card sized aide mémoires.

9.3   Quality Assurance

There is a need to provide assurance that the MAH's pharmacovigilance obligations are being met and also to identify any deficiencies in the pharmacovigilance system. A mechanism must, therefore, be in place to provide assurance that activities are being performed in accordance with the pharmacovigilance legislation, guidelines, the MAH's procedures and good pharmacovigilance practice (GPvP).

The scope of the QA activities, for example auditing, should include all activities that are in place in the MAH to meet the pharmacovigilance legislation and guidelines, for example activities in drug-safety functions and functions that interface with drug safety. For global systems, this would include all relevant geographical sites that are involved in the collection, processing or analysis of safety data. QA activities are also required where the MAH has contracted out any pharmacovigilance tasks or functions.

The frequency and scope of QA activities, for example auditing, should be commensurate with the extent and complexity of the pharmacovigilance system. A risk-based approach may be appropriate provided that the MAH is able to provide a rationale to its approach. QA audits must be performed by personnel who are independent from the pharmacovigilance system and who are appropriately trained. Some scenarios below provide examples of the expectations with regard to QA audits.

SCENARIO 1

A small organisation does not have the appropriate experience and resource to enable it to carry out pharmacovigilance activities. Therefore, it is decided to outsource all activities to a specialised pharmacovigilance contractor(s). In this situation, outsourcing is an appropriate option. However, the MAH needs to gain assurance that the service and facilities offered by the contractor(s) are fit for purpose and will meet the needs of the MAH. It is expected that the MAH arranges for a pre-agreement assessment or vendor audit to be conducted, prior to commencing work with the contractor(s). Periodic audits may be appropriate after work has started. Without relevant pharmacovigilance experience, it may be difficult for the MAH to undertake these checks themselves, but it is not acceptable for the MAH to assume that the contractor is able to fulfil all of their pharmacovigilance requirements. A sophisticated website or glossy promotional magazine does not necessarily equate to a high-quality organisation. Ultimately, the MAH retains legal responsibility for fulfilling pharmacovigilance obligations and should be confident that the organisation is getting the service it requires from the contractor.

SCENARIO 2

The MAH has personnel with pharmacovigilance experience, but there is insufficient resource to undertake all of the pharmacovigilance activities required. Therefore, some aspects of the pharmacovigilance activities are contracted to a third party. As with scenario 1, it is expected that the MAH provides themself with assurance that the contractor is able to meet the needs. The scope and frequency of ongoing audits may depend on the type of activities being conducted by the contractor.

It is important to note that the contractor, in effect, becomes part of the MAH's pharmacovigilance system and therefore contractors should be held to the same standards.

SCENARIO 3

Where the MAH has contractual agreements with licensing partners, the MAH should have adequate oversight of the activities of the licensing partner, for example through QA audits, provision of reports or regular documented meetings.

An example of poor practice observed during pharmacovigilance inspections is that when procedures are audited, the auditor is looking to ensure that personnel work according to SOPs, but there is no check to ensure that the procedures are compliant with the applicable legislation and guidance. Although the content of a procedure may be under the responsibility of the author, this is something that should be reviewed during audits. The issue of whether or not a member of staff is working in compliance with SOPs becomes irrelevant to a certain degree if the procedure does not enable the MAH to meet the legislative requirements.

Another issue that is seen with pharmacovigilance audits relates to the choice of auditor. It is important that an auditor has appropriate understanding of the pharmacovigilance legislation in order to be able to assess whether the MAH is meeting the requirements of the legislation and is independent of the activities being audited.

In some areas of good practice issues (GxP), self-audits are recommended. With regard to pharmacovigilance systems, this can be a very useful exercise in terms of QC checks but is not considered to be an independent check and on its own would not be considered to provide sufficient assurance to the MAH that the system is functioning properly.

Records of audits that are planned and conducted should be distributed to the appropriate personnel, including the QPPV. Following issue of the report, there should be a system in place to monitor that appropriate corrective and preventative action has been taken. The system should also allow for escalation of issues to appropriate personnel if, for example, there is a dispute over an audit finding or corrective and preventative action has not been taken. Records of audits that are planned and conducted should be retained.

9.4 Record Retention

The MAH is required to maintain detailed records of all suspected adverse reactions occurring either in the EC or in a third country.

Facilities should be provided for the secure storage and retrieval of pharmacovigilance documentation. Archive design and archive conditions should protect contents from untimely destruction (e.g. protection from damage by water, fire, light and pests).

Competent Authorities may request pharmacovigilance data at any time and, therefore, data must be stored for an indefinite period. If the MAH wishes to destroy pharmacovigilance documentation, or to destroy paper records after transferring the information into an electronic format, the MAH should first perform an appropriate risk assessment and should document this assessment. If paper copy records are being transferred to electronic media, sufficient evidence should exist that the process retains all the information present in the original in a legible manner and that the media used for storage will remain readable over time.

Where questions relating to the evaluation of benefits and risks may arise in relation to a product for which a MAH holds a marketing authorisation (or held a marketing authorisation in the past), it is inadvisable for the MAH to destroy pharmacovigilance documentation relating to the product.

The MAH is required to provide a description of the locations of the different types of pharmacovigilance source documents, including archiving arrangements (in the DDPS).

9.5 Examples of Inspection Findings

Examples of areas of concern that have been identified during inspections are provided below. This is not an exhaustive list but serves to summarise some of the key points from this chapter and highlights areas that can be problematic. It is anticipated that examples will prove useful to help MAHs to address such issues.

(i)   Key pharmacovigilance activities and processes are not detailed in formal management approved procedures.
(ii) Pharmacovigilance training has not been provided to all personnel working for, or on behalf of, the MAH. As a result, there is no assurance that staff would know what to do if someone were to report an adverse drug reaction involving a company product to them.
(iii) Not all aspects of the pharmacovigilance system have been included in the scope of audits performed of the central safety group: for example the role of the QPPV and interface groups, such as regulatory affairs.
(iv) The MAH has no documented policy for the retention of pharmacovigilance documentation.

Current metrics relating to MHRA pharmacovigilance inspection findings can be found on our website. The exact nature of findings will vary from company to company and findings are graded on a case-by-case basis, taking into account the evidence relating to the issue and the impact of the findings on, for example, public safety or other areas of the pharmacovigilance system.

10

Interactions between Pharmacovigilance and Other Functions

<table>
<tr>
<td>Editor's
note</td>
<td>The responsibility for GPvP involves all personnel of the MAH. Staff performing certain functions will be more involved than others, although any individual may receive a report of an AE relating to the products for which the company holds marketing authorisations. GPvP should be a company-wide concept spanning the whole life-cycle of a product.

The aim of this chapter is to identify and provide guidance on the types of interaction that may occur between the pharmacovigilance department and other personnel within the company (Fig. 10.1). These interactions are not limited to the transfer of AEs to the pharmacovigilance department. For example, data that contribute to the overall safety evaluation of a product may be generated by other departments, and notification of information to HCPs and patients to ensure the safe use of a medicinal product will often involve other functions.

This chapter should not be viewed as an exhaustive list or definitive tool. Each organisation is structured differently and chooses to perform similar tasks in different ways to meet regulatory requirements. The functional areas have been loosely placed into specific "departments"; however, in reality this will vary from company to company. Particular personnel may perform one or more of these functions, and activities sited in one "department" in one organisation may actually be performed by another department(s) in certain organisations.</td>
</tr>
</table>

10.1 All Personnel

Any person within a company may receive an AE report or other safety information relating to the company's products. While it is accepted that customer-facing personnel are most likely to receive such reports (such as medical representatives, clinical research, medical information, customer services and product quality), sources of AE reports can extend to friends and family, the lay press and other media, and so these reports could potentially be received by any employee. All

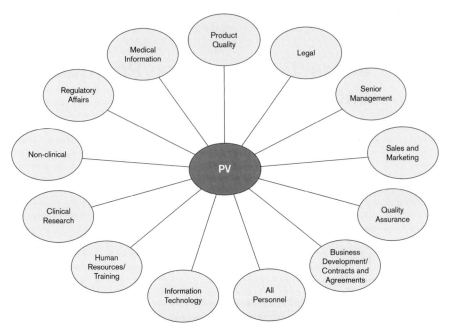

Figure 10.1 Interactions between pharmacovigilance (PV) and other functions.

personnel should, therefore, receive basic pharmacovigilance training on the receipt and subsequent transfer of safety information to the pharmacovigilance department (Section 9.2). This will help to ensure that all reports that are notified to the MAH are collected and collated appropriately.

Once personnel have received initial training, it is important to ensure that this is periodically refreshed and updated. The periodicity will be dependent upon the role of the employee within the organisation; for example, customer-facing personnel will require more frequent training than staff who are less likely to receive AE reports. Personnel such as switchboard operators, those involved with the contact system out of office hours (which could include security guards) and those responsible for receiving enquiries through the company's website (that is via a "Contact us" function) should also be identified and appropriate training provided.

Other triggers for refresher training could be a significant change in legislation, an update to the company's procedures for AE receipt and transfer to the pharmacovigilance department or the emergence of a significant product issue that may trigger enquiries to the company.

10.2 Medical Information

Directive 2001/83/EC (as amended) Article 98 states that, "The marketing authorisation holder shall establish, within his undertaking, a scientific service in charge of information about the medicinal products that he places on the market." In addition, Paragraph 40 of the same Directive also states that, "The provisions governing the information supplied to users should provide a high degree of consumer protection, in order that medicinal products may be used correctly on the basis of full and comprehensible information." The scientific service referred to in the Directive is commonly called the medical information department. This is likely to receive a large proportion of the AEs and other safety-related information reported to the company, since it is often the first port of call for both HCPs and patients. Training of those who work in this area should, therefore, be extensive so that they are able to recognise and capture safety information appropriately.

The interaction between medical information and pharmacovigilance is a key relationship in the pharmacovigilance system, and in some cases both functions will be covered by the same personnel. When separate departments exist, there should be a clear system in place for transfer of AEs from the medical information department to pharmacovigilance, as well as a reconciliation mechanism to ensure all relevant safety information has been transferred (Section 2.2.1).

The medical information team may also be involved with the "out-of-office hours" procedure for handling the receipt of medical information enquiries and AEs. They may receive a request to speak to the QPPV and should, therefore, be kept informed of who the QPPV is and their contact details, and also of the back-up procedure should the QPPV be unavailable.

Medical information personnel may be involved in RMPs. This could involve the provision of specific risk-minimisation information to enquirers who have either a product-specific or issue-specific question. They may also provide information to HCPs on PASS that are ongoing with a product, should this be requested. In such situations, notification to the medical information department of what risk-management activities have been agreed with the Competent Authorities is important in order to meet these obligations, to ensure that there is a uniform, company-wide approach to risk management and that all relevant personnel are aware of their respective responsibilities with regard to risk management and minimisation. Any updates to ongoing PASS or other post-marketing commitments should also be communicated to medical information personnel.

Safety information provided to HCPs and consumers should nearly always be based on the approved product information (SPCs and PILs).

Medical information personnel should be informed of all ongoing safety issues as well as any approved updates to product information, since this may well alter the information supplied to HCPs. Updates to product information may also be required to be notified to various external organisations such as the eMC website, and the medical information department may be responsible for performing this task (Chapter 8). Medical information staff should also be involved in all urgent safety restrictions and DHPCs in order for them to provide up-to-date information to HCPs and patients.

Pharmacovigilance staff may periodically be involved in the training of medical information personnel on the safety profile of products, as well as any specific safety issues of which they should be aware. For example, there may be certain events of interest that require targeted questions to be raised with reporters or enquirers. If medical information personnel are aware of these questions, they will be able to raise them with the reporter/enquirer on first contact.

In turn, medical information personnel may train others, such as medical representatives, on the company's products. It is, therefore, important that any specific safety information or concerns are communicated to the medical information department so they can be included in any training they provide.

A useful source of information on desirable standards for medical information departments and guidance on how best they can meet their pharmacovigilance obligations can be found on the website of the Pharmaceutical Information and Pharmacovigilance Association (www.aiopi.org.uk/about/guidelines.jsp).

10.3 Sales and Marketing

As detailed in Article 93 of Directive 2001/83/EC (as amended), "Medical sales representatives must be adequately trained and shall have sufficient scientific knowledge to be able to provide information that is precise and as complete as possible about the medicinal products which they promote. During each visit, medical sales representatives shall give the persons visited, or have available for them, summaries of the product characteristics of each medicinal product they present. Medical sales representatives shall transmit to the scientific service any information about the use of the medicinal products they advertise, with particular reference to any adverse reactions reported to them by the persons they visit."

As previously described, medical representatives have a key role to play in terms of collection of AE reports (Section 3.1.4). In some companies, medical representatives pay regular visits to HCPs and so establish a working relationship with them. This may make it more likely that a HCP would report a problem with the product or an adverse reaction to a company's medical representative rather than contacting their medical information or pharmacovigilance department.

The training of sales and marketing personnel on pharmacovigilance procedures is a key activity in terms of what they should do if they become aware of an AE or other safety issue. A useful source of information on the role of the medical representative can be found under the professional publications' section of the website of the Association of the British Pharmaceutical Industry (www.abpi.org.uk).

Particularly for patent-protected products, companies may be keen to initiate market research programmes or organisations may perform market research on a company's products with a view to selling such data upon completion to the MAH. Additional guidance relating to collecting AEs and product quality complaints from market research programmes can again be found under the professional publications' section of the website of the Association of the British Pharmaceutical Industry.

Medical representatives also have an important role to play in the communication of medical product information to ensure safe and effective use of the product. They should, therefore, be kept informed of all updates to product information and promotional material in a timely manner so that they can supply accurate and up-to-date product information to HCPs. Medical representatives should specifically be aware of the procedure for being notified of/receiving updated SPCs and associated promotional material containing abbreviated prescribing information, as well as the destruction/return of out-of-date SPCs and promotional material (Section 8.5.3).

In relation to DHPCs, members of the sales and marketing departments are the ideal individuals to consult with in order to help to identify the target groups for communication of these documents (Competent Authorities may specify who the recipients should be). They will be able to highlight the main prescribers of the product and can help to facilitate such communications, which may reduce the time from identification of any issue to provision of new information to the end user (Section 6.5.1).

10.4 Regulatory Affairs

There will be continual interaction between the pharmacovigilance and regulatory affairs departments throughout the life-cycle of a product and the topics that will involve both departments are extensive. A discussion of some of these topics is given below.

10.4.1   Safety variations and urgent safety restrictions

It is expected that there is a documented procedure for handling of safety variations and urgent safety restrictions. The procedure(s) should cover the responsibilities of regulatory and pharmacovigilance personnel. In the event that the MAH has identified a requirement for a variation to be submitted for safety reasons (urgent safety restriction or not), it should be clear who within the organisation will be involved and what the timelines should be, including the timeframe in which the variation will be submitted to Competent Authorities.

In the event that a Competent Authority has requested a variation to be submitted for safety reasons, there should be a mechanism in place to ensure that (1) the request is notified to the QPPV in a timely fashion so that he or she can have oversight of the response to the request, and (2) the variation application is submitted within the requested timeframe.

10.4.2   Responses to requests for information from regulatory authorities

The MAH should have in place a mechanism by which requests for information from Competent Authorities are responded to in an appropriate manner and which is described in a documented procedure. Similar to the request by a Competent Authority to submit a safety variation, the process should outline the notification of key personnel including the QPPV and a mechanism to ensure that timeframes for submission of the relevant information are adhered to. Responsibilities for collating the relevant information and submission should also be defined.

10.4.3   Post-marketing commitments

It would usually be the role of the regulatory affairs department to implement a mechanism to ensure that all post-marketing commitments are tracked and are reported within specified timeframes, as agreed with Competent Authorities (this could include ongoing provision of PASS progress reports and RMP updates). The regulatory affairs personnel should ensure that other post-marketing commitments for which pharmacovigilance may not be directly responsible are also notified to the pharmacovigilance department, since these can affect other activities; for example, completion of a non-clinical study may affect product labelling or RMPs and require inclusion in PSURs.

10.4.4   Periodic Safety Update Reports

The regulatory affairs department may have a role to play in PSUR production in terms of the provision of information on regulatory authority actions and worldwide marketing authorisation status. Submission of type II safety variations may be required at the time of the PSUR (or a plan to submit a variation) and so the regulatory affairs department needs to be informed at an early stage should conclusions of this nature be likely within the PSUR. The regulatory affairs department also routinely receives the PSUR assessment report provided back to the MAH following review by the Competent Authority. It is important that this report is shared with pharmacovigilance personnel, particularly if there is a request for further information or for clarification/amendments to future PSUR submissions. Consideration could be given to implementing a mechanism to track actions required and key milestones following the receipt of assessment reports, particularly when a company has a large product portfolio.

10.4.5   Product labelling

The regulatory affairs department will generally be the document owner for approved product labelling, including SPCs and PILs. There should be a robust system in place so that all relevant personnel, including pharmacovigilance, are notified of all updates to product labelling. When a MAH is operating on a global basis and there are a number of local approved labels for a product, there should be a mechanism in place so that local changes to labels for safety reasons are notified to the pharmacovigilance department as this could trigger a re-evaluation of the risk–benefit profile of the product and/or an update to the CCSI.

10.4.6   Worldwide marketing authorisation status

Pharmacovigilance staff must be kept informed of any approvals, any regulatory authority or MAH actions taken for safety reasons (including suspensions and withdrawals), divestments, change in MAH name, as well as voluntary revocation of marketing authorisations and loss of marketing authorisation because of the so-called "Sunset Clause", since all have some implication on pharmacovigilance processes. The "Sunset Clause" refers to Article 24 (4–6) of Directive 2001/83EC, as inserted by Article 1(23) of Directive 2004/27EC, whereby "any marketing authorisation which, within three years of granting, is not followed by the placing on the market of the authorised product will cease to be valid". An authorised product previously placed on the market in an authorising Member State but subsequently ceasing to be actually present on the market for a period of three consecutive years will also cease to have valid authorisation.

Any actions taken for safety reasons must be assessed against all other marketing authorisations for related products (containing the same active substance or an active substance in the same therapeutic class) for which the MAH is responsible and appropriate measures taken. A Competent Authority may contraindicate a specific patient population on the grounds of an unacceptable risk–benefit assessment as part of the conditions of marketing authorisation approval. Should the MAH have indications for those contraindicated patient populations approved in other territories, a re-assessment of risk–benefit would be required. The regulatory affairs department must ensure that all such information is communicated to the pharmacovigilance department to determine what risk–benefit assessments/actions are required.

10.4.7   Preparation for marketing authorisation submission

A DDPS is now required as part of a marketing authorisation application in the EU. Pharmacovigilance departments are normally the document owners for the DDPS and it is important that there is a process in place so that the most up-to-date version is submitted with each application. The regulatory affairs department may be involved in notifications of updates to this document, particularly if a variation submission is required.

Regulatory affairs personnel must ensure appropriate pharmacovigilance input into RMPs, as the pharmacovigilance department may have an active role to play in meeting post-marketing commitments.

10.5   Non-clinical Staff

Data from *in vivo* and *in vitro* experiments relating to toxicology, pharmacology and pharmacokinetics can all provide important safety information (positive and negative) on a product. Indeed, preclinical data may provide safety signals requiring further evaluation and/or action.

Non-clinical data can be generated at any time in a product's life-cycle. Interactions may first occur between pharmacovigilance and non-clinical experts when the safety specification is being compiled (as part of a RMP) for a marketing authorisation application. Decisions to address non-clinical safety findings may require a multidisciplinary team including non-clinical, clinical and pharmacovigilance personnel.

At the time of marketing authorisation approval, there may still be ongoing long-term studies (e.g. carcinogenicity) that will require analysis on completion and may require an update to the RMP. Again, the relevance of findings (and potential impact on the RMP and product information) requires input from non-clinical experts.

A mechanism should be in place for non-clinical personnel to notify the QPPV or delegate of completed studies that may contribute safety data. More specifically, PSURs should include discussion of relevant non-clinical studies; this not only includes completed studies but also those that are planned or in progress.

Should a signal be generated from non-clinical data (this could be identified from the scientific literature for studies not performed by the MAH), non-clinical experts will play an important role in the discussions regarding the impact on the risk–benefit profile of the product. Even if a potential safety issue is identified that is not derived from non-clinical work, it may be prudent to consult such personnel to assist in identifying ways of investigating the issue, such as specific *in vitro* or *in vivo* laboratory experiments.

10.6 Product Quality

Product technical complaints and other information concerning potentially defective medicines notified to the MAH may also be associated with AEs. In turn, reports received by pharmacovigilance personnel may indicate a pharmaceutical quality problem; for example, lack of efficacy reports. As discussed above, it is important that there is a mechanism in place to identify AEs received as part of a product technical complaint, and vice versa, and to ensure the transfer of this information to the appropriate personnel.

Upon analysis of a product complaint, a critical safety concern may be detected (for example, incorrect amount of an active ingredient) and urgent action may be required. A multidisciplinary team including personnel from at least pharmacovigilance and product quality departments is likely to be involved with the evaluation and subsequent action. Such situations may require a product recall (and almost certainly the QPPV would be notified and/or involved).

Other multidisciplinary teams may be required to deal with issues relating to counterfeits, which are discussed in Chapter 6.

10.7 Legal Department

The interactions between the pharmacovigilance and legal departments in terms of contracts and agreements are covered in Chapter 11.

The other main interaction that legal personnel may have with pharmacovigilance staff relates to receipt of complaints by customers and perhaps receipt of a claim for compensation relating to an adverse reaction. This information should be passed on to pharmacovigilance personnel for processing and evaluation. Input can be provided for any legal proceedings, as necessary. The legal and pharmacovigilance departments may also closely interact in the event of a product withdrawal, which could lead to civil action cases being filed against the MAH.

10.8 Human Resource Department or Those Responsible for Training

Topics that may require interactions with the human resources department and/or the personnel responsible for training include:

- obtaining up-to-date lists of personnel to identify training needs or to facilitate identifying appropriate personnel to discuss a specific issue (e.g. a toxicologist to discuss non-clinical findings);
- system for storage of job descriptions, CVs (including higher-level education certificates to verify qualifications) and personal training files;
- information regarding the company-wide system for training and/or conducting the pharmacovigilance training on behalf of the department;
- high-level organisational charts (for inclusion in the DDPS);
- discussion with the QPPV of whether individuals are suitably qualified and trained to carry out specific tasks delegated by the QPPV; the human resources department may also have a role to play in formalisation of this delegation through updates to job descriptions and/or contracts;
- discussion of training plans for pharmacovigilance personnel (including external courses).

10.9 Senior Management

The interaction between pharmacovigilance staff and senior management is important in a number of areas:

- formally to appoint a QPPV;
- to promote awareness and understanding of the MAH's responsibility for pharmacovigilance and the support required by the QPPV from the MAH;
- during identification of a serious safety issue that may require action such as a recall, suspension or withdrawal (including briefing personnel who deal with the press);

- to discuss budgetary requirements for the department (e.g. database implementation and resource).

There are requirements placed upon the MAH with regard to pharmacovigilance that must be communicated to senior management in order to promote awareness and to ensure appropriate personnel, systems and support are available to fulfil legal obligations. Failure to comply with pharmacovigilance obligations can have a considerable negative impact on a MAH, and senior management should be aware of this. The greater the awareness that senior management has of pharmacovigilance requirements, the more likely that pharmacovigilance activities will be supported adequately to fulfil these requirements.

10.10 Information Technology

It is inevitable that pharmacovigilance personnel (as with all personnel in a company) will interact with the IT department. How extensively the two will interact depends on what electronic applications are used within pharmacovigilance, such as a safety database.

Considerations that should be discussed with the IT department include access to safety data. The IT department will be able to restrict access to electronic information that should only be viewed and amended by specific safety personnel. Access to data may extend to laptop security: does IT operate a "virtual private network" access or are there similar security mechanisms in place to protect pharmacovigilance data when operating remotely?

There is a need for the MAH to plan for business continuity in the event of a major disruption to the IT system. Pharmacovigilance staff should be familiar and/or have input into procedures for disaster recovery mechanisms in order to ensure that requests for safety information and regulatory reporting timelines can be met, and that safety data can be analysed within a reasonable timeframe. Pharmacovigilance personnel must be provided with adequate means to continue their key tasks throughout such periods of disaster.

In situations where there is a safety database in place, the involvement of IT will be more extensive. Some companies may have bespoke databases designed and developed by the internal IT department. If the company has purchased a commercial safety database, the IT department would invariably be involved with vendor selection, audit and validation processes (including change control). The IT department may also be involved in an advisory role with regard to electronic reporting of ICSRs even if no database is involved (e.g. use of the EVWeb tool).

As with all MAH personnel, it is important that IT staff have a level of understanding of pharmacovigilance (both in terms of its regulatory framework and its practical aspects) appropriate for their role so that they can adequately support and advise the pharmacovigilance function.

11

Contracts and Agreements

11.1   General Considerations for Contracts and Agreements

This chapter discusses the various types of third party with which a MAH may have an association and gives guidance on what may need to be included in contracts and agreements with these third parties in order to fulfil pharmacovigilance obligations.

The MAH should have formal contracts in place for any of the following situations:

- outsourcing of pharmacovigilance activities and use of service providers for pharmacovigilance activities;
- use of third party distributors and manufacturers;
- co-marketing, co-licensing and co-promotion of products.

In order to monitor the safety of their products and have the ability to take appropriate action when required, a MAH needs access to all available safety data on their products, including data received by third parties. Detailed contracts or agreements allow the MAH to define exactly which data need to be transferred, how they should be transferred, reconciliation procedures for data exchange and the timelines for the transfer. Contracts or agreements should also describe the information that the MAH will share with other parties, in order to allow the other parties to fulfil the tasks that have been contracted to them.

The legal department and/or legal representative of a MAH will almost certainly be involved with all contracts and agreements between the MAH and external organisations (e.g. contract manufacturers, distributors, clinical research organisations, external consultants). Such personnel should be aware of the need to ensure that adequate pharmacovigilance provisions are in place. It may be that the best of way of ensuring pharmacovigilance requirements are adequately addressed in contracts and agreements is for the legal department to notify someone from pharmacovigilance upon drafting of a new agreement to assess what needs to be put in place. Alternatively, a MAH could develop templates for each type of agreement, although the final draft of the agreement may still need to be reviewed by pharmacovigilance personnel.

11.1.1 Points to consider for contracts and agreements

Irrespective of the type of contract or agreement in place, the MAH should consider the following points.

- Do formal contracts and agreements exist where they should?
- Are they signed and dated by all parties?
- Are contracts and agreements reviewed periodically and is there a mechanism for updating them?
- Who is responsible for maintenance, regular review and updates?
- Do they reflect current legislative requirements and guidelines?
- Is there a mechanism in place to review and update contracts and agreements in response to a major revision to the legislation and guidance?
- Do they reflect current practice?

● Does a procedural document exist that describes the creation and maintenance of all contracts and agreements, and does this document specify the routine inclusion of pharmacovigilance obligations?

11.2 Outsourcing of Pharmacovigilance Activities

A MAH may potentially outsource all pharmacovigilance activities or a specific function to third parties, which can range from large contract research organisations to individual consultants. It should be noted that the MAH maintains the legal responsibility for pharmacovigilance even if activities are outsourced. The MAH must, therefore, have adequate oversight of the activities of the contractor, for example through QA audits, provision of reports or regular meetings (Section 9.3).

Examples of activities that could be outsourced include but are not limited to:

● the role of the QPPV;
● management of clinical trial safety including receipt and processing of serious AEs (see Chapter 12);
● receipt and processing of pharmacovigilance data;
● submission of expedited reports to regulatory authorities (electronic or paper);
● literature searching;
● medical information service;
● preparation of PSURs;
● preparation of ASRs;
● medical input into pharmacovigilance;
● signal detection and trend analysis;
● audits of the pharmacovigilance system;
● co-ordination of post-authorisation initiatives (e.g. management of MAH sponsored registries).

The MAH may also use a third party to provide a service that is not a specific pharmacovigilance activity but still forms part of the pharmacovigilance system. These services include, but are not limited to:

● provision and support of computerised databases, including hosted systems;
● archiving of data.

Contracts in the situations listed above have the potential to be complex, and it is not possible to provide guidance on detailed contents within the scope of this guidance.

11.2.1   Points to consider for outsourcing agreements

- Where the role of the QPPV has been outsourced, the contract should detail exactly what tasks the QPPV will be performing, detail the information that will be provided to the QPPV and describe how the QPPV will have oversight of the system. The contract should also detail how the QPPV will be available to the MAH 24-hours a day and describe the back-up procedures that apply during periods of unavailability, such as holidays.

- If external consultants are used for providing medical input into the system, the contract should include which duties will be performed, for example provision of seriousness and causality assessments and review of PSURs and ASRs. It is recommended that the availability of the consultant should also be clearly outlined.

- When a MAH uses a database hosted by a third party, a contract should exist with that third party. It may also be appropriate for a service-level agreement to be written as part of the contract, which details the disaster recovery and back-up procedures that apply when the system is unavailable. The service-level agreement may also detail, for example, what will happen if electronic reporting of ICSRs is not possible or who has responsibility for providing training on the use of the database. Where relevant, issues relating to data protection may also need to be addressed.

- Where third parties are used for archiving of pharmacovigilance data, the contract should include, as a minimum, statements about the period of record retention, conditions of storage, a requirement for the MAH to be notified in advance before their documents are transferred to another site, retrieval arrangements and control of access to the data.

- If a third party is used to provide a medical information service, the contract should detail the mechanism for transferring medical enquiries associated with AEs to the MAH and should state what information the MAH will provide to the contractor to support their activities. Details of the operating hours of the medical information service and which products are covered should also be considered for inclusion.

- Where literature searching has been outsourced, the contract should specify all the active substances for which the contractor will be responsible, including in the search the terms that are to be searched and the procedure for managing the output of searches (Chapter 4).

- If PSUR production has been outsourced, the contract should state as a minimum how, when and what information is to be exchanged in order for this function to be performed (e.g. that all non-serious AE reports received within the reporting period of a PSUR should be exchanged in time for inclusion in that PSUR), the QC and assurance procedures that will be implemented, and the review and approval process.

● Where signal detection has been outsourced, the contract could indicate what the inputs into the process are, the system that is to be used and how and when the outputs will be shared with the MAH.

11.3 Third-party Distributors and Manufacturers

A MAH may use a third party to manufacture and distribute products on its behalf, and it is possible that the name of the manufacturer and/or distributor could be included in the product information or on the outer packaging. Therefore, a HCP or consumer may contact the manufacturer or distributor with a medical enquiry or to report an adverse reaction or product complaint.

It is a common pharmacovigilance inspection finding that contract manufacturing or distribution agreements do not contain statements as to what the expectations are in terms of the exchange of medical enquiries, pharmacovigilance data or product technical complaints. The contracts and agreements should address all products that the third party is manufacturing or distributing.

11.4 Co-licensing/Co-marketing and Co-promotion of Products

Co-licensing, co-marketing and co-promotion agreements are common in the pharmaceutical industry and allow companies to share resources and knowledge. When companies agree to co-license, co-market or co-promote products, contracts need to detail which party is responsible for fulfilling specific pharmacovigilance tasks and functions. Since these types of agreement can be complex, consideration should be given to involving pharmacovigilance personnel in the process. Where these types of alliance exist, a documented agreement for safety data exchange should be in place for each company and/or product.

A brief description of the nature of the agreements the company establishes with co-marketing partners and contractors for pharmacovigilance activities should be provided in the DDPS.

Co-licensing or co-marketing arrangements should be identified for products authorised in the EU and the distribution of the major responsibilities between the parties made clear.

11.4.1   Points to consider in co-licensing/co-marketing/co-promotion agreements

The following may need to be considered for inclusion in co-operative agreements:

- definitions;
- mechanism for exchanging safety information and frequency of reconciliation;
- maintenance of the global safety database;
- responsibility for specific tasks such as:
  - reporting and follow-up of ICSRs,
  - production of PSURs,
  - handling of product quality complaints, exposure during pregnancy, misuse, abuse, lack of efficacy, medication error and overdose,
  - literature searching,
  - signal detection and/or trend analysis,
  - management of RSI and escalation procedures for disputes over labelling,
  - handling of urgent safety restrictions,
  - management of product recalls,
  - retention of pharmacovigilance records;
- responsibility for responding to regulatory authority enquiries;
- frequency and scope of mutual audits;
- frequency of meetings between the parties;
- identity of the key contact people for each party;
- method for termination and review.

If the first company has sole responsibility for fulfilling regulatory reporting requirements in one or more countries, then the contract or agreement should specify exactly how an AE received by the second company would be transferred to it. Lack of sufficient detail in contracts may potentially lead to a lack of compliance with regulatory reporting if neither party submits ICSRs or PSURs, or a duplication of effort if both parties perform the same submissions.

11.5   Other Types of Contracts and Agreements

11.5.1   Agreements with local affiliates

It is common practice within the pharmaceutical industry for certain pharmacovigilance activities, such as case processing or PSUR production, to be centralised to one or more sites. In this scenario, local country sites tend to have the responsibility for local receipt of adverse reaction reports and their subsequent transfer to the central pharmacovigilance group. Local country offices may also retain the responsibility for local expedited reporting. It can be useful in such instances to have in place agreements between the central group and local affiliates that set out the exact responsibilities of each party. If a formal agreement is not considered appropriate, these responsibilities may be captured in the form of a procedure. As previously discussed, the MAH must have in place a system to ensure such agreements are kept up to date and accurately reflect both the legislation and the internal standards for pharmacovigilance.

11.5.2 Transfer of a marketing authorisation

It is not unusual for ownership of a marketing authorisation to be transferred from one MAH to another company. At the time of transfer of a marketing authorisation, it may be useful for the companies to come to an agreement with regard to the exchange of existing pharmacovigilance information. Such information could take the form of PSURs, line listings, case files, etc. In this way valuable information on the safety of the product is not lost and the new MAH has a more advanced starting point for their pharmacovigilance activities.

11.6 Examples of Inspection Findings

Examples of areas of concern that have been identified during inspections are provided below. This is not an exhaustive list but serves to summarise some of the key points from this chapter and highlights areas that can be problematic. It is anticipated that examples will prove useful to help MAHs to address such issues.

(i) Signed contracts are not in place with all applicable third parties. It has also been seen that a contractor has starting providing a service to the MAH prior to the contract been signed by all parties.

(ii) The contracts in place do not define all services that are being provided to the MAH.

(iii) The agreement with company X does not document the timeframes in which safety information is to be exchanged.

(iv) The contract with company X includes a 90-day timeframe for the exchange of non-serious AEs. This could result in certain AEs not being included in PSURs, as if an unlisted non-serious AE was received by company X up to one month before DLP of the PSUR, the AE report may not be transferred to the MAH in time.

(v) The agreements in place with contract manufacturers do not clearly define the manufacturer's responsibilities with respect to safety, for example notifying the MAH of any adverse reactions that may be associated with product complaints.

Current metrics relating to MHRA pharmacovigilance inspection findings can be found on our website. The exact nature of findings will vary from company to company and findings are graded on a case-by-case basis, taking into account the evidence relating to the issue and the impact of the findings on, for example, public safety or other areas of the pharmacovigilance system.

Requirements for Solicited Reports

Editor's note	The previous chapters of this guide have primarily been concerned with pharmacovigilance in the post-authorisation phase of the product life-cycle. Collection and collation of pharmacovigilance data on a medicinal product does not begin after first authorisation, as safety information is also gathered during the pre-authorisation clinical development phase. In addition, clinical development on a product can continue following the granting of a marketing authorisation, either via interventional trials or via non-interventional studies. This can either be in the indication for which an authorisation is already held or a new indication.
	This chapter will focus upon the pharmacovigilance reporting obligations for solicited reports. These obligations are largely driven by whether the report arises in an interventional or non-interventional setting. The topics in this chapter will, therefore, include the distinction between interventional trials and non-interventional studies and their reporting requirements. It will also include safety reporting requirements for PASS, registries and investigator-led studies.

12.1 Relevant Terminology

12.1.1 Trial/study definitions

In order to establish the safety reporting requirements that apply to a study, one must determine whether the study is (1) an interventional clinical trial or (2) a non-interventional study. The following definitions should assist with this decision.

CLINICAL TRIAL (DIRECTIVE 2001/20/EC)

Any investigation in human subjects intended to discover or verify the clinical, pharmacological and/or other pharmacodynamic effects of one or more investigational medicinal product(s), and/or to identify any adverse reactions to one or more investigational medicinal product(s) and/or to study absorption, distribution, metabolism and excretion of one or more investigational medicinal product(s) with the object of ascertaining its (their) safety and/or efficacy.

NON-INTERVENTIONAL STUDY (DIRECTIVE 2001/20/EC)

A study where the medicinal product(s) is (are) prescribed in the usual manner in accordance with the terms of the marketing authorisation. The assignment of the patient to a particular therapeutic strategy is not decided in advance by a trial protocol but falls within current practice and the prescription of the medicine is clearly separated from the decision to include the patient in the study. No additional diagnostic or monitoring procedures shall be applied to the patients and epidemiological methods shall be used for the analysis of the collected data.

INTERVENTIONAL TRIAL

If the study does not fulfil the above definition, then it should be considered as an interventional study. Interventional trials fall within the remit of Directive 2001/20/EC. If there is doubt about whether the study in question is an interventional clinical trial, it is recommended that readers refer to the following: Volume 10, Notice to Applicants, Chapter V: Question & Answers – Clinical Trial Documents; in particular refer to the algorithm "Is it a clinical trial of a medicinal product". This is also available from the Clinical trials section of the MHRA website.

12.1.2   Other definitions that may clarify safety reporting requirements

The following definitions may further assist in the clarification of safety reporting requirements.

SOLICITED REPORTS (VOLUME 9A AND ICH E2D)

Solicited reports are those derived from organised data-collection schemes, such as clinical trials, registries, post-approval named-patient use programmes, other patient support and disease-management programmes, and surveys of patients or healthcare providers. Solicited reports may also originate from MAH efforts to gather information on efficacy or patient compliance.

AEs obtained from any of the above should not be considered as spontaneous reports. For the purposes of safety reporting, solicited reports should be classified as study reports and, therefore, where possible, should have an appropriate causality assessment by a HCP or a MAH.

INVESTIGATIONAL MEDICINAL PRODUCT (EU DIRECTIVE 2001/20/EC)

An investigational medicinal product is a pharmaceutical form of an active substance or placebo being tested or used as a reference in a clinical trial, including products already with a marketing authorisation but used or assembled (formulated or packaged) in a way different from the authorised form, or when used for an unauthorised indication, or when used to gain further information about the unauthorised form.

NON-INVESTIGATIONAL MEDICINAL PRODUCT (MEDICINAL PRODUCTS FALLING OUTSIDE THE DEFINITION OF AN INVESTIGATIONAL MEDICINAL PRODUCT)

Products that are not the object of investigation (i.e. other than the tested product, placebo or active comparator) may be supplied to subjects participating in a trial and used in accordance with the protocol. For instance, some clinical trial protocols require the use of medicinal products such as support or rescue/escape medication for preventive, diagnostic or therapeutic reasons and/or to ensure that adequate medical care is provided for the subject. They may also be used in accordance with the protocol to induce a physiological response. These medicinal products do not fall within the definition of investigational medicinal products (IMPs) in Directive 2001/20/EC and are called non-investigational medicinal products (NIMPs). They may be supplied by the sponsor, who provides details of these NIMPs and their proposed use in the trial protocol and ensures that they are of the necessary quality for human use. A NIMP may also be supplied by the investigator site.

POST-AUTHORISATION STUDY

A post-authorisation study can include any study conducted within the conditions laid down in the SPC and other conditions laid down for the marketing of the product or under normal conditions of use. A post-authorisation study may, therefore, be defined as a clinical trial, a non-interventional study or a PASS (see below).

POST-AUTHORISATION SAFETY STUDY

A PASS is a pharmacoepidemiological safety study or a clinical trial carried out in accordance with terms of the marketing authorisation, conducted with the aim of identifying or quantifying a safety hazard relating to an authorised medicinal product (Volume 9A).

REGISTRY (VOLUME 9A, PART I, TABLE I.7.A (PASS) AND ICH E2E)

A registry is a list of patients presenting with the same characteristic(s). This characteristic may be a disease or an outcome (disease registry) or a specific exposure (exposure or drug registry). Both types of registry, which only differ by the type of patient data of interest collated, may collect a battery of information using standardised questionnaires in a prospective fashion. Disease/outcome registries, such as registries for blood dyscrasias, severe cutaneous reactions, or congenital malformations, may help to collect data on drug exposure and other factors associated with a clinical condition.

12.1.3　Summary of study categorisation

Figure 12.1 summarises the way in which studies can be categorised. From this it can be seen that post-authorisation studies can either be interventional or non-interventional in nature and that PASS are a subset of post-authorisation studies. Therefore, PASS can either be interventional clinical trials or non-interventional studies. The segments within the figure are explained in Table 12.1.

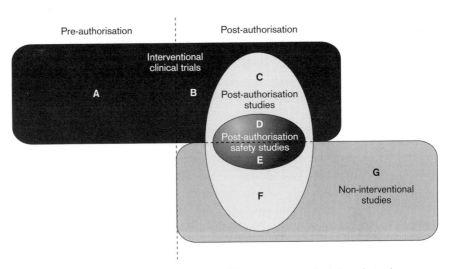

Figure 12.1 Venn diagram illustrating different types of trial and study.

It should be noted that a product is often authorised in one region before another and so there may be reports from either post-marketing studies or spontaneous sources that require reporting in a region where the product has not yet been approved. For example, if a product is authorised in the USA but is still in the pre-authorisation phase and

Table 12.1 Explanation of the areas within figure 12.1

Section A	Interventional clinical trials that are being conducted when no marketing authorisation exists in any territory worldwide
Section B	Interventional clinical trials that are being conducted in the post-authorisation period. For example, if a product is already approved for one indication, trials may be conducted to obtain data to support an application for a different indication
Section C	Interventional post-authorisation studies; that is, studies conducted within the conditions laid down in the SPC and other conditions laid down for the marketing of the product or under normal conditions of use and meeting the definition of an interventional clinical trial
Section D	Interventional PASS, which is a subset of both interventional studies and post-authorisation studies
Section E	Non-interventional PASS, which is a subset of non-interventional studies and post-authorisation studies
Section F	Non-interventional post-authorisation studies; that is, studies conducted within the conditions laid down in the SPC and other conditions laid down for the marketing of the product or under normal conditions of use, but which do not meet the definition of an interventional clinical trial
Section G	Non-interventional studies, those that do not meet the definition of an interventional clinical trial, for example a study to collect data on patient demographics

SPC, Summary of Product Characteristics; PASS, post-authorisation safety study.

undergoing clinical trials in the EU, SUSARs arising from the US will require expedited reporting (Section 6.4).

12.2 Safety Reporting for Non-interventional Studies

Reporting requirements for non-interventional post-authorisation studies are included in Directive 2001/83/EC (as amended), Regulation (EC) 726/2004 and the pharmacovigilance responsibilities are outlined in Volume 9A (Annex 2). The requirements generally follow those for reports from spontaneous sources but differ with respect to reporting in PSURs. Once the study has been defined as a non-interventional study, it must also be assessed as to whether it fulfils the definition of a PASS (Section 12.1) in order to determine exact reporting requirements.

12.2.1 Expedited reporting of adverse reactions

SARs within the EU and SUSARs outside the EU from non-interventional studies are subject to the same reporting criteria and timelines as for spontaneous cases reported by HCPs (Section 3.5 and Annex 2).

12.2.2   Ongoing safety evaluation

There may be other adverse reactions that, although they do not qualify for expedited reporting, when assessed are likely to affect the safety of trial subjects and/or patients prescribed the product. In accordance with MAH obligations, these should be notified immediately to the Competent Authorities to discuss appropriate action.

In addition, all safety information obtained from non-interventional studies, including non-serious adverse reactions, should form part of the ongoing safety evaluation of the medicinal product (Chapter 6). The MAH should, therefore, consider how non-serious cases are collected and collated to ensure these are taken into account when evaluating the risk–benefit profile of the product.

12.2.3   Periodic Safety Update Reports

All SARs (those attributable to the medicinal product by either investigator or MAH) from non-interventional studies should be included in PSUR line listings.

All studies sponsored by the MAH, including all non-interventional studies that yield safety information with a potential impact on the safety profile of the product, should be discussed in the Studies section of the PSUR, and other appropriate sections (Annex 2).

12.2.4   Annual Safety Reports

Interventional clinical trial ASRs do not have to be produced for non-interventional studies. However, Part 1 of an ASR for an interventional clinical trial(s) may contain data from non-interventional studies if the studies involve the same IMP and new and relevant findings may impact on the safety profile of that product.

12.2.5   Final study reports

In addition to inclusion in PSURs and ASRs (where appropriate), all adverse reactions/events from non-interventional studies, including those that are considered non-serious, should be summarised in the final study report in the form of frequency tables.

12.3   Interventional Clinical Trials

Interventional clinical trials may be conducted at various times throughout the life-cycle of a product. Interventional clinical trials may be designed to look at the safety and tolerability of a single drug. Others may be more complex in design, such as those designed to look at the efficacy of a product in comparison with similar treatments or placebo, or those designed to look at interactions with commonly co-prescribed drugs. More than one drug may be used in a clinical trial in order to meet the objectives of that trial; however, in terms of subject safety, all drugs are of interest. This makes it clear that all drugs, even those with a marketing authorisation, that are used in a trial as comparators are considered IMPs. Such comparator drugs are, therefore, subject to the same reporting requirements as the test drug. There are some products that may be used in the trial according to the protocol but fall outside the definition of an IMP; these are the NIMPs, non-investigational medicinal products. There are situations where NIMPs are subject to reporting requirements.

The reporting requirements for interventional clinical trials are described below and primarily relate to reporting of SUSARs. In a similar way to reporting requirements for spontaneous reports, as described in Chapter 3, reporting requirements for interventional clinical trials are dependent on certain assessments, including causality and expectedness. Issues relating to these assessments are discussed below.

12.3.1 Causality assessments

Sponsors may use different scales to assess the causality of an event. For example, a simple two-point scale may be used where the options for a suspected causal relationship are "yes" or "no". Alternatively, more complex scales can be used that include terms such as definitely related, probably related, possibly related, unlikely to be related, not related or not assessable. The protocol should include advice for investigators about the causality scale. Where more than two options are available, a definition for each option should be provided together with details of which options equate to a suspected adverse reaction versus an AE. If the investigator states that the event is not related, it is recommended that the SAE form should prompt the investigator to provide details of an alternative explanation for the event. If the investigator assigns the causality as "not assessable", the sponsor should adopt a conservative approach in which the event is deemed a suspected adverse reaction until follow-up information is received from the investigator. This scenario also applies should the investigator not supply a causality assessment on initial reporting: that is, the event should be considered as causally related.

The sponsor is also required to make an assessment of causality, as he or she will have greater knowledge of the product upon which to base the causality assessment, such as preclinical information and knowledge of the product's use in other trials and/or patient populations (ENTR/CT3:

Detailed guidance on the collection, verification and presentation of adverse reaction reports arising from clinical trials on medicinal products for human use, April 2006, Section 4.2.4).

12.3.2   Investigator's brochure

The reference document used for a clinical trial should be identified in the protocol. It should be consistent throughout all the Member States concerned; the same reference document must be used across the trial, regardless of where trial sites are based. For IMPs without a marketing authorisation, the reference document for safety and assessment of expectedness should be an IB.

For those IMPs that have an EU marketing authorisation, and the IMP is to be used according to the marketing authorisation, a SPC should be used. For marketed products where more than one EU SPC exists, the sponsor must select the most appropriate one for that trial. For a trial that is being run across multiple sites, and where each site may source the IMP from different suppliers, the sponsor should identify a common SPC to be used as the reference document at all sites.

For those IMPs that have a marketing authorisation but are not being used in accordance with that marketing authorisation, for example in a different indication, the sponsor should decide whether it is appropriate to use a SPC or whether an IB should be produced as a reference document. When there are significant differences in the description of those events considered to be expected in the SPC versus the IB (for an IMP with an EU marketing authorisation), the sponsor must have a rationale for these differences based on available data. This rationale should be documented. A rationale for classifying events as expected should take into account factors such as the type of event and possible causal relationship. In addition, the frequency with which the event is seen in the general population or population under study together with the frequency with which the event is reported in subjects receiving the IMP compared with subjects receiving placebo are both considerations when assessing whether to list an event as expected.

There should be appropriate procedures in place to ensure that SPCs and IBs are reviewed for safety information to ensure consistency. Signal generation activities that trigger changes to a SPC should lead to consideration of whether equivalent changes are required to the IB and the PIL.

Sponsors should carefully consider how IBs are used to determine the expectedness of an event. If it is not clear which sections of the IB are to be used to determine expectedness, and the sponsor lists all SAEs in the IB as they occur (regardless of causality), the first report of a related event could be classified as expected if previous unrelated SAEs had been received. This could result in reduced expedited SUSAR reporting from

clinical trials to Competent Authorities. If the adverse reaction is significant enough to be referred to as expected in the IB, the MAH should also
consider whether it is appropriate to update the SPC. Sponsors of trials
with marketed products used outside the licensed indication and who are
not the MAHs should monitor any changes to the SPC of the MAH and
review the IB accordingly.

Some sponsors choose to inform investigators in the IB of all AEs that
have been reported with the product, for general information. A clear
distinction should be made between events that are included for general
information and reactions that are considered by the sponsor to be
expected for the product. This could be achieved by appending the
DCDS/DCSI to the IB, as these documents describe the current safety
profile of the product under investigation based on suspected adverse
reaction data: that is, what the sponsor considers to be related to the
product. Alternatively a tabulation of expected events could be provided
within the IB.

It is a requirement that the IB is reviewed annually (Directive
2005/28/EC, Chapter 2, Article 8). Any updates to the reference safety
documents, either IBs or SPCs, should be communicated in a timely
manner to concerned investigators. Consideration should also be given to
review of the informed consent and communication with patients in relation to new safety information. If no changes are required to the IB at the
time of the annual review, then this should be documented by the sponsor.

12.3.3 What is a SUSAR?

The obvious answer to this question is that a SUSAR is a "suspected
unexpected serious adverse reaction". However, there are some subtleties
that need to be considered. As seen above, the decision regarding whether
an event or reaction is expected is based upon the information provided
in the reference document for the trial. As such, the process by which the
reference document is updated can greatly influence those terms that
would be considered as unexpected and therefore potentially qualify for
expedited reporting.

There is no hard and fast rule about when an event/reaction should be
included in the reference document and/or considered expected. Indeed,
in practice, it would not be feasible to do this, as every drug is different
and has to be considered in its own context (indication for treatment,
mode of action, etc.).

However, the responsibility for sponsors and/or MAHs to determine
what is expected has an impact on the data that are submitted to
Competent Authorities and ethics committees and also the data that are
recorded on EudraVigilance.

Consider the scenario where one occurrence of a particular reaction results in an update to the reference document, and then additional reports for the same reaction are received. The initial report would be assessed as unexpected and submitted to EudraVigilance (provided it met all of the other criteria for an expedited report). However, subsequent reports would be assessed as expected and would not require expedited reporting to EudraVigilance. Compare this with the scenario where a single report of a reaction is received but does not trigger the process to update the reference document. In this case, subsequent reports of the same reaction would be assessed as unexpected and, therefore, qualify for expedited reporting until there was sufficient information to update the reference document. Sponsors may also over-report expected reactions if assessments of expectedness are ineffective.

The inconsistencies between these approaches raises concern about whether data are reliable and how useful they can be. Over-reporting or incorrect reporting does not assist Competent Authorities to develop an understanding of the safety profile of the IMP. Both under- and over-reporting (such as submitting expected reports or those considered to be not related) can skew the data and potentially dilute safety signals. It would be considered to be good practice for the expected events listed in the IB for a trial to contribute to the development of the undesirable effects section in the SPC, should the IMP obtain a marketing authorisation. This should be borne in mind when including events as expected within the IB.

12.3.4   Reporting requirements for investigational medicinal products

Investigators must report all SAEs to the sponsor in accordance with the approved protocol (see Annex 2). It is expected that the protocol demands immediate reporting of SAEs by investigators, which in practice usually means within 24 hours. Typically, this would involve faxing the SAE form, but if fax facilities are not available the protocol should describe back-up procedures and include SAE reporting contacts within the sponsor organisation or designated clinical research organisation.

Certain events that meet the definition of a SAE may be excluded from such reporting, upon agreement of the Competent Authorities. Examples of such events are those that are classed as end points or disease-defining events, or events that are considered to be "expected" as part of the treatment and/or trial procedures, unless the frequency or severity of such events is unusual. Such exceptions must be stated in either the protocol or the IB. Laboratory parameters may also require reporting within the same timeframes as SAEs. These should be specified in the protocol and made clear to the laboratory concerned.

SUSARs must be reported to Competent Authorities in whose territory the trial is taking place within seven days of the sponsor becoming aware of the event for fatal or life-threatening events (any relevant follow-up information should be subsequently communicated within an additional eight days) and within 15 days of the sponsor becoming aware of the event for all other SAEs. SUSARs must also be reported to the ethics committees that have approved the trial in the same timescale. The reporting requirements for ethics committees vary in Member States; therefore, sponsors of international trials should familiarise themselves with the applicable local requirements.

The sponsor is also required to inform all concerned investigators of SUSARs. A concerned investigator is any investigator in trials sponsored by the same sponsor who is using the same IMP (irrespective of whether the IMP is used for a different indication). The legislation does not provide timelines for this and the sponsor must decide what is appropriate. For example, it may be appropriate to inform investigators of SUSARs on a monthly or even quarterly basis. This will be dependent on the type of trial and the nature of the potential adverse reactions. It is expected that the risk-assessment decision for frequency of reporting to concerned investigators is documented by the sponsor. Note that any immediate safety concerns must be communicated to all concerned investigators on an expedited basis.

Consideration should be given to the number of potential SUSARs that could be generated and the method of communicating those SUSARs to concerned investigators. For example, if an investigator is receiving SUSARs on an individual and potentially daily basis, are they likely to give each SUSAR their full attention? It may be useful for the sponsor to provide an evaluation of the SUSAR data as this can help investigators to put the data into context.

The sponsor is required to report to all relevant parties all SUSARs that originate outside the EU for all clinical trials conducted by the sponsor with the same IMP. For non-commercial organisations this may mean that lead investigators would require knowledge of those other investigators within their organisation who are conducting trials with the same medicinal product, even if it is being used in a different indication.

Expedited reporting requirements for SUSARs that occur within the concerned trial and outside the concerned trial are clearly described in the Volume 10 guidance documents entitled "ENTR/CT3 Detailed guidance on the collection, verification and presentation of adverse reaction reports arising from clinical trials on medicinal products for human use" and "ENTR/CT4 Detailed guidance on the European database of Suspected Unexpected Serious Adverse Reactions (EudraVigilance – Clinical Trial Module)". In particular, the tables contained in ENTR/CT4 are of assistance to sponsors when deciding which reports need to be submitted, by what route and to which parties.

As previously described, comparator products are defined as IMPs, and so the requirements described above are applicable. In addition, if the MAH for the product is not the sponsor of the trial, then these events should be notified by the sponsor to the MAH in order that this information may be included in the MAH's ongoing safety-monitoring procedures.

12.3.5   Reporting requirements for non-investigational medicinal products

Examples of products used in a trial according to the protocol, but falling outside the definition of an IMP (NIMPs), are "challenge agents" used to induce a physiological effect (e.g. epinephrine or certain allergens), rescue medication for preventative action, radiolabelled ligands used for scanning and diagnostic purposes, or concomitant medications required by the protocol.

Further guidance on NIMPs can be found in Volume 10, Chapter V "Guidance on IMPs and other Medicinal Products used in Clinical Trials".

In relation to Directive 2001/20/EC, it is important to clarify the requirements that apply to NIMPs (see Annex 2). These are summarised in Table 12.2.

The following are scenarios when an adverse reaction to a NIMP would require reporting according to Directive 2001/20/EC.

● If the adverse reaction is suspected to be linked to an interaction between a NIMP and an IMP and is serious and unexpected (according to the reference document for the IMP), the sponsor should report in accordance with 2001/20/EC (Article 17).
● If a SUSAR is reported and it might be linked to either a NIMP or an IMP but cannot be attributed to only one of these, the sponsor should report in accordance with 2001/20/EC (Article 17).
● If an adverse reaction associated with the NIMP is likely to affect the safety of the trial subjects, the sponsor should report to Competent Authorities and concerned ethics committees in accordance with 2001/20/EC Article 10(b).

In terms of the third scenario, the question arises, when is something likely to affect the safety of the trial subjects and when will it not? The inference is that all other SARs involving a NIMP (other than those listed previously) do not require to be notified per 2001/20/EC (Article 17), but this is something for the sponsor to decide. However, the event may need to be reported in accordance with post-authorisation pharmacovigilance

Table 12.2 Summary of the requirements of Directive 2001/20/EC that apply to non-investigational medicinal products

Article	Requirement	Rationale
17	The requirement to submit serious adverse reactions	The definition of an adverse reaction only applies to IMPs. A NIMP does not fall within the definition of an IMP; therefore, there is no requirement to submit serious adverse reactions associated with NIMPs (there are some exceptions, which are explained in the text)
10(b)	Should a new event relating to the conduct of the trial that is likely to affect the safety of the subjects occur, the requirement for investigators and sponsors to take appropriate urgent safety measures to protect the subjects against any immediate hazard The requirement for sponsors to inform Competent Authorities and ethics committees of such new events and the measures taken	This refers to trial-related events, not specifically IMP-related events
16	The requirement for investigators to notify the sponsor of serious adverse events	Adverse events are not specifically related to the IMP; therefore, investigators should report serious adverse events associated with both the IMP and any NIMP

IMP, investigational medicinal product; NIMP, non-investigational medicinal product.

requirements if the NIMP has an EU MAH and the MAH becomes aware of the event.

For some clinical trials it is possible that the sponsor of the trial is the MAH for the NIMP, but this may not always be the situation. In any case, it is recommended that SARs associated with a NIMP are reported to the MAH in order that this information may be used in the MAH's ongoing safety-monitoring procedures.

If the sponsor of a trial is also the MAH for the NIMP used in that trial, the reporting requirements defined in Directive 2001/83 (as amended) and Regulation 726/2004 apply for any SARs associated with the NIMP.

If the NIMP does not have a marketing authorisation in the UK, it is considered an unlicensed "special" and the licensing authority must be notified by the sponsor of any SARs associated with the NIMP that originates from the UK, as per SI 1994/3144.

12.3.6 Electronic reporting

The electronic reporting of SUSARs came into force with effect from 1 May 2004. The legal basis for this requirement is provided in Directive 2001/20/EC and the implementing texts. SUSARs reported as required by the Directive should be submitted to the EudraVigilance Clinical Trial Module.

It is expected that sponsors are capable of reporting electronically. For the latest information about how to report electronically please refer to the EudraVigilance website (http://EudraVigilance.emea.europa.eu/human/index.asp). Additional requirements are also provided on the MHRA website.

12.3.7 Considerations for blinded trials

SUSARs must be reported unblinded to Competent Authorities and ethics committees. Blinded data is of limited value to Competent Authorities, as it does not enable meaningful evaluation of data. The sponsor should consider how best to manage such unblinding so that those involved with the trial (outside of pharmacovigilance) do not become aware of the result, thereby avoiding any possible bias in the trial. For example, two reports may be produced, one unblinded for expedited reporting to Competent Authorities and ethics committees, and one blinded for forwarding to the project team and concerned investigators.

For the purpose of triage of a SAR in a blinded trial, expectedness may be assessed initially using the assumption that the test drug has been given. If it is assessed as unexpected against the test drug reference document, it should be unblinded. If, following unblinding, it is seen that the clinical trial subject received the comparator drug, but the event still meets the criteria for a SUSAR, in that it is unexpected according to the comparator reference document (which should be defined in the protocol), then it should be expedited according to the requirements set out in Section 12.3.4 and notified to the company that holds the marketing authorisation for the comparator drug. If, following unblinding, it is discovered that the IMP was a placebo, then this event will not require expedited reporting, unless in the opinion of the investigator or sponsor the event was related to a reaction to the placebo, for example an allergic reaction to an excipient. This is summarised in Figure 12.2.

If a subject has been administered multiple test drugs as part of a trial, then an assessment should be made against each test drug reference document. If the reaction is assessed as unexpected for any of the test drugs the subject potentially received, then it should be unblinded. When the result of the break of blind is known, and if the reaction is still unexpected for

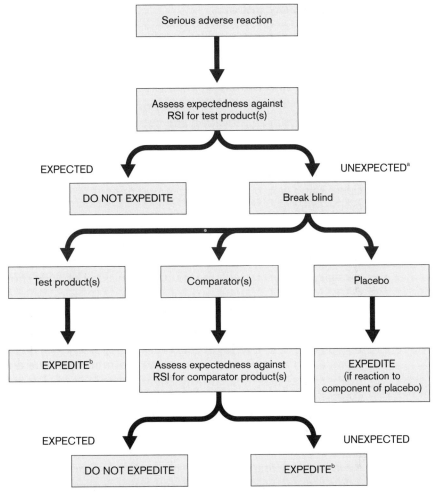

^aFor any of the test products administered to that subject. ^bIf the reaction is unexpected for the actual test or comparator product administered to that subject.

Figure 12.2 Considerations for blinded trials. RSI, Reference Safety Information.

the actual test drug administered, then this will be required to be reported as a SUSAR. The same logic will apply for subjects administered multiple comparator products during a blinded trial.

For details on how to manage SARs from blinded trials in PSURs, please refer to Section 5.5.

12.3.8 Annual Safety Reports

It is a requirement of EU Directive 2001/20/EC that the Competent Authorities and ethics committees are provided with a safety report on an annual basis throughout a trial. This includes line listings of all SARs and a report on subjects' safety. Detailed guidance on the format and content of these reports is provided in Volume 10, Chapter II "Detailed guidance on the collection, verification and presentation of adverse reaction reports arising from clinical trials on medicinal products for human use". The purpose of the report is to highlight any new safety information and review the safety profile of the IMP, taking into account all available safety data. For blinded trials, no additional unblinding is required for expected SARs.

The DLP for ASRs is one year after the first authorisation of the trial in any Member State. ASRs must be submitted within 60 days of the DLP. Where sponsors conduct more than one clinical trial with the same IMP, a single, combined ASR should be produced. The ASR should include a global analysis of the safety profile of the IMP and should also include a safety report and line listings of SARs in relation to each trial.

For marketed products, where the sponsor is the MAH, the DLP should coincide with the international birth date. The latter should also be used as the DLP if an EU marketing authorisation is granted for the IMP for the first time in any Member State during a time when the IMP is still under clinical investigation. The period covered by this particular ASR should cover the time period between the last ASR and the marketing authorisation approval date, and so will cover a period of less than one year. For clarifications relating to specific ASRs, it is recommended that the advice of the Competent Authority is sought.

Early-phase trials may start and finish within a year. An ASR is not expected for these trials. However, notification of the end of trial is required. In this notification, the sponsor should include an analysis of subject safety along with line listings of SARs and summary tables, if appropriate. If an ASR is produced that describes multiple trials, it is recommended that details of such short-running trials are included for completeness.

The guidance states that all available safety data must be taken into account within an ASR, and so consideration should be given to discussion of relevant safety information from outside of the clinical trial, such as spontaneous reactions and any investigator-sponsored studies of which the MAH is aware. All new and relevant findings should be discussed in the report.

The CIOMS VII working group has published a report entitled "Development Safety Update Report (DSUR): Harmonizing the Format and Content for Periodic Safety Reporting During Clinical Trials".

Recognising that regulatory authorities in the EU, USA and other locations require periodic reports during the conduct of clinical trials (e.g. the ASR in the EU) but that the requirements for these reports differ across the regions, CIOMS VII has proposed an internationally harmonised document that is modelled on the PSUR for marketed products.

Following on from this report, ICH is developing a common format for periodic reporting of safety information arising during the conduct of clinical trials, ICH E2F. If adopted, it is likely that this would replace the ASR in the EU. The provisional timeline for implementation of E2F is June 2009.

12.3.9 Safety monitoring boards

Clinical trials may also involve a data safety monitoring board (DSMB) or committee. Generally, a safety board is used in blinded trials studying diseases with high morbidity or mortality. The DSMB may review unblinded data in order to monitor the safety of the drug under investigation and make recommendations to the trial sponsor, such as requests for further information, amendment of the protocol or even termination of the trial on safety grounds. The ability to review unblinded data is a huge advantage, as the DSMB can make decisions without impacting the integrity of the trial.

The composition and remit of the DSMB must be clear, and referenced in the trial protocol. The DSMB should have a charter that dictates how often they will meet and how they will communicate with the sponsor, such as production of open minutes for the sponsor and closed minutes for the DSMB for blinded trials. The DSMB must commit to the charter; this is particularly important for IMPs where the safety profile may be unknown or poorly defined. As the DSMB may make a recommendation for amendment or termination of the trial, it is also important that the board remains independent of the sponsor in order to reduce any possible bias.

There should be procedures in place to ensure that any recommendations made by the DSMB are promptly addressed by the sponsor and appropriate and timely action is taken. In case of urgent safety measures, these will also need to be communicated, as appropriate, to Competent Authorities and ethics committees (in the UK this should be done within three days), and also to concerned investigators and patients.

Any recommendations from the DSMB should also be included and discussed in the ASR. Further guidance on data monitoring committees is available from the EMEA website (Annex 2).

12.3.10 Safety reporting to ethics committees

The reporting requirements for ethics committees have already been included in relevant sections above, but are summarised here for reference.

SUSARs that are fatal or life threatening must be reported to ethics committees within seven days (with any relevant follow-up information subsequently communicated within an additional eight days). All other SUSARs must be reported to ethics committees within 15 days of the sponsor becoming aware of the event. SUSAR reports sent to ethics committees should be unblinded, as detailed in Volume 10, ENTR/CT3, Section 5.1.8.

The sponsor is also required to submit to ethics committees at regular intervals (e.g. six-monthly) all SUSARs from clinical trials with the same IMP, and the same sponsor, that originate outside of the EU. For further information and guidance about reporting to ethics committees in the UK, please refer to the National Research Ethics Service website (www.nres.npsa.nhs.uk).

Ethics committees must also be provided with a copy of the ASR in parallel with the Competent Authority. This is not the same as the annual progress report that is required by ethics committees. The safety update provided in a progress report to the main research ethics committee cannot be submitted as an ASR, as the template for the safety update to the research ethics committee does not include sufficient detail to meet the needs of the ASR for the Competent Authorities, such as the requirement for aggregate summary tabulations or the review of all available safety data.

12.4 Post-authorisation Safety Studies

The definition of a PASS is provided in Section 12.1. Detailed guidance on PASS is provided in Part I, Section 7 of Volume 9A. PASS may be necessary if safety concerns have been noted during the clinical development of a medicinal product or if a signal has been identified during post-authorisation use. Additionally, PASS can be useful in confirming the safety profile of a product under normal conditions of use, which may lead to the identification of unknown adverse reactions. PASS may either be requested by a Competent Authority or initiated by the MAH. In either case, a PASS should form part of the MAH's RMP, if one is available (Chapter 7).

PASS can either be interventional or non-interventional in nature. If a PASS is interventional, then it must be conducted in accordance with Directive 2001/20/EC, including safety reporting requirements (Section 12.3). If the PASS is non-interventional, then the safety reporting requirements are generally in line with those for spontaneous adverse reactions (Section 12.2).

In certain scenarios, expedited reporting of ICSRs may not be required, for example in retrospective cohort studies where it is not possible to assess causality at an individual case level. In such scenarios, the MAH is encouraged to discuss the requirements with the appropriate Competent Authority.

12.4.1 Progress reports from Post-authorisation Safety Studies

Progress reports must be submitted to Competent Authorities for PASS being performed by the MAH. The periodicity of submission will depend on whether the study is requested by the Competent Authority or whether it is being performed at the MAH's initiative (see Part I, Section 7 of Volume 9A).

In addition to progress reports, safety information from the PASS will need to be included in:

- ASRs (if the PASS is an interventional study; see Section 12.3.8);
- PSURs
- RMPs.

Safety information from non-interventional PASS (and other non-interventional studies) may also need to be included in ASRs (as required under Directive 2001/20/EC) if such findings are relevant to subjects participating in interventional clinical trials. If the sponsor and/or MAH is aware of such findings, these should be discussed in Part 1 of the applicable ASR (Annex 2).

12.5 Investigator-led Studies

After a marketing authorisation has been granted, the MAH may be involved in studies that it is not directly sponsoring, for example those that are led by clinicians employed by NHS trusts or academic institutions. The level of involvement of the MAH in these studies may vary. For example, post-authorisation studies may be entirely led or organised by the principal investigator, with the MAH only providing the product. Alternatively, the MAH may be more involved, such as providing support with pharmacovigilance functions (e.g. collecting and collating safety data).

For interventional trials being sponsored by organisations other than the MAH, the sponsor remains responsible for the trial, not the MAH. It is expected, however, that if the MAH is supporting the trial by providing funding or supplying the IMP, then there is an agreement in place that includes the requirement for the investigator to report safety information to the MAH. This should be a two-way agreement, such that if the MAH becomes aware of significant new safety information relating to the IMP, this is shared with the sponsor–investigator. If the MAH is supplying IMP to the investigator, the MAH should consider whether the sponsor has applied for a clinical trials authorisation.

It is possible that principal investigators may carry out post-authorisation studies using products already in stock (in the NHS in the UK), in which case the MAH has no knowledge of the study. It is acknowledged that the MAH may find it difficult to collect safety information from these types of study, and such information may only become available via literature searches if the study results are published in scientific journals.

12.6   Registries

Studies performed using registry data are usually classified as non-interventional studies. Registry data may also be used to perform PASS. The use of standardised questionnaires to collect registry data does not usually alter the "non-interventional" classification of the study.

Registries may be established and managed by a MAH, by a contract company on behalf of the MAH, or by an organisation independent of the MAH. In all of these situations, a MAH may use registry data to perform studies, such as PASS. Competent Authorities may request the MAH to perform a registry study and supply updates on registry data as part of a RMP commitment.

Considerations for safety reporting of registry data include the following:

- For the purposes of safety reporting, reports from registries are classified as solicited reports and, where possible, should have an appropriate causality assessment by a HCP or by the MAH.
- If the registry is managed by the MAH, then the MAH is responsible for reporting adverse reactions (expedited reports and in PSURs) identified from registry data in accordance with Regulation (EC) 726/2004, Directive 2001/83/EC (as amended) and Volume 9A.
- If the registry is managed by a contract company on behalf of the MAH, then, depending on the terms of the agreement between the two parties, either the contract company or the MAH is responsible for reporting adverse reactions identified from registry data in accordance with Regulation (EC) 726/2004, Directive 2001/83/EC (as amended) and Volume 9A. The agreement should clearly state the responsibilities of each party. In addition, the MAH would be expected to assess the

contract company and/or registry at appropriate intervals to ensure that adverse reactions have been identified, managed and reported in accordance with the agreement.

- If the registry is managed by an organisation independent of the MAH and it contains adverse reaction reports that are associated with a MAH's product, the MAH would be expected to report these adverse reactions in accordance with applicable legislation only if the MAH becomes aware of the cases. It is common practice for independent registries to publish annual reports, which MAHs may become aware of (e.g. through literature search procedures). However, information obtained from an annual report may contain a paucity of information relating to individual adverse reaction reports and may not include causality confirmation. It may also be difficult for the MAH to perform follow up on these cases. The MAH may attempt to establish an agreement with the independent organisation for exchange of safety data relating to product(s) for which the MAH holds authorisations.

12.7 Examples of Inspection Findings

Examples of areas of concern that have been identified during inspections are provided below. This is not an exhaustive list but serves to summarise some of the key points from this chapter and highlights areas that can be problematic. It is anticipated that examples will prove useful to help MAHs to address such issues.

(i)   There is evidence of failing to identify all AEs and SAEs occurring to patients, particularly during the follow-up period. Patients may be followed up for lengthy periods but there is often not appropriate consideration in the protocol for the recording and management of safety information during the follow-up period.

(ii)   There are errors in the decision-making process regarding reports that qualify for expedited reporting; for example, over-reporting to Competent Authorities of deaths that are not unexpected and/or causally related.

(iii)   SUSARs are being reported to Competent Authorities in a blinded fashion, when they should be unblinded prior to submission.

(iv)   There is a general lack of discussion of the risk–benefit evaluation for the IMP within the ASR.

(v)   For authorised medicinal products, which are also being used in interventional trials, there is a lack of cross-referencing between the ASR and the PSUR.

(vi)   There is no evidence that the MAH has assessed the impact of major changes in legislation on the company's processes and procedures, with particular reference to Council Directive 2001/20/EC, the provisions of which were applicable from 1 May 2004.

(vii) The procedures for the management of safety information over extended holiday periods are insufficiently detailed; for example, who checks the dedicated fax, and what is the potential impact upon patient safety and regulatory reporting timelines?

(viii) There is no procedure to describe the process for handling urgent safety measures.

(ix) There are deficiencies in the safety reporting sections of the protocol; for example, lack of clarity regarding who should be sent what reports and/or information and when.

(x) In non-commercial research, there are inadequate mechanisms to share safety information with investigators if more than one study uses the same IMP.

(xi) There is inadequate or inappropriate ongoing review of safety data (e.g. for review of non-serious as well as serious data) by the sponsor during the conduct of a trial or of a programme of trials.

(xii) The sponsor has failed to take timely action in response to the recommendations of a DSMB.

Current metrics relating to MHRA pharmacovigilance inspection findings can be found on our website. The exact nature of findings will vary from company to company and findings are graded on a case-by-case basis, taking into account the evidence relating to the issue and the impact of the findings on, for example, public safety or other areas of the pharmacovigilance system.

Introduction to Pharmacovigilance Inspections

Editor's note	The MHRA Pharmacovigilance Inspectorate is part of the Inspection, Enforcement and Standards Division of the MHRA. The function of the Pharmacovigilance Inspectorate is to assess compliance with UK and EU legislation relating to the monitoring of the safety of medicines given to patients as part of the MHRA's mission to safeguard public health. This is mainly achieved through carrying out inspections of UK MAHs. The MHRA initiated a voluntary pharmacovigilance inspection programme in October 2002 to develop the inspection methodology. In July 2003, the MHRA introduced a statutory pharmacovigilance inspection programme.
	Further details on the Pharmacovigilance Inspectorate, including details of the current level of fees for national pharmacovigilance inspections can be accessed via the GPvP page of the MHRA website.

Inspectors' Rights

Inspectors have rights conferred under the Medicines Act 1968 sections 111 (1 to 3) and 112 (1 to 4 and 7) as well as subordinate legislation applying the Act. These include the right to enter any premises covered by the Act to carry out inspections, take samples, require the production of books and documents, and to take copies of, or copies of entries in, such books and documents, and seize and detain substances, articles and documents. It is a criminal offence under section 114 (2 and 3) of the Medicines Act 1968 to obstruct an inspector during the conduct of an inspection covered by the Act.

European legislation includes the rights of Member States to inspect MAHs: Article 111 of Directive 2001/83/EC, as amended by 2004/27/EC, Section 1 states:

> *Such inspections shall be carried out by officials representing the competent authority that shall be empowered to:*

*(d) inspect the premises, records and documents of marketing author-
isation holders or any firms employed by the marketing authorisation holder to perform the activities described in Title IX
[Pharmacovigilance], and in particular Articles 103 and 104.*

In addition, in relation to centrally authorised products, Article 19 of
Regulation (EC) No 726/2004 states:

*1. The supervisory authorities shall be responsible for verifying on
behalf of the Community that the holder of the marketing authorisation for the medicinal product for human use or the manufacturer or
importer established within the Community satisfies the requirements
laid down in Titles IV, IX [Pharmacovigilance] and XI of Directive
2001/83/EC.*

Types of Pharmacovigilance Inspection

(i) *Routine national inspections.* These are scheduled inspections that
UK MAHs undergo on a periodic basis. MAHs are notified of these
inspections in advance. These inspections are generally systems based,
meaning that inspectors examine the systems and procedures used by
a MAH to comply with existing EU and national pharmacovigilance
regulations and guidance.

(ii) *"For cause" national inspections.* These are ad hoc inspections that
are triggered as a result of, for example, safety issues, suspected
violations of legislation relating to the monitoring of the safety of
medicines, or referrals by other Member States. In rare circumstances,
MAHs may not be notified of these inspections in advance.

(iii) *CHMP-requested inspections.* The CHMP may request inspections
of MAHs in association with specific centrally authorised products.
These can either be routine or triggered. The EMEA co-ordinates
these inspections and together with the Member States is developing
a plan for routine inspections of MAHs with centralised authorised
products. The general organisation and process for CHMP-requested
pharmacovigilance inspections is described in Volume 9A, Part 1,
Section 2.4. The procedures for EU pharmacovigilance inspections
requested by the CHMP can be found on the EMEA web site at
http://www.emea.europa.eu/Inspections/GCPproc.html.

Scope of Inspections

In some circumstances, such as a CHMP-requested inspection, third-country sites may be subject to inspection by the MHRA if they are involved in monitoring the safety of medicines marketed in the EU. The MHRA performs routine pharmacovigilance inspections of UK MAHs. If, however, a MAH has delegated important pharmacovigilance activities to a contract company, then the contract company or individual contractors may also be included in the inspection.

The Inspection Schedule

The MHRA's original intention was to inspect every UK MAH on a three-yearly cycle; however, the inspectorate has moved towards a more risk-based approach to inspection scheduling. This will help to focus resources to improve the protection of public health where there is a potentially higher risk, in line with Hampton principles.[1] Factors which may affect inspection scheduling include:

- number of MAs held;
- product portfolio;
- QPPV details not provided to MHRA;
- number of "black triangle" products (intensive monitoring);
- number of products with known safety risks;
- non-compliance with 15-day reporting requirements or PSUR submissions;
- companies placing their first product on the market.

Phases of the Inspection Process

There are three main phases of each pharmacovigilance inspection:

(i) planning;
(ii) conduct of inspection;
(iii) reporting and follow-up.

---

[1] Further information on the Hampton Review "Reducing Administrative Burdens" can be accessed at http://www.hm-treasury.gov.uk/independent_reviews/hamptonreview/hampton_index.cfm.

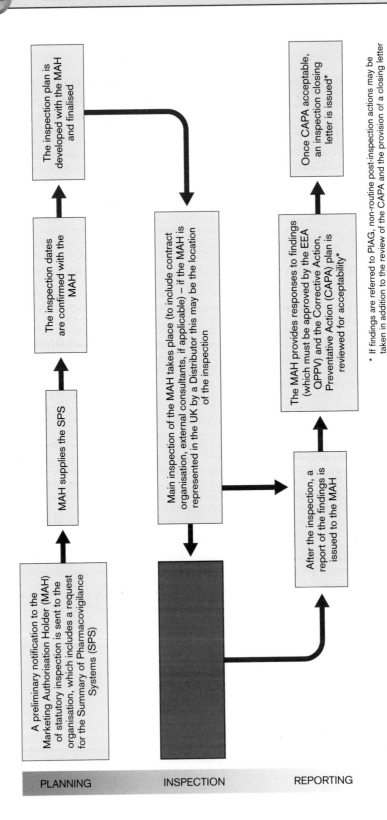

Figure A1.1 Overview of the inspection process. CAPA, corrective action, preventative action; EEA, European Economic Area; MAH, Marketing Authorisation Holder; PIAG, Pharmacovigilance Inspection Action Group; QPPV, Qualified Person for Pharmacovigilance; SPS, Summary of Pharmacovigilance Systems.

1 Planning

For routine, national inspections, the company will be contacted (usually by the lead inspector) and will be notified of the inspection. The company will be requested to provide a Summary of Pharmacovigilance Systems (SPS). This provides information to assist both the MAH and the Inspectorate in preparing for the inspection. The most up-to-date version of the SPS template is available from the MHRA GPvP website. It is recognised that there are areas of overlap and/or duplication between the SPS and the DDPS. Where appropriate, a DDPS could be used to provide some of the information required in the SPS if agreed in advance with the Inspectorate. It would be necessary to submit additional information required for the SPS that is not present in the DDPS in a format agreeable to the Inspectorate.

The proposed inspection dates will be discussed and agreed. On receipt of the SPS, a draft inspection plan will usually be provided to the company for review and confirmation of personnel involved in interview sessions. A detailed inspection plan may not be provided prior to a "for cause" inspection. It is important that personnel who actually perform the activities are included in interview sessions in order to gain most value from the inspection from both the Inspectorate's and the company's perspective. Although face-to-face interviews are most effective, it is permissible to use tele- or video-conferences to overcome availability issues and to prevent personnel travelling unnecessarily long distances. Time zones in different countries need to be considered if this is the case.

Prior to the inspection, a MAH may be requested to provide additional documents to be made available either prior to the site visit or for the first day of the inspection. Requested documents may include:

- CVs, job descriptions and training records for interviewees;
- organisation charts/organograms (with names and job titles);
- procedural documents (e.g. SOPs, working instructions, etc.);
- standard training material and presentations;
- individual case files for selected products;
- PSURs for selected products;
- contracts and agreements with co-marketing partners, contractors, distributors;
- RMPs;
- meeting minutes;
- line listings of adverse reaction reports;
- validation documentation for computerised systems;
- audit plans (internal audit reports will not routinely be reviewed, but may be requested in exceptional circumstances).

2 Conduct of the inspection

An opening meeting will be held on the first day of the inspection, during which the scope and conduct of the inspection will be described.

The inspections themselves consist of site visits during which interviews and reviews of document and computer systems (including searches of any pharmacovigilance databases) are performed. A review of various areas, for example the archive facility, may also be included.

In general, a closing meeting will be held on the last day of the inspection to provide oral feedback on any deficiencies identified.

The following points should be considered in relation to the conduct of an inspection.

- In general, the company is free to choose which members of staff attend both the opening and closing meetings.
- The MHRA has its own system for managing document requests, the details of which will be described during the opening meeting.
- No documents provided by the MAH will be removed from site without prior notification.
- Documents may be requested that are located at sites outside the EU. These sites may be in different time zones from the inspected site. Any difficulties in obtaining documents during the inspection should be discussed with the inspection team at an early stage. Arrangements for providing documents post-inspection can be negotiated.
- Note-takers or observers are free to sit in on interview sessions as long as they do not disrupt the interview process.
- Companies are free to take their own notes during the inspection, but recording of interviews or meetings is not permissible.

3 Reporting

Deficiencies found during MHRA pharmacovigilance inspections are graded as follows.

Critical. A deficiency in pharmacovigilance systems, practices or processes that adversely affects the rights, safety or well-being of patients or that poses a potential risk to public health or that represents a serious violation of applicable legislation and guidelines.

Major. A deficiency in pharmacovigilance systems, practices or processes that could potentially adversely affect the rights, safety or well-being of patients or that could potentially pose a risk to public health or that represents a violation of applicable legislation and guidelines.

Other. A deficiency in pharmacovigilance systems, practices or processes that would not be expected to adversely affect the rights, safety or well-being of patients.

In general, preliminary findings will be communicated verbally at the closing meeting. An inspection report is then prepared and reviewed internally to ensure consistency of classification of deficiencies prior to issue of the final report. The report is sent to the MAH, usually within 30 working days of the site visit or the date of the provision of the last document requested, whichever is the latest. It should be noted that the factual matter contained in the inspection report relates only to those things that the inspection team sees and hears during the inspection process. The inspection report is not to be taken as implying a satisfactory state of affairs in documentation, premises, equipment, personnel or procedures not examined during the inspection.

Responding to Findings

Following the issue of the inspection report, the MAH is requested to respond to any deficiencies identified and to provide the MHRA with an appropriate "corrective and preventative action" plan. The lead inspector will set the deadline for provision of responses. In practice, this is usually 30 working days. Note that, in some circumstances, the MAH may be required to take immediate action to address a critical or major finding, for the protection of patients.

In relation to completing the responses:

- The EEA QPPV should indicate his or her approval of the responses by signing the document containing the responses.
- Each inspection finding is numbered. A response should be produced for each inspection finding and the finding number should be referenced next to the response. Responses are not required in relation to recommendations or observations.
- If the accuracy of information contained in the inspection report is challenged or if findings are disputed, then the respondent should enclose relevant documentary evidence supporting the responses. If a finding is not disputed, then documentary evidence is not required.

When the deficiency is reviewed by the MAH, consideration should be given not only to correcting the specific examples cited in the inspection report but also to identifying and correcting the root cause of the deficiency, where appropriate.

Other points to consider when responding to inspection findings are:

- the action must address the finding in terms of immediate corrective action and future preventative actions;
- the company should not make promises it cannot deliver;
- timelines should be clearly stated for each action;
- responses should be clear and succinct.

Consequences of Inadequate Systems

Critical findings are routinely referred to the MHRA's Pharmacovigilance Inspection Action Group (PIAG), a non-statutory, multi-disciplinary group constituted to advise the Director of Inspection, Enforcement and Standards, the Director of Vigilance and Risk Management of Medicines and the Director of Licensing on any recommendation for referral or enforcement action appropriate to their divisions that arises from non-compliance detected during pharmacovigilance inspections. The PIAG provides advice in cases where critical findings are identified during inspection and/or serious non-compliance is identified that could affect the rights, safety or well-being of patients.

The group meets regularly, usually monthly, to deal with ongoing business and to consider new referrals. Ad hoc meetings may be convened to address serious and urgent issues.

The PIAG recommendations for action to date have consisted of the following:

- Early re-inspection has been the most common recommendation to date. In most cases on re-inspection, adequate progress has been observed. In some cases, a further re-inspection has been required and a minority of cases have been referred back to PIAG for consideration of other actions.
- Sharing of information with other Competent Authorities and the EMEA, where appropriate (e.g. in relation to applications that may be under consideration). In one case, this led to a CHMP request for an EU pharmacovigilance inspection.
- Sending a "warning letter" to remind the MAH of their legal obligations and of the consequences of continued non-compliance.
- Meetings with senior MAH representatives to discuss the issues and the consequences of non-compliance.
- Referral to the MHRA Enforcement Group for investigation with a view to criminal prosecution.

Potential additional actions that may be considered in the future include the following:

- Macrory administrative fines (following the implementation of the Hampton principles).[2]
- Referral to the EMEA and Commission in accordance with the EU infringement procedure (fines) for centrally authorised products.[3]
- Particular scrutiny of new marketing authorisation applications to confirm the status of the pharmacovigilance system on the basis that the DDPS included in the application is inadequate, where the MAH's pharmacovigilance system is known from inspection to be non-compliant.

In relation to clinical trials, additional actions are available in accordance with EU and UK clinical trial legislation, for example, issuing of infringement notices, suspension of Clinical Trial Authorisations or rejection of applications for Clinical Trial Authorisation.

Re-inspections

For the national inspection programme, there are a number of different types of re-inspection:

- for cases referred to PIAG, re-inspections are normally required within 6–12 months;
- periodic inspections performed as part of UK and EU routine inspection programmes (frequency dependent upon risk assessment);
- UK and EU triggered inspections.

Re-inspections could be unannounced if persistent non-compliance is detected or suspected. The focus of the inspection may be different from that of a routine systems inspection depending on the reason for the re-inspection.

One focus will be the improvement of the system resulting from the deficiencies identified in the previous inspection. A lack of action by the MAH will be taken into consideration when classifying inspection findings. Some areas may receive closer evaluation during re-inspection; for example, areas in which significant problems were previously identified. Some areas may not be evaluated to the same extent. For example, computer system validation may not be evaluated in depth if there have not been any upgrades or changes to the system.

---

[2] For further information visit http://bre.berr.gov.uk/regulation/reviewing_regulation/penalties/index.asp.
[3] Commission Regulation (EC) No 658/2007.

Tips for Preparing for a Regulatory Authority Inspection

- Remember that inspections are a chance for the company to demonstrate regulatory compliance and an opportunity to improve its pharmacovigilance system.
- Be honest.
- Communicate any issues or non-compliances that have already been identified by the MAH to the inspectors, at an early stage.
- Expect the unexpected!
- Do not waste time and effort prior to the inspection making quick fixes. These may often not be appropriate or may need to be changed after the inspection.
- Communicate promptly to the inspection team if there are any problems or difficulties in fulfilling inspection requests or if requests are unclear or ambiguous.
- The MAH may need to assign specific resource to assist with the co-ordination of the inspection. The individual or team assigned to do this must have good co-operations from other areas of the organisation.
- Ensure that everyone knows their role and responsibilities.
- Be prepared for deviations from the inspection plan at short notice.
- Ensure that interviewees and backroom staff are appropriate. Specific resource may need to be dedicated to address requests for documentation during the course of the inspection.
- Ensure that sufficient resources are made available to meet requests; for example, photocopiers, printer toner, fax machines and adequate meeting rooms or offices.
- Ensure that the interview environment is suitable.
- Ensure that documentation is clearly labelled as per the inspector's request and that it is logged on the document request form.
- Establish a communication plan:
  - who: contact list local and/or global;
  - single contact point for co-ordination of requests coming from the inspection room.
- Ensure that relevant departments and sites are informed to ensure that documents can be obtained from them if required.
- Ensure that there is a mechanism to obtain the relevant documentation, wherever it resides within the organisation, in a prompt manner.
- Ensure that tele- or video-conference facilities are working and have been tested, and that technical people are available if problems arise.
- Check that the documents provided are complete and fulfil the request(s). Inadequate responses to requests may lead to additional requests and prolong the process.
- Finally remember that the goals of the company and inspectors are the same – *to protect public health.*

Relevant Legislation and Guidance

European Legislation

Regulation (EC) No 726/2004 of the European Parliament and of the Council of 31 March 2004 laying down Community procedures for the authorisation and supervision of medicinal products for human and veterinary use and establishing a European Medicines Agency.

Commission Regulation (EC) No 540/95 of 10 March 1995 laying down the arrangements for reporting suspected unexpected adverse reactions which are not serious, whether arising in the Community or in a third country, to medicinal products for human or veterinary use authorized in accordance with the provisions of Council Regulation (EEC) No 2309/93.

Directive 2001/83/EC of the European Parliament and of the Council of 6 November 2001 on the Community code relating to medicinal products for human use.

Directive 2004/27/EC of the European Parliament and of the Council of 31 March 2004 amending Directive 2001/83/EC on the Community code relating to medicinal products for human use.

Directive 2004/24/EC of the European Parliament and of the Council of 31 March 2004 amending, as regards traditional herbal medicinal products, Directive 2001/83/EC on the Community code relating to medicinal products for human use.

Commission Directive 2003/63/EC of 25 June 2003 amending Directive 2001/83/EC of the European Parliament and of the Council on the Community code relating to medicinal products for human use.

Directive 2001/20/EC of the European Parliament and of the Council of 4 April 2001 on the approximation of the laws, regulations and administrative provisions of the Member States relating to the implementation of good clinical practice in the conduct of clinical trials on medicinal products for human use.

Regulation (EC) No 1901/2006 of the European Parliament and of the Council of 12 December 2006 on medicinal products for paediatric use and amending Regulation (EEC) No 1768/92, Directive 2001/20/EC, Directive 2001/83/EC and Regulation (EC) No 726/2004.

Regulation (EC) No 1902/2006 of the European Parliament and of the Council of 20 December 2006 amending Regulation 1901/2006 on medicinal products for paediatric use.

Commission Regulation (EC) No 658/2007 of 14 June 2007 concerning financial penalties for infringement of certain obligations in connection with marketing authorisations granted under Regulation (EC) No 726/2004 of the European Parliament and of the Council.

Full text of the above can be accessed at http://ec.europa.eu/enterprise/pharmaceuticals/index_en.htm.

UK Legislation

UK Medicines Act 1968 and the updates contained in applicable Statutory Instruments, including:

The Medicines for Human Use (Marketing Authorisations Etc.) Regulations 1994, SI No. 3144.

The Medicines (Codification Amendments Etc.) Regulations 2002, SI No. 236.

The Medicines for Human Use (Fees and Miscellaneous Amendments) Regulations 2003, SI No. 2321.

The Medicines (Marketing Authorisations and Miscellaneous Amendments) Regulations 2004, SI No. 3224.

The Medicines (Provision of False or Misleading Information and Miscellaneous Amendments) Regulations 2005, SI No. 1710.

The Medicines (Marketing Authorisations Etc.) Amendment Regulations 2005, SI No. 2759.

The Medicines for Human Use (Clinical Trials) Regulations 2004, SI No. 1031.

The Medicines for Human Use (Clinical Trials) Amendment Regulations 2006, SI No. 1928.

The Medicines for Human Use (Clinical Trials) Amendment (No.2) Regulations 2006, SI No. 2984.

Full text of UK Statutory Instruments and Explanatory Memoranda can be obtained from the Office of Public Sector Information http://www.opsi.gov.uk/stat.htm.

Guidance Documents and Other Useful Reference Texts

A2.1 International Conference on Harmonisation (ICH) documents

CPMP/ICH/377/95	E2A	Note for Guidance on Clinical Safety Data Management: Definitions and Standards for Expedited Reporting
CPMP/ICH/287/95	E2B (M)	Note for Guidance on Clinical Safety Data Management: Data Elements for Transmission of Individual Case Safety Reports
CHMP/ICH/166783/05	E2B (R3)	Note For Guidance on Data Elements for Transmission of Individual Case Safety Reports – DRAFT DOCUMENT
CPMP/ICH/288/95	E2C (R1)	Note for Guidance on Clinical Safety Data Management: Periodic Safety Update Reports for Marketed Drugs
CPMP/ICH/3945/03	E2D	Post-approval Safety Data Management: Note for Guidance on Definitions and Standards for Expedited Reporting
CPMP/ICH/5716/03	E2E	Pharmacovigilance Planning: Note for Guidance on Planning Pharmacovigilance Activities
CPMP/ICH/135/95	E6	Note for Guidance on Good Clinical Practice
CPMP/ICH/2711/99	E11	Note For Guidance on Clinical Investigation of Medicinal Products in the Paediatric Population

Available from the ICH website: (http://www.ich.org/cache/compo/276–254–1.html).

A2.2 Eudralex documents

Volume 9A		The rules governing medicinal products in the European Union: guidelines on "Pharmacovigilance for Medicinal Products for Human Use"
Volume 10	ENTR/CT3	Detailed guidance on the collection, verification and presentation of adverse reaction reports arising from clinical trials on medicinal products for human use
Volume 10	ENTR/CT4	Detailed guidance on the European database of Suspected Unexpected Serious Adverse Reactions (Eudravigilance – Clinical Trial Module)

Available from the European Commission website (http://ec.europa.eu/enterprise/pharmaceuticals/eudralex/index.htm).

A2.3 EMEA Scientific Guidelines for Human Medicinal Products

EMEA/192632/2006	Template for EU Risk Management Plan (EU-RMP)
EMEA/CHMP/313666/05	Exposure to Medicinal Products during Pregnancy: Need for Post-authorisation Data
EMEA/CHMP/235910/05	Guideline on conduct of pharmacovigilance for medicines used by the paediatric population
EMEA/CHMP/EWP/5872/03 Corr	Guideline on Data Monitoring Committees

Available from the European Medicines Agency website (http://www.emea.europa.eu/).

UK Pharmacovigilance Offences

Table A3.1 Enforcement provisions under Statutory Instrument 1994/3144 [The Medicines for Human Use (Marketing Authorisations Etc.) Regulations 1994 as amended by Statutory Instruments 2002/236, 2003/2321, 2004/3224, 2005/1710, 2005/2759, 2006/1952] SCHEDULE 3

Offence	Provisions
Failure to comply with the conditions attached to a marketing authorisation	Without prejudice to any other sanction which may be available for the enforcement of conditions attaching to marketing authorizations, any holder of a marketing authorization for a relevant medicinal product who contravenes any condition of the authorization shall be guilty of an offence
Failure to implement urgent safety restrictions	**3A** Any person who is the holder of a marketing authorization who fails to implement an urgent safety restriction imposed on him by the licensing authority under Regulation 6A or by the European Commission under Commission regulation (EC) No. 1085/2003 shall be guilty of an offence
	5 Any person who is or, immediately before its revocation or suspension, was the holder of a marketing authorization who fails to comply with a notice given to him under regulation 6(5) (notice to take all reasonably practicable steps to publish information concerning revocation or suspension or to recover possession of products affected) shall be guilty of an offence

Failure to inform the UK licensing authority of amendments to the DDPS, any prohibition or restriction imposed by the Competent Authorities of any country in which the medicinal product is marketed and of any other new information which might influence the evaluation of the benefits and risks of the medicinal product	**6** Any holder of a marketing authorization who fails promptly to: update information concerning the product or any connected matter as required by Article 8.3 of the Directive, Article 6 of Regulation (EC) No 726/2004 or, in the case of a holder of an authorisation for a national homeopathic product, Article 8.3 of the 2001 Directive as applied by paragraph 1(3) of Part 1 of Schedule 1A; or
	
	(cc) provide information to the licensing authority as required by—
	    (i) the third paragraph of Article 23 of the 2001 Directive or, in the case of a holder of an authorisation for a national homeopathic product, that paragraph read in accordance with the modifications in regulation 1(8)(c),
	    (ii) the fourth paragraph of Article 23 of the 2001 Directive, or
	    (iii) the first paragraph of Article 23a of the 2001 Directive, or
	(d) provide information to the EMEA, the Commission or the licensing authority as required by Article 16.2 of Regulation (EC) No. 726/2004,
	(dd) provide information to the EMEA as required by the first or second paragraphs of Article 13(4) of Regulation No. 726/2004, or

	(e) submit any application to the licensing authority or the Community to make any changes or variation as required by Article 23 of the 2001 Directive or Article 16.3 of Regulation (EC) No. 726/2004, shall be guilty of an offence
Failure to provide information requested by the UK licensing authority, which might influence the evaluation of the benefits and risks of the medicinal product	6A Any holder of a United Kingdom marketing authorization who fails to forward to the licensing authority any data requested by the authority pursuant to the final paragraph of Article 23 or of Article 23a of the 2001 Directive: (a) where the licensing authority have served a written notice on the holder under regulation 7(5) in relation to the request, within the time specified in that notice; or (b) where there is no such notice, promptly, shall be guilty of an offence
Failure to provide the EMEA with data relating to the volume of sales of the medicinal product at Community level, broken down by Member State, and any data in the holder's possession relating to the volume of prescriptions, in the context of pharmacovigilance, or to provide specific pharmacovigilance data from targeted groups of patients on request of the EMEA	6D Any person who is the holder of a Community marketing authorization who fails to provide the EMEA with any data requested pursuant to the final paragraph of Article 13(4) or the final paragraph of Article 26 of Regulation (EC) No. 726/2004: (a) within the time specified in the request, if a time within which to provide the data to the EMEA is so specified, or (b) promptly, if no such time is specified, shall be guilty of an offence
Failure to communicate information about pharmacovigilance concerns to the UK licensing authority and the EMEA, where applicable, at the same time or before communicating these concerns to the public	6E Any person who is the holder of a Community or United Kingdom marketing authorization who communicates to the general public information: (a) relating to pharmacovigilance concerns about the product to which the authorization relates, (b) without having previously communicated, or without simultaneously communicating, such information to the EMEA, in the case of a product for which there is a Community marketing authorization, or otherwise the licensing authority, shall be guilty of an offence

Table A3.1 (*cont.*)

Failure to communicate pharmacovigilance concerns to the UK licensing authority, EMEA or the public in a way that is objective and is not misleading	6F (a) (b)	Any person: (a) who is the holder of a Community or United Kingdom marketing authorization; and (b) who fails to ensure that the information which he communicates to the general public, the licensing authority or the EMEA relating to pharmacovigilance concerns about the product to which his authorization relates is presented objectively and is not misleading, shall be guilty of an offence
Failure of the marketing authorisation holder to appoint an appropriate QPPV	7	Any person responsible for placing on the market a relevant medicinal product authorized by the Community or by the licensing authority who, at any time, does not have at his disposal an appropriately qualified person responsible for pharmacovigilance as required by Chapter 3 of Title II of Regulation (EC) No. 726/2004 or Title IX of the 2001 Directive shall be guilty of an offence
Failure to report adverse reactions in accordance with Community legislation (as expedited reports and in PSURs)	8	Any person responsible for placing a relevant medicinal product on the market who fails to report to the licensing authority any suspected adverse reaction, or to submit to the licensing authority any records of suspected adverse reactions as required by Chapter 3 of Title II of Regulation (EC) No. 726/2004 or Title IX of the 2001 Directive, shall be guilty of an offence
Failure to keep records of adverse reaction reports as required by Community legislation		Any person responsible for placing a relevant medicinal product on the market who fails to make or maintain a detailed record of any suspected adverse reaction as required by Chapter 3 of Title II of Regulation (EC) No. 726/2004, or Title IX of the 2001 Directive shall be guilty of an offence.
Failure of the QPPV to fulfil their obligations in accordance with Community legislation, including failure to establish and maintain a system, prepare specific reports and provide information necessary for the evaluation of benefits and risks	10	Any person who, while employed or engaged as an appropriately qualified person responsible for pharmacovigilance for the purposes of Chapter 3 of Title II of Regulation (EC) No. 726/2004, or Title IX of the 2001 Directive fails to: (a) establish or maintain a system for collecting and collating information about suspected adverse reactions; (b) prepare for the licensing authority a report on any such reactions; or (c) ensure that a request from the licensing authority for the provision of additional information necessary for the evaluation of the benefits and risks afforded by a relevant medicinal product is answered fully and promptly; or (d) provide to the licensing authority any other information relevant to the evaluation of the benefits and risks afforded by a medicinal product, including appropriate information on post authorization safety studies, as required by any provision of any such Chapter or Title, shall be guilty of an offence

Provision to the UK licensing authority (including by the QPPV) of information relating to product safety, which is false and misleading *Added to Schedule 3 in Statutory Instrument 2005 No. 1710: "The Medicines (Provision of False or Misleading Information and Miscellaneous Amendments) Regulations 2005"*	10A (1) Any person who in the course of an application for the grant, renewal or variation of a marketing authorization for a relevant medicinal product: (a) fails to provide to the licensing authority any information which is relevant to an evaluation of the safety, quality or efficacy of the relevant medicinal product as required by point (7) or (11) of the introduction to Annex I to the 2001 Directive; or (b) provides to the licensing authority any information which is relevant to an evaluation of the safety, quality or efficacy of the relevant medicinal product but which is false or misleading in a material particular, shall be guilty of an offence (2) Any person who: (a) is responsible for placing a relevant medicinal product on the market; (b) is the marketing authorization holder for a relevant medicinal product; or (c) while employed or engaged as an appropriately qualified person responsible for pharmacovigilance for the purposes of Chapter 3 of Title II of Council Regulation (EEC) No 2309/93 [sic; this should read 726/2004] or Title IX of the 2001 Directive is required to provide information to the licensing authority about a relevant medicinal product; who provides to the licensing authority any information which is relevant to an evaluation of the safety, quality or efficacy of the relevant medicinal product but which is false or misleading in a material particular shall be guilty of an offence
Failure to retain adverse reaction records from compassionate use or to make these records available for inspection	13 Any person who fails to keep any record required under paragraph 6 of Schedule 1, or to give notice or make it available for inspection as and when required under paragraph 7 of that Schedule, shall be guilty of an offence
Provision to the UK licensing authority of information relating to product safety for compassionate use, which is false and misleading.	13A Any person who: (a) sells or supplies a relevant medicinal product in accordance with any of paragraphs 1 to 4 of Schedule 1; or (b) provides a specification for such a product for the purposes of paragraph 1 of that Schedule; who provides to the licensing authority any information which is relevant to an evaluation of the safety, quality or efficacy of the relevant medicinal product but which is false or misleading in a material particular shall be guilty of an offence

Table A3.1 (cont.)

Added to Schedule 3 in SI 2005 No. 1710: "The Medicines (Provision of False or Misleading Information and Miscellaneous Amendments) Regulations 2005".	

For all offences committed under the Medicines Act, the listed penalties apply. The differences in the offences relate to whether the case is tried in a Magistrate's Court or in a Crown Court	**Penalties**
	
	14 Any person guilty of an offence under any of the preceding paragraphs shall be liable:
	  (a) on summary conviction, to a fine not exceeding the statutory maximum;
	  (b) on conviction on indictment, to a fine or to imprisonment for a term not exceeding two years or
	      to both

Liability of employers (including senior management and board members)	**Miscellaneous** 15 (1) Where an offence is committed under any of paragraphs 8, 9, 10 or 10A by a person mentioned in those paragraphs who is acting as the employee or agent of another person, the employer or principal of that person shall be guilty of the same offence
The defence of due diligence	17 (1) A person does not commit an offence under paragraph 6B, 6C, 10A or 13A if he took all reasonable precautions and exercised all due diligence to avoid the commission of that offence (2) Where evidence is adduced which is sufficient to raise an issue with respect to that defence, the court or jury shall assume that the defence is satisfied unless the prosecution proves beyond reasonable doubt that it is not

DDPS, detailed description of the pharmacovigilance system; EMEA, European Medicines Agency; PSUR, Periodic Safety Update Report; QPPV, Qualified Person for Pharmacovigilance.

Table A3.2 Other enforcement provisions[a]

Provision	Offences
UK clinical trial legisation relating to safety reporting: SI 2004/1031: "The Medicines for Human Use (Clinical Trials) Regulations 2004" SI 2006/1928: "The Medicines for Human Use (Clinical Trials) Amendment Regulations 2006"	49 (1) Offences exist for any person who contravenes any of the following provisions. . . : (ee) **Notification of serious breaches – Regulation 29A** (1) The sponsor of a clinical trial shall notify the licensing authority in writing of any serious breach of (a) the conditions and principles of good clinical practice in connection with that trial; or (b) the protocol relating to that trial, as amended from time to time in accordance with Regulations 22 to 25, within 7 days of becoming aware of that breach. (2) For the purposes of this regulation, a "serious breach" is a breach which is likely to effect [sic] to a significant degree: (a) the safety or physical or mental integrity of the subjects of the trial; or (b) the scientific value of the trial (f) **Urgent safety measures — Regulation 30(2).** An exemption for Regulation 29 exists for urgent safety measures in order to protect the subjects of a clinical trial against any immediate hazard to their health or safety. However, the sponsor shall immediately and in any event no later than 3 days from the date the measures are taken, give written notice to the licensing authority and the relevant ethics committee of the measures taken and the circumstances giving rise to those measures (g) **Notification of adverse events – Regulation 32(1), (3), and (5) to (9).** (1) An investigator shall report any serious adverse event which occurs in a subject at a trial site at which he is responsible for the conduct of a clinical trial immediately to the sponsor. . . . (3) Following the immediate report of a serious adverse event, the investigator shall make a detailed written report on the event. (5) Adverse events, other than those to which paragraphs (1) to (3) apply, that are identified in the protocol as critical to evaluations of the safety of the trial shall be reported to the sponsor in accordance with the reporting requirements, including the time periods for such reporting, specified in that protocol. (6) The reports made under paragraphs (1), (3) and (5) shall identify each subject referred to in the report by a number assigned to that subject in accordance with the protocol for the trial. (7) The number assigned to a subject in accordance with the protocol must be different from the number of any other subject in that trial, including any subject at a trial site outside the UK. (8) Where the event reported under paragraph (1) or (5) consists of, or results in, the death of a subject, the investigator shall supply the sponsor; and in any case where the death has been reported to the relevant ethics committee, that committee, with any additional information requested by the sponsor or, as the case may be, the committee. (9) The sponsor shall keep detailed records of all adverse events relating to a clinical trial which are reported to him by the investigators for that trial

Table A3.2 (cont.)

(h) **SUSAR reporting – Regulation 33(1) to (5).** (1) A sponsor shall ensure that all relevant information about a suspected unexpected serious adverse reaction which occurs during the course of a clinical trial in the UK and is fatal or life-threatening is recorded and reported as soon as possible to the licensing authority, the competent authorities of any EEA State, other than the UK, in which the trial is being conducted, and the relevant ethics committee, and in any event not later that [sic – should read than] 7 days after the sponsor was first aware of the reaction. (2) A sponsor shall ensure that within 8 days of a report in accordance with paragraph (1) (b), any additional relevant information is sent to the persons or bodies listed in that paragraph. (3) A sponsor shall ensure that a suspected unexpected serious adverse reaction which occurs during the course of a clinical trial in the UK, other than those referred to in paragraph (1), is reported as soon as possible to the licensing authority; the competent authorities of any EEA State, other than the UK, in which the trial is being conducted; and the relevant ethics committee; and in any event not later that [sic] 15 days after the sponsor is first aware of the reaction. (4) For the purposes of paragraphs (1) to (3), the sponsor may fulfil his obligations to report or provide information to the licensing authority and the competent authorities of any EEA State, other than the UK, by entering the report or information in the European database established in accordance with Article 11 of the Directive. (5) A sponsor shall ensure that, in relation to each clinical trial in the UK for which he is the sponsor, the investigators responsible for the conduct of a trial are informed of any suspected unexpected serious adverse reaction which occurs in relation to an IMP used in that trial, whether that reaction occurs during the course of that trial or another trial for which the sponsor is responsible

(i) **SUSAR reporting – Regulation 34.** If a clinical trial is being conducted at a trial site in a third country in addition to sites in the UK, the sponsor of that trial shall ensure that all suspected unexpected serious adverse reactions occurring at that site are entered into the European database established in accordance with Article 11 of the Directive

(j) **Annual Safety Reports – Regulation 35(1).** As soon as practicable after the end of the reporting year, a sponsor shall, in relation to each IMP tested in clinical trials in the UK for which he is the sponsor furnish the licensing authority and the relevant ethics committees with a list of all the suspected serious adverse reactions which have occurred during that year in relation to those trials, whether at trial sites in the UK or elsewhere, or any other trials relating to that product which are conducted outside the UK and for which he is the sponsor, including those reactions relating to any IMP used as a placebo or as a reference in those trials; and a report on the safety of the subjects of those trials

False or misleading information

50 (1) Any person who in the course of:

(a)   making an application for an ethics committee opinion;

(b)   making a request for authorisation to conduct a clinical trial; or

(c)   making an application for the grant or variation of a manufacturing authorisation;

provides to the licensing authority or an ethics committee any relevant information which is false or misleading in a material particular shall be guilty of an offence

(2) Any person who:

(a)   is conducting a clinical trial authorised in accordance with these Regulations;

(b)   is a sponsor of such a clinical trial;

(c)   while acting under arrangements made with a sponsor of such a clinical trial, performs the functions of that sponsor; or

(d)   holds a manufacturing authorisation;

and who, for the purposes of these Regulations, provides to the licensing authority or an ethics committee any relevant information which is false or misleading in a material particular shall be guilty of an offence

(3) Any person who, for the purpose of being engaged as a qualified person in accordance with Regulation 43, provides to the licensing authority or to the holder of a manufacturing authorisation any information which is false or misleading in a material particular shall be guilty of an offence

(4) In this regulation, "relevant information" means any information which is relevant to an evaluation of:

(a)   the safety, quality or efficacy of an IMP;

(b)   the safety or scientific validity of a clinical trial; or

(c)   whether, with regard to a clinical trial, the conditions and principles of good clinical practice are being satisfied or adhered to

Defence of due diligence

51 (1) A person does not commit an offence under these Regulations if he took all reasonable precautions and exercised all due diligence to avoid the commission of that offence.

(2) Where evidence is adduced which is sufficient to raise an issue with respect to that defence, the court or jury shall assume that the defence is satisfied unless the prosecution proves beyond reasonable doubt that it is not

Penalties

52   A person guilty of an offence under these Regulations shall be liable:

on summary conviction to a fine not exceeding the statutory maximum or to imprisonment for a term not exceeding three months or to both;

on conviction on indictment to a fine or to imprisonment for a term not exceeding two years or to both

Table A3.2 (cont.)

Scientific service: **SI 1994/1932 "The Medicines** **(Advertising) Regulations 1994"**	4 Any person who holds a product licence relating to a relevant medicinal product shall: (a) establish a scientific service to compile and collate all information, whether received from medical sales representatives employed by him or from any other source, relating to that product; (b) ensure that, in relation to any such product which medical sales representatives promote, those medical sales representatives are given adequate training and have sufficient scientific knowledge to enable them to provide information which is as precise and as complete as possible about that product **Penalties** 23 (1) Any person who contravenes Regulations 3(1), 4, 6(1) or (3), 7, 8, 10(1), 14(1), 15(1), 16, 18(1), (2) or (3), 20(2) or (3), 21(1) or (3), or 22(1)(a) shall be guilty of an offence and shall be liable: (a) on summary conviction, to a fine not exceeding the statutory maximum; (b) on conviction on indictment, to a fine or to imprisonment for a term not exceeding two years or to both
UK Fraud Act 2006	**Fraud** (1) A person is guilty of fraud if he is in breach of any of the sections listed in subsection (2) (which provide for different ways of committing the offence) (2) The sections are: (a) section 2 (fraud by false representation), (b) section 3 (fraud by failing to disclose information), and (c) section 4 (fraud by abuse of position) (3) A person who is guilty of fraud is liable: (a) on summary conviction, to imprisonment for a term not exceeding 12 months or to a fine not exceeding the statutory maximum (or to both); (b) on conviction on indictment, to imprisonment for a term not exceeding 10 years or to a fine (or to both) **Fraud by false representation** (1) A person is in breach of this section if he: (a) dishonestly makes a false representation, and (b) intends, by making the representation: (i) to make a gain for himself or another, or (ii) to cause loss to another or to expose another to a risk of loss

(2) A representation is false if:
    (a) it is untrue or misleading, and
    (b) the person making it knows that it is, or might be, untrue or misleading
(3) "Representation" means any representation as to fact or law, including a representation as to the state of mind of:
    (a) the person making the representation, or
    (b) any other person
(4) A representation may be express or implied
(5) For the purposes of this section a representation may be regarded as made if it (or anything implying it) is submitted in any form to any system or device designed to receive, convey or respond to communications (with or without human intervention)

Fraud by failing to disclose information

A person is in breach of this section if he:
    (a) dishonestly fails to disclose to another person information which he is under a legal duty to disclose, and
    (b) intends, by failing to disclose the information
        (i) to make a gain for himself or another, or
        (ii) to cause loss to another or to expose another to a risk of loss

EU infringement procedure: Commission Regulation (EC) No 658/2007

For centrally authorised products lays down financial penalties for the infringement of specific obligations in Regulation 726/2004, including infringements of the following obligations:

5 the supply of any new information which may entail a variation to the terms of the marketing authorisation, the notification of any prohibition or restriction imposed by the competent authorities of any country in which the medicinal product is marketed, or the supply of any information that may influence the evaluation of the risks and benefits of the product, as referred to in Article 16(2) and Article 41(4) of Regulation (EC) No 726/2004;

8 placing on the market in accordance with the content of the Summary of the Product Characteristics and the labelling and package leaflet as contained in the marketing authorisation;

9 the specific obligations referred to in Article 14(7) of Regulation (EC) No 726/2004 or in any other provisions adopted pursuant thereto;

12 the appropriately qualified person responsible for pharmacovigilance, as referred to in Article 48 of Regulation (EC) No 726/2004;

13 recording and reporting of suspected serious adverse reactions and, in the case of veterinary medicinal products, human adverse reactions, as referred to in Article 23 and Article 24(1) and Article 49(1) of Regulation (EC) No 726/2004;

Table A3.2 *(cont.)*

14 reporting of suspected serious unexpected adverse reactions, suspected transmission of infectious agents and, in the case of veterinary medicinal products, human adverse reactions, as referred to in Article 24(2) and Article 49(2) of Regulation (EC) No 726/2004;

15 detailed recording of all suspected adverse reactions and submission of such records in the form of Periodic Safety Update Reports, as referred to in Article 24(3) and Article 49(3) of Regulation (EC) No 726/2004;

16 communication of information relating to pharmacovigilance concerns to the general public, as referred to in Article 24(5) and Article 49(5) of Regulation (EC) No 726/2004;

17 collation and assessment of specific pharmacovigilance data, as referred to in the fourth paragraph of Article 26 and the fourth paragraph of Article 51 of Regulation (EC) No 726/2004

EEA, European Economic Area; IMP, investigational medicinal product; SUSAR, suspected unexpected serious adverse reaction.
aThis table is current at the time of production of this Guide, but as new Statutory Instruments are adopted, new offences may be adopted or existing offences may be amended. Other UK offences that apply to marketing authorisation holders that do not directly relate to pharmacovigilance are not included in this table.

4

Safety Reporting Requirements for Clinical Studies

Table A4.1

	Interventional clinical trials	Non-investigational medicinal products	Non-interventional studies
How to report a new event likely to affect the safety of trial subjects	**Article 10(b) of Directive 2001/20/EC:** if a SUSAR associated with an IMP "is likely to affect the safety of the subjects, the sponsor and the investigator shall take appropriate urgent safety measures to protect the subjects against any immediate hazard. The sponsor shall forthwith inform the competent authorities of those new events and the measures taken and shall ensure that the Ethics Committee is notified at the same time" *NB The reporting requirements also apply to contract research organisations/contractors, if the task has been formally delegated to a contract research organisation/contractor*	**Eudralex Volume 10, Chapter V** ("Guidance on Investigational Medicinal Products (IMPs) and other medicinal products used in Clinical Trials"): "If the medicinal product reaction due to the NIMP is likely to affect the safety of the trial subjects, the sponsor should report it to each competent authority and Ethics Committee concerned in accordance with Article 10(b) of Directive 2001/20/EC and section 5.1.1.2 of the 'Detailed guidance on the collection, verification and presentation of adverse reaction reports'" **Article 10(b) of Directive 2001/20/EC** applies to both IMPs and NIMPs: if a SUSAR associated with a NIMP "is likely to affect the safety of the subjects, the sponsor and the investigator shall take appropriate urgent safety measures to protect the subjects against any immediate hazard. The sponsor shall forthwith inform the competent authorities of those new events and the measures taken and shall ensure that the Ethics Committee is notified at the same time"	**Regulation 726/2004 and Directive 2001/83/EC (as amended):** this post-authorisation legislation applies for non-interventional studies on products with an EU marketing authorisation if the sponsor is the MAH. The MAH "shall forthwith inform the Agency, the Commission and the Member States of any prohibition or restriction imposed by the competent authorities of any country in which the medicinal product for human use is marketed and of any other *new information* which might influence the evaluation of the benefits and risks of the medicinal product for human use concerned" **Eudralex Volume 9A:** "A safety concern may be unexpectedly identified in the course of performing a study on an authorised medicinal product that would normally fall outside the scope of this guidance. In that case, the Marketing Authorisation Holder and specifically the QPPV are expected to inform the relevant Competent Authorities immediately and to provide a brief report on progress at intervals and at study end as requested by the Authorities" If the sponsor is not the MAH, but the MAH directly supplies the product for use in a study, it is recommended that there should be an agreement in place for exchange of relevant safety

	information between the MAH and sponsor. In other circumstances, routine post-authorisation processes should be used, e.g. reporting via the yellow card scheme in the UK	For non-interventional studies on products with an EU marketing authorisation, post-authorisation legislation applies if the sponsor is the MAH or if the MAH becomes aware of the adverse reaction, i.e. Regulation 726/2004 and Directive 2001/83/EC (as amended) **Eudralex Volume 9A, Part I, 7.4.2:** "For non-interventional post-authorisation safety studies (PASS), conducted inside and outside the EU, the usual regulatory requirements for reporting of adverse reactions should be fulfilled according to Chapters I.4. and I.6" For all non-interventional PASS on products with an EU marketing authorisation, if the MAH becomes aware of the reaction, the MAH is required to: • "report all serious adverse reactions *(this includes any suspected transmission via a medicinal product of an infectious agent)* arising from within the EU on an expedited basis (i.e. within 15 days), to the Competent Authority of the Member State on whose territory the incident occurred, and in addition, for products authorised through the mutual recognition or decentralised procedures and for products which have been the subject of a referral procedure, to the
How to report adverse events, adverse reactions and serious adverse reactions	**Article 16 of Directive 2001/20/EC:** "The investigator shall report all serious adverse events immediately to the sponsor except for those that the protocol or investigator's brochure identifies as not requiring immediate reporting. The immediate report shall be followed by detailed, written reports. The immediate and follow-up reports shall identify subjects by unique code numbers assigned to the latter. The sponsor shall keep detailed records of all adverse events which are reported to him by the investigator or investigators Adverse events and/or laboratory abnormalities identified in the protocol as critical to safety evaluations shall be reported to the sponsor according to the reporting requirements and within the time periods specified in the protocol For reported deaths of a subject, the investigator shall supply the sponsor and the Ethics Committee with any additional information requested The sponsor shall keep detailed records of all adverse events which are reported to him by the investigator or investigators. These records shall be submitted to the Member States in	Articles 16 and 17 of Directive 2001/20/EC apply to both IMPs and NIMPs, but only in relation to the types of SUSAR described below **Volume 10 Eudralex, Chapter V** ("Guidance on Investigational Medicinal Products (IMPs) and other medicinal products used in Clinical Trials"): "Article 16 of Directive 2001/20/EC requires the investigator to notify to the sponsor any adverse events occurring in the clinical trial which may be related to the use of IMPs or NIMPs. It also requires the sponsor to keep detailed records of all adverse events which are reported to him by the investigator(s). If the adverse reaction is suspected to be linked to an interaction between a NIMP and an IMP, and is serious and unexpected, the sponsor should report it as a suspected unexpected serious adverse reaction (SUSAR) according to Article 17 of Directive 2001/20/EC If an adverse reaction (serious and unexpected) is suspected and might be linked to either a NIMP or an IMP and cannot be attributed to only one of these, then the sponsor should report it as a SUSAR in accordance with Article 17 of Directive 2001/20/EC" It follows that if the SUSAR is definitely attributed to the NIMP and is not

Table A4.1 (cont.)

Interventional clinical trials	Non-investigational medicinal products	Non-interventional studies
whose territory the clinical trial is being conducted, if they so request" **Articles 17 of Directive 2001/20/EC:** "(a) The sponsor shall ensure that all relevant information about suspected serious unexpected adverse reactions that are fatal or life-threatening is recorded and reported as soon as possible to the competent authorities in all the Member States concerned, and to the Ethics Committee, and in any case no later than seven days after knowledge by the sponsor of such a case, and that relevant follow-up information is subsequently communicated within an additional eight days. (b) All other suspected serious unexpected adverse reactions shall be reported to the competent authorities concerned and to the Ethics Committee concerned as soon as possible but within a maximum of fifteen days of first knowledge by the sponsor. (d) The sponsor shall also inform all investigators" **National Research Ethics Service:** For current procedures for SUSAR reporting to UK research ethics committees see http://www.nres.npsa.nhs.uk. The sponsor should have a documented rationale to describe when and how	considered to be related in any way to an IMP, and is not likely to constitute a hazard to the safety of other trial subjects, it should note be reported under the EU clinical trial legislation. However, in this situation, if the NIMP has an EU marketing authorisation, the sponsor and/or investigator should consider whether the SUSAR should be reported in accordance with routinepost- authorisation processes (e.g. the yellow card scheme in the UK). In addition, if the sponsor is also the MAH for the NIMP, the SUSAR should be reported in accordance with applicable post-authorisation legislation (e.g. Regulation 726/2004, Directive 2001/83/EC (as amended)) **"Specials":** If a NIMP is a "special" supplied on a compassionate use basis, the UK requirements contained in Statutory Instrument 1994/3144, Schedule 1, paragraph 7 apply in relation to the adverse reaction reporting requirements for sellers or suppliers of the product	Reference Member State. These reports should also be included in the PSURs (see Chapter I.6); • report all unexpected serious adverse reactions *(this includes any suspected transmission via a medicinal product of an infectious agent)* arising from outside the EU on an expedited basis (i.e. within 15 days) to the Agency (EMEA) and to all Member States where the medicinal product is authorised These reports should also be included in the PSURs (see Chapter I.6); • report on expected serious adverse reactions occurring outside the EU in accordance with Chapter I.6 on PSURs" All adverse reactions/events including those which are considered non-serious, should be summarised in the final study report in frequency tables *[NB In general terms, reports from studies should have a causality assessment by a healthcare professional or the marketing authorisation holder.]* "In certain study designs, such as case-control or retrospective cohort studies (see Data Sources in Table I.7.A), in which it is not feasible or appropriate to make an assessment of causality between medical events recorded and the medicinal products at individual case level, expedited reporting of Individual Case Safety Reports

SUSAR reports are submitted to other concerned investigators (this should include investigators using the same IMP irrespective of whether the IMP is being used in a different indication in a trial sponsored by the same sponsor)

(ICSRs) is not required. In case of doubt, the Marketing Authorisation Holder should clarify the reporting requirements through the contact point referred to in Chapter I.7, Section 4.1.a, according to the authorisation procedure of the product"

What to report in ASRs		

Articles 17 of Directive 2001/20/EC:
"2. Once a year throughout the clinical trial, the sponsor shall provide the Member States in whose territory the clinical trial is being conducted and the Ethics Committee with a listing of all suspected serious adverse reactions which have occurred over this period and a report of the subjects' safety"

Eudralex Volume 10, Chapter II ("Detailed guidance on the collection, verification and presentation of adverse reaction reports arising from clinical trials on medicinal products for human use") provides guidance on the format and content of ASRs. The ASR for an interventional clinical trial should have three parts:

Part 1: Analysis of the subjects' safety in the concerned clincal trial.

Part 2: A line listing of all suspected serious adverse reactions (including all SUSARs) that occurred in the concerned trial, including also serious adverse reactions from third countries.

Eudralex Volume 10, Chapter V ("Guidance on Investigational Medicinal Products (IMPs) and other medicinal products used in Clinical Trials") does not make specific reference to the inclusion of NIMP safety data in ASRs. However, cases reported as SUSARs, where the SUSAR is suspected to be linked to an interaction between a NIMP and an IMP, or where the SUSAR might be linked to either a NIMP or an IMP and cannot be attributed to only one of these, should be included in ASR line listings (Part 2) and aggregate summaries (Part 3). In addition, Part 1 of the ASR "should describe in a concise way, all new and relevant findings, known by the sponsor, related to the safety of the subjects in the concerned trial, including all new findings related to the safety of investigational medicinal product treatments or other treatments used in the trial and any other findings related to clinical trial procedures." New safety findings related to NIMPs may need to be discussed in this part irrespective of whether or not the findings are associated with an IMP interaction

Interventional clinical trial ASRs *do not* have to be produced for non-interventional studies. However, Part 1 of an interventional clinical trial ASR "should describe in a concise way, all new and relevant findings, known by the sponsor, related to the safety of the subjects in the concerned trial, including all new findings related to the safety of investigational medicinal product treatments or other treatments used in the trial and any other findings related to clinical trial procedures". Safety findings from non-interventional studies may be relevant to subjects participating in interventional clinical trials. If the sponsor is aware of such findings, the findings should be discussed in Part 1 of the interventional trial ASR

Eudralex Volume 9A, Part I, 7.4.3: for PASS states "a) Studies requested by Competent Authorities Marketing Authorisation Holders should provide a study progress report *annually*, or more frequently as requested by the Competent Authorities (e.g. according to the Risk Management Plan milestones) or on their own initiative. If the study is discontinued, a final report should also be

Table A4.1 (cont.)

Interventional clinical trials	Non-investigational medicinal products	Non-interventional studies
Part 3: An aggregate summary tabulation of suspected serious adverse reactions that occurred in the concerned trial **National Research Ethics Service:** For current procedures for ASRs for UK research ethics committees see http://www.nres.npsa.nhs.uk		submitted, which will include the reasons for stopping the study. The content of the progress report should follow a logical sequence and should include all the available data which is [sic] judged relevant for the progress of the study, e.g. number of patients who have entered the study according to their status (exposure, outcome, etc.), problems encountered and deviations from the expected plan After review of the report, Competent Authorities may request additional information. A final study report should be submitted according to an agreed timetable (e.g. Risk Management Plan milestones) . . . Both progress and final reports should be sent to the Competent Authorities of the Member States in which the study is being conducted and to the Competent Authority that requested the study. In case of products authorised through the mutual recognition or decentralised procedures, these reports should also be sent to the Reference Member State and, in case of centrally authorised products, to the Agency, the Rapporteur and Co-Rapporteur . . . b) Studies performed at the Marketing Authorisation Holder's initiative Progress and final reports should be included or updated in the corresponding PSUR and/or Risk Management Plan.

| What to report in PSURs | In accordance with post-authorisation legislation (i.e. Regulation 726/2004 and Directive 2001/83/EC (as amended)), and the guidance contained in Eudralex Volume 9A, MAHs are required to produce and submit PSURs for products with EU marketing authorisations

When an interventional clinical trial is conducted on a product with an EU marketing authorisation, the following information relating to the trial may need to be included in PSURs for the product if the MAH is aware of the information (if the MAH is not the sponsor for the trial, the MAH may not have access to this information except via agreements with the sponsor or via searches of published literature)

Executive summary: details of urgent safety restrictions and particular safety concerns identified during clinical trials

Update of Regulatory Authority or MAH actions taken for safety reasons: details of clinical trial suspensions or urgent safety restrictions | Where the NIMP is a product with a marketing authorisation in the EU and the MAH of the NIMP becomes aware of new safety information arising from the use of the NIMP in clinical trials, that information should be included in PSURs for the NIMP as described in column 2

In addition, cases reported as SUSARs, where the SUSAR is suspected to be linked to an interaction between a NIMP and an IMP, or where the SUSAR might be linked to either a NIMP or an IMP and cannot be attributed to only one of these, should be included in PSUR line listings for the IMP if the IMP is a product with a marketing authorisation in the EU and the MAH of the IMP becomes aware of the information | In accordance with post-authorisation legislation (i.e. Regulation 726/2004 and Directive 2001/83/EC (as amended)), and the guidance contained in Eudralex Volume 9A, MAHs are required to produce and submit PSURs for products with EU marketing authorisations

When a non-interventional study is conducted on a product with an EU marketing authorisation, the following information relating to the study may need to be included in PSURs

Executive summary: details of urgent safety restrictions and particular safety concerns identified during studies

Update of Regulatory Authority or MAH actions taken for safety reasons: details of study suspensions or urgent safety restrictions

Patient exposure: when adverse reaction data from clinical studies are included in the PSUR, the relevant denominator(s) should be provided. For ongoing studies, an estimation of patient exposure may be made

Cases presented as line listings: All serious adverse reactions (attributable to the medicinal product by either | When a safety concern is raised, a report should be submitted immediately to the relevant Competent Authorities (including the Agency and (Co-) Rapporteur for centrally authorised products and the Reference Member State for products authorised through the mutual recognition or decentralised procedures)" |

Table A4.1 (*cont.*)

Interventional clinical trials	Non-investigational medicinal products	Non-interventional studies
Patient exposure: when adverse reaction data from clinical studies are included in the PSUR, the relevant denominator(s) should be provided. For ongoing and/or blinded studies, an estimation of patient exposure may be made **Cases presented as line listings:** all serious adverse reactions (attributable to the medicinal product by either investigator or sponsor) available from PASS and other studies (including those which are part of the RMP) **Cases presented as summary tabulations:** unless the number of cases is very small, when a narrative description may suffice, an aggregate summary for each of the line listings should usually be presented **MAH's analysis of individual case histories:** relevant cases from clinical trials may need to be discussed in this section **Studies:** all studies (non-clinical, clinical and epidemiological) yielding safety information (this includes lack of efficacy data) with a *potential impact on product information*, studies specifically planned, in progress and those published with a discussion of any interim or final results. The MAH should *not routinely*		investigator or sponsor) available from PASS and other studies (including those which are part of the RMP) or named-patient/compassionate use **Cases presented as summary tabulations:** unless the number of cases is very small, when a narrative description may suffice, an aggregate summary for each of the line-listings should usually be presented **MAH's analysis of individual case histories:** relevant cases from non-interventional studies may need to be discussed **Studies:** all studies (non-clinical, clinical and epidemiological) yielding safety information (this includes lack of efficacy information) with a *potential impact on product information*, studies specifically planned, in progress and those published that address safety concerns should be included with a discussion of any interim or final results. The MAH should *not routinely* catalogue or describe all the studies. Studies that are part of the RMP should be mentioned **Newly analysed studies:** all relevant studies containing *important safety information* and newly analysed during the reporting period should be described, including those from epidemiological, toxicological or laboratory investigations. Reference should be made to the RMP, where applicable. Copies of full study

catalogue or describe all the studies. Studies that are part of the RMP should be mentioned

Newly analysed studies: all relevant studies containing *important safety information* and newly analysed during the reporting period should be described, including those from epidemiological, toxicological or laboratory investigations. Reference should be made to the RMP, where applicable. Copies of full study reports should be appended (e.g. in case of PASS and for other studies with a significant safety finding) only if deemed appropriate

[NB discussion of studies yielding safety information with a potential impact on product information applies whether or not the study was conducted in a licensed indication].

Targeted new safety studies: new studies specifically planned or conducted to examine a safety concern (actual or hypothetical) should be described (e.g. objective, starting date, projected completion date, number of subjects, protocol abstract). When possible and relevant, if an interim analysis was part of the study plan, the interim results of ongoing studies may be presented. When the study is completed and analysed, the final results should be presented in a subsequent PSUR. Copies of full reports should be appended for PASS and for other studies with a significant safety finding) only if deemed appropriate

Targeted new safety studies: new studies specifically planned or conducted to examine a safety concern (actual or hypothetical) should be described (e.g. objective, starting date, projected completion date, number of subjects, protocol abstract). When possible and relevant, if an interim analysis was part of the study plan, the interim results of ongoing studies may be presented. When the study is completed and analysed, the final results should be presented in a subsequent PSUR. Copies of full reports should be appended for PASS and for other studies with a significant safety finding only if deemed appropriate

Planned studies: should be discussed in the RMP and if relevant in the related PSUR section

Published studies: reports in the scientific and medical literature, including relevant published abstracts from meetings, containing important safety findings (positive or negative) should be summarised and publication reference(s) provided

Other studies: the MAH should provide any relevant information from the data collected by pregnancy exposure registries and a discussion of the positive and negative experience of use of the medical product during pregnancy

Table A4.1 (cont.)

Interventional clinical trials	Non-investigational medicinal products	Non-interventional studies
and for other studies with a significant safety finding only if deemed appropriate **Planned studies:** should be discussed in the RMP and if relevant in the related PSUR section **Published studies:** reports in the scientific and medical literature, including relevant published abstracts from meetings, containing important safety findings (positive or negative) should be summarised and publication reference(s) provided **Overall safety evaluation:** experience in special patient groups (e.g. children, elderly, organ impaired, a qualitative description of off-label use) should be given. A subsection of the PSUR should deal with use of the medicinal product in children if the product has a paediatric indication, if there is evidence of significant off-label use in children or if there are adverse reactions reported in the paediatric population. Data from completed or ongoing clinical trials should be presented separately from spontaneous reports [NB when blinded clinical trials on products authorised in the EU are unblinded, updates on serious		**Overall safety evaluation:** experience in special patient groups (e.g. children, elderly, organ impaired, a qualitative description of off-label use) should be given. A subsection of the PSUR should deal with use of the medicinal product in children if the product has a paediatric indication, if there is evidence of significant off-label use in children or if there are adverse reactions reported in the paediatric population. Data from completed or ongoing clinical trials should be presented separately from spontaneous reports

expected adverse reactions that were reported during the trial may need to be provided in a PSUR produced subsequent to unblinding]

ASR, Annual Safety Report; EMEA, European Medicines Agency; EU, European Union; IMP, investigational medicinal product; MAH, Marketing Authorisation Holder; NIMP, non-investigational medicinal product; PASS, post-authorisation safety studies; PSUR, Periodic Safety Update Report; QPPV, Qualified Person for Pharmacovigilance; RMP, Risk Management Plan; SUSAR, suspected unexpected serious adverse reaction.

5

Pharmacovigilance Initiatives

The Better Regulation of Medicines Initiative

The Better Regulation of Medicines Initiative (BROMI) is a broad-ranging strategy group, led by the MHRA, bringing together representatives from the Proprietary Association of Great Britain, the non-proprietary sector, the National Pharmacy Association, the UK Department of Health and the Cabinet Office. The aim of the initiative is to develop regulation that is accountable, proportionate, targeted, consistent and transparent.

The initial BROMI workstreams related to leaflets and labels and MHRA processes (variations, copy licenses and change of ownership). At the October 2006 BROMI meeting, a further workstream regarding pharmacovigilance was proposed.

The vigilance subgroup was set up in early 2007 to look at the BROMI principles, with a risk-based approach to lifting regulatory burdens in the area of pharmacovigilance, where safe to do so. The focus of activities has been reducing workload in the areas of literature searching, PSUR production and ASPRs.

Ways of reducing the duplication of effort in the area of literature searching have been considered, particularly in relation to generic medicines. Of particular interest has been a literature service provided in Germany, which was established to meet the needs of a large number of pharmaceutical companies. Weekly screening of worldwide scientific literature databases is undertaken by a third party for a set list of chemically defined and herbal substances. Companies subscribe to the service and define the substances for which they require literature searching. Scientific assessment of the results of the search is undertaken by physicians and PhDs and the results are classified into four categories. Potential ICSRs are then made available to all relevant companies. The service is supported by documented procedures and contractual agreements and is overseen by a steering committee. The BROMI vigilance subgroup has considered whether a similar model could be utilised by UK MAHs.

In relation to ASPRs, the MHRA has proposed rationalisation of the ASPR process, which would lessen the resource burden by reducing the number of ASPRs sent out to companies. Methods of reducing the number of duplicate reports are also high on the agenda. In December 2007, two changes to the ASPR generation programme were implemented: first, the seriousness criteria upon which ASPRs are sent out is now limited to the ICH definition of seriousness (previously ASPRs were also sent out if the report contained a term which was defined as dictionary-serious by the MHRA); second, for reports submitted to the MHRA by a MAH, an ASPR is no longer sent back to the MAH. These changes have resulted in a smaller number of ASPRs being sent out to MAHs. At the time of writing, additional changes are under consideration to reduce further the burden imposed by ASPRs.

A working group was set up to look at a model for PSUR work sharing, taking into account the European PSUR work-sharing project being operated under the Heads of Medicines Agencies. A pilot scheme for production of common PSURs was commenced in October 2007 involving a small number of active substances.

European Commission Strategy for Pharmacovigilance

During 2007, proposals were announced to amend the legal framework for pharmacovigilance in the EU as part of the Commission strategy. Key proposals include:

- amendments to Directive 2001/83/EC and Regulation 726/2004;
- establishment of the concept of good vigilance practices;
- simplification of the process for a DDPS and introduce the concept of a Pharmacovigilance System Master File;
- inclusion of key risk-management measures in the marketing authorisation application;
- expedited reporting of serious third-country and EU domestic reports to EudraVigilance only;
- EMEA to take on the role of scanning of the scientific literature and case entry of reports onto EudraVigilance;
- establishment of a EU list of medicines under intensive monitoring;
- linking of the periodicity of PSUR submissions to knowledge of the safety of the product;
- introduction of patient reporting throughout the EU.

These proposals could have a major impact on the pharmacovigilance systems of both MAHs and Competent Authorities and will most likely necessitate a revision of this Guide.

Glossary

ABUSE (OF A MEDICINAL PRODUCT), SYNONYM: DRUG ABUSE

Eudralex Volume 9A: Persistent or sporadic, intentional excessive use of medicinal products which is accompanied by harmful physical or psychological effects (Article 1(16) of Directive 2001/83/EC).

ADVERSE EVENT

Eudralex Volume 9A: Any untoward medical occurrence in a patient or clinical-trial subject administered a medicinal product and which does not necessarily have to have a causal relationship with this treatment (Article 2(m) of Directive 2001/20/EC). An adverse event can, therefore, be any unfavourable and unintended sign (e.g. an abnormal laboratory finding), symptom or disease temporally associated with the use of a medicinal product, whether or not considered related to the medicinal product.

ADVERSE REACTION, SYNONYMS: ADVERSE DRUG REACTION, SUSPECTED ADVERSE (DRUG) REACTION

Eudralex Volume 9A: A response to a medicinal product which is noxious and unintended and which occurs at doses normally used in man for the prophylaxis, diagnosis or therapy of disease or for the restoration, correction or modification of physiological function (Article 1(11) of Directive 2001/83/EC).

Response in this context means that a causal relationship between a medicinal product and an adverse event is at least a reasonable possibility (see ICH E2A Guideline).

Adverse reaction also includes adverse clinical consequences associated with use of the product outside the terms of the Summary of Product Characteristics or other conditions laid down for the marketing and use of the product (including prescribed doses higher than those recommended, overdoses or abuse).

AUDIT

ISO 9000: Systematic, independent and documented process for obtaining evidence and evaluating it objectively to determine the extent to which audit criteria are fulfilled. (Audit criteria are a set of policies, procedures or requirements against which collected audit evidence is compared.)

AUDIT TRAIL

ICH E6: Documentation that allows reconstruction of the course of events.

BLINDING

ICH E6: A procedure in which one or more parties to the trial are kept unaware of the treatment assignment(s). Single blinding usually refers to the subject(s) being unaware, and double blinding usually refers to the subject(s), investigator(s), monitor, and, in some cases, data analyst(s) being unaware of the treatment assignment(s).

CLINICAL TRIAL

Directive 2001/20/EC: Any investigation in human subjects intended to discover or verify the clinical, pharmacological and/or other pharmacodynamic effects of one or more investigational medicinal product(s), and/or to identify any adverse reactions to one or more investigational medicinal product(s), and/or to study absorption, distribution, metabolism and excretion of one or more investigational medicinal product(s) with the object of ascertaining its (their) safety and/or efficacy.

COMPARATOR

ICH E6: An investigational or marketed product (i.e. active control), or placebo, used as a reference in a clinical trial.

COMPANY CORE DATA SHEET

Eudralex Volume 9A: A document prepared by the Marketing Authorisation Holder containing, in addition to safety information, material relating to indications, dosing, pharmacology and other information concerning the product.

COMPANY CORE SAFETY INFORMATION

Eudralex Volume 9A: All relevant safety information contained in the Company Core Data Sheet prepared by the Marketing Authorisation Holder and which the Marketing Authorisation Holder requires to be listed in all countries where the company markets the product, except when the local regulatory authority specifically requires a modification. It is the reference information by which listed and unlisted are determined for the purpose of periodic reporting for marketed products, but not by which expected and unexpected are determined for expedited reporting.

CONSUMER

Eudralex Volume 9A: A person who is not a healthcare professional, such as a Patient, lawyer, friend or relative/parents/children of a Patient.

CONTRACT RESEARCH ORGANISATION

ICH E6: A person or an organisation (commercial, academic or other) contracted by the sponsor to perform one or more of a sponsor's trial-related duties and functions.

DATA LOCK POINT

Eudralex Volume 9A: The date designated as the cut-off date for data to be included in a Periodic Safety Update Report.

DRUG ABUSE

See abuse.

EU BIRTH DATE

Eudralex Volume 9A: The date of the first marketing authorisation for a medicinal product granted in the EU to the Marketing Authorisation Holder:

- for medicinal products authorised through the centralised procedure, the EU Birth Date is the date of the marketing authorisation granted by the European Commission, i.e. the date of the Commission Decision;
- for medicinal products authorised through the mutual recognition or decentralised procedure, the EU Birth Date is the date of the marketing authorisation granted by the Reference Member State;
- for medicinal products authorised through purely national procedures (outside the mutual recognition or decentralised procedure), the Marketing Authorisation Holder may propose a birth date, which can be applied to reporting requirements across the Member States.

HEALTHCARE PROFESSIONAL

Eudralex Volume 9A: For the purposes of reporting suspected adverse reactions, healthcare professionals are defined as medically qualified persons, such as physicians, dentists, pharmacists, nurses and coroners.

In addition, the MHRA accepts reports from the following healthcare professionals: coroners, midwives, health visitors, radiographers and optometrists.

INDEPENDENT ETHICS COMMITTEE

ICH E6: An independent body (a review board or a committee, institutional, regional, national, or supranational), constituted of medical professionals and non-medical members, whose responsibility it is to ensure the protection of the rights, safety and well-being of human subjects involved in a trial and to provide public assurance of that protection, by, among other things, reviewing and approving/providing favourable opinions on the trial protocol, the suitability of the investigator(s), facilities, and the methods and material to be used in obtaining and documenting informed consent of the trial subjects.

The legal status, composition, function, operations and regulatory requirements pertaining to independent ethics committees may differ among countries, but should allow the independent ethics committee to act in agreement with good clinical practice.

INDIVIDUAL CASE SAFETY REPORT

Eudralex Volume 9A: A document providing the most complete information related to an individual case at a certain point of time. An individual case is the information provided by a primary source to describe suspected adverse reaction(s) related to the administration of one or more medicinal products to an individual patient at a particular point of time.

INTERNATIONAL BIRTH DATE

Eudralex Volume 9A: The date of the first marketing authorisation for a medicinal product granted to the Marketing Authorisation Holder in any country in the world. For a medicinal product for which the International Birth Date is not known, the Marketing Authorisation Holder can designate an International Birth Date to allow synchronisation of submission of Periodic Safety Update Reports.

INVENTED NAME

Eudralex Volume 9A: The name of a medicinal product as it appears in the Product Information, or the common or scientific name together with a trademark or the name of the Marketing Authorisation Holder followed by the strength and the pharmaceutical form of the product.

The common name is the international non-proprietary name (INN) recommended by the World Health Organization, or if one does not exist, the usual common name.

INVESTIGATIONAL MEDICINAL PRODUCT

Directive 2001/20/EC: A pharmaceutical form of an active substance or placebo being tested or used as a reference in a clinical trial, including products already with a marketing authorisation, but used or assembled (formulated or packaged) in a way different from the authorised form, or when used for an unauthorised indication, or when used to gain further information about the unauthorised form.

INVESTIGATOR'S BROCHURE

ICH E6: A compilation of the clinical and nonclinical data on the investigational product(s) which is relevant to the study of the investigational product(s) in human subjects.

LISTED ADVERSE REACTION

Eudralex Volume 9A: An adverse reaction whose nature, severity, specificity and outcome are consistent with the information in the Company Core Safety Information.

MEDICINAL PRODUCT

Eudralex Volume 9A:
- Any substance or combination of substances presented as having properties for treating or preventing disease in human beings; or
- Any substance or combination of substances which may be used in or administered to human beings either with a view to restoring, correcting or modifying physiological functions by exerting a pharmacological, immunological or metabolic action, or to making a medical diagnosis (Art 1(2) of Directive 2001/83/EC).

NON-INTERVENTIONAL TRIAL

Directive 2001/20/EC: A study where the medicinal product(s) is (are) prescribed in the usual manner in accordance with the terms of the marketing authorisation. The assignment of the patient to a particular therapeutic strategy is not decided in advance by a trial protocol but falls within current practice and the prescription of the medicine is clearly separated from the decision to include the patient in the study. No additional diagnostic or monitoring procedures shall be applied to the patients and epidemiological methods shall be used for the analysis of the collected data.

PERIODIC SAFETY UPDATE REPORT

Eudralex Volume 9A: Periodic safety update reports mean the periodical reports containing the records referred to in Article 104 of Directive 2001/83/EC and in Article 24(3) of Regulation (EC) No 726/2004.

POST-AUTHORISATION STUDY

Eudralex Volume 9A: Any study conducted within the conditions laid down in the Summary of Product Characteristics and other conditions laid down for the marketing of the product or under normal conditions of use. A post-authorisation study falls within the definitions of either a clinical trial or a non-interventional study and may also fall within the definition of a post-authorisation safety study.

POST-AUTHORISATION SAFETY STUDY

Eudralex Volume 9A: A pharmacoepidemiological study or a clinical trial carried out in accordance with the terms of the marketing authorisation, conducted with the aim of identifying or quantifying a safety hazard relating to an authorised medicinal product (Article 1(15) of Directive 2001/83/EC).

QUALITY ASSURANCE

ISO 9000: Part of quality management focused on providing confidence that quality requirements are fulfilled.

QUALITY CONTROL

ISO 9000: Part of quality management focused on fulfilling quality requirements. (Quality requirement is the requirement for inherent characteristics of a product, process or system.)

QUALITY MANAGEMENT

ISO 9000: Coordinated activities to direct and control an organisation with regard to quality.

QUALITY MANAGEMENT SYSTEM

ISO 9000: Management system to direct and control an organisation with regard to quality.

REPORTER

ICH E2B(R3): Reporter is the primary source of the information, that is the person who initially reports the facts.

RISK–BENEFIT BALANCE

Eudralex Volume 9A: An evaluation of the positive therapeutic effects of the medicinal product in relation to the risks (any risk relating to the quality, safety or efficacy of the medicinal product as regards Patients' health or public health) (Article 1(28a) of Directive 2001/83/EC).

RISK MANAGEMENT SYSTEM

Eudralex Volume 9A: A risk management system shall comprise a set of pharmacovigilance activities and interventions designed to identify, characterise, prevent or minimise risks relating to medicinal products, including the assessment of the effectiveness of those interventions (Article 34 of Regulation (EC) No 1901/2006).

RISKS RELATED TO USE OF A MEDICINAL PRODUCT

Eudralex Volume 9A: Any risk relating to the quality, safety or efficacy of the medicinal product as regards Patients' health or public health and any risk of undesirable effects on the environment (Article 1(28) of Directive 2001/83/EC).

SERIOUS ADVERSE REACTION

Eudralex Volume 9A: Serious adverse reaction means an adverse reaction which results in death, is life-threatening, requires in-patient hospitalisation or prolongation of existing hospitalisation, results in persistent or significant disability or incapacity, or is a congenital anomaly/birth defect (Article 1(12) of Directive 2001/83/EC).

Life threatening in this context refers to a reaction in which the patient was at risk of death at the time of the reaction; it does not refer to a reaction that hypothetically might have caused death if more severe.

Medical and scientific judgement should be exercised in deciding whether other situations should be considered serious reactions, such as important medical events that might not be immediately life threatening or result in death or hospitalisation but might jeopardise the patient or might require intervention to prevent one of the other outcomes listed above. Examples of such events are intensive treatment in an emergency room or at home for allergic bronchospasm, blood dyscrasias or convulsions that do not result in hospitalisation or development of dependency or abuse.

Any suspected transmission via a medicinal product of an infectious agent is also considered a serious adverse reaction.

SOLICITED SOURCE OF INDIVIDUAL CASE SAFETY REPORTS

Eudralex Volume 9A: Organised data collection schemes which include clinical trials, registries, named-patients use programmes, other patient support and disease management programmes, surveys of patients or healthcare providers or information gathering on efficacy or patient compliance.

For the purpose of safety reporting, solicited reports should be classified as Individual Case Safety Reports from studies and, therefore, should have an appropriate causality assessment by a healthcare professional or the Marketing Authorisation Holder.

SPONSOR

ICH E6: An individual, company, institution, or organisation which takes responsibility for the initiation, management, and/or financing of a clinical trial.

SPONTANEOUS REPORT

Eudralex Volume 9A: An unsolicited communication by a healthcare professional or consumer to a company, regulatory authority or other organisation (e.g. WHO, a regional centre, a poison control centre) which fulfils the following three conditions:

- it describes one or more suspected adverse reactions in a patient;
- the patient was given one or more medicinal products;
- it does not derive from a study or any organised data collection scheme.

Healthcare professionals or consumers may be stimulated to report a suspected adverse reaction by several situations including:

- a Direct Healthcare Professional Communication;
- Early Post-Marketing Phase Vigilance (EPPV), e.g. in Japan;
- a report in the press;
- direct questioning of healthcare professionals by company representatives.

In these circumstances, provided the report meets the three conditions above, it should be considered a spontaneous report.

UNEXPECTED ADVERSE REACTION

Eudralex Volume 9A: An adverse reaction, the nature, severity or outcome of which is not consistent with the Summary of Product Characteristics (SPC) (Article 1(13) of Directive 2001/83/EC). This includes class-related reactions which are mentioned in the SPC but which are not specifically described as occurring with this product. For products authorised nationally, the relevant SPC is that approved by the Competent Authority in the Member State to whom the reaction is being reported. For centrally authorised products, the relevant SPC is the SPC authorised by the European Commission. During the time period between a CHMP Opinion in favour of granting a marketing authorisation and the Commission Decision granting the marketing authorisation, the relevant SPC is the SPC annexed to the CHMP Opinion.

UNLISTED ADVERSE REACTION

Eudralex Volume 9A: An adverse reaction that is not specifically included as a suspected adverse effect in the Company Core Safety Information (CCSI). This includes an adverse reaction whose nature, severity, specificity or outcome is not consistent with the information in the CCSI. It also includes class-related reactions which are mentioned in the CCSI but which are not specifically described as occurring with this product.

URGENT SAFETY RESTRICTION

Eudralex Volume 2, Chapter 5: An interim change to product information concerning particularly one or more of the following items in the summary of product characteristics, the indications, posology, contra-indications, warnings, target species and withdrawal periods due to new information having a bearing on the safe use of the medicinal product. The urgent safety restriction may be imposed by the marketing authorisation holder or by the competent authorities.

Index

Page number in *italics* refer to figures or tables.

A

abstracts
  literature searching 52
  reporting from 58
abuse of drugs
  definition 191
  reports 36
access
  databases 7
  pharmacovigilance data 22, 117
adolescents, definition 68
adverse drug reactions 9–10
  clinical trials, legislation 169, *177–9*
  in compassionate use
    failure to report 167
    in PSURs 65
  consumer reports *see* consumer reports,
    adverse drug reactions
  databases for reports 7
  deficiencies in reporting 47–8
  definitions 191
  expectedness *see* expectedness
  failure to report 166
  literature searches, reports found 57, 58, 59
  to NIMPs 138
  non-serious
    delays in transfer to other companies
      125
    literature searching 59
  out-of-hours receipt of reports 109
  pharmacovigilance data types 18–19
  review of reports 74–5
  selection for PSURs 64–5
  serious *see* serious adverse drug reactions
    (SARs)
  severity change 77
  special patient populations, reports in
    PSURs 68
  from 'specials' 47
  unexpected 196–7
    suspected serious *see* suspected
      unexpected serious adverse drug
      reactions (SUSARs)
  valid 34
    reclassification 18–19, 22
  see also adverse events
adverse events
  clinical trials
    legislation 169, *177–9*
  definitions, causality 189
  follow-up 34–7
    by Marketing Authorisation Holders 35
    missed 147
  reports
    registries 147
    sources 107
  training on 101–2
  see also adverse drug reactions
age groups, PSURs and 67–9
agreements 8, 119–26
algorithms, expediting of reports 42, *43*
annual reports, from registries 147
Annual Safety Reports (ASRs) 142–3
  clinical trials 12, 142, *179–81*
  copies to ethics committees 144
  information from PASS 145
  legislation 170
  non-interventional studies 132
  Periodic Safety Update Reports 147
Anonymised Single Patient Reports (ASPRs) 32
  proposed rationalisation 187–8
appointment of Qualified Persons for
    Pharmacovigilance 1–3
archiving 105
  outsourcing, contracts 122
articles, found in literature searches 56–7
Association of the British Pharmaceutical
    Industry, website, on medical sales
    representatives 111

audits
    computer systems in 25
    definition 191–2
    inspections 153
    of pharmacovigilance 103–5, 106
        management of reports 105
    quality control 7–8, 103

B

back-ups, QPPV 2, 4, 12
    information to 12
    place of residence 5
Bayesian methods, signal detection 76
benefits and risks
    balance, definition 195
    information handling on 12
    literature screening for 51
    impact of potential signals 79–80
Better Regulation of Medicines Initiative
    (BROMI) 187–8
    on duplication in literature searching 58–9
biosimilars, timing of PSURs 62
birth dates
    definition 191
    harmonised, PSURs and 63
    international
        Annual Safety Reports 142
        definition 192
'black triangle' products 42, 97
blinded trials 140–1
    data safety monitoring boards 143
    definition 190
    SAR reports in PSURs 66
    SUSARs 147
    see also unblinding
brand names, in reports from Competent
    Authorities 32
breast milk exposure, expedited case reporting
    45
business continuity plans 24

C

case reference numbers, duplicate report
    management 22
causality
    assessment 39, 133–4
        literature reports 57
    definitions of adverse reactions 189
centrally authorised products, PSURs for 62

children
    definition 68
    Periodic Safety Update Reports 67–8,
        184
CIOMS VII working group, "Development
    Safety Update Report" 142–3
claims for compensation 116
class effects, literature screening 51
clinical trials
    Annual Safety Reports and 12, 142,
        179–81
    categorisation 130–1
    definition 127–8, 190
    information to QPPV 12
    legislation 168–71
    notification of end of 142
    in PSURs 65
    reporting requirements 136–7
    RSI availability 92
    safety reporting 175–85
    written procedures 100
    see also interventional trials
clock start see day zero
co-licensing agreements 123–4
co-marketing agreements 123–4
co-promotion agreements 123–4
coding, Individual Case Safety Reports 33
cohort studies, retrospective 145
collation of pharmacovigilance data 20–2
collection of pharmacovigilance data 20–2
combination products, PSURs for 67
Commission Directive 2003/63/EC 159
Commission Regulations
    540/95 159
    658/2007 160
        infringement procedure 173–4
Committee for Medicinal Products for Human
    Use (CHMP)
    commitments to 13
    guidance on Risk Management Plans 85
    inspections requested by 150
committee meetings, on safety 12
companies see Marketing Authorisation
    Holders
Company Core Data Sheet, definition 190
Company Core Safety Information (CCSI) 91,
    92
    amendment, PSURs and 71
    definition 190–1
    expectedness of adverse drug reaction and
        40

comparator drugs
  definition 190
  interventional trials 133, 138
compassionate use, adverse drug reactions
  failure to report 167
  in PSURs 65
compensation, claims 116
Competent Authorities
  benefits and risks
    information on 12
  checking reports from, duplicate prevention 58
  commitments of MAHs to 13
  mechanisms for responses to 112
  reports from 32
  requests for information 10–11, 23
  requiring changes in RSI 93
  safety variations and 112
  urgent communications from DSMB 143
complaints *see* product technical complaints
completed studies, pharmacovigilance plans in RMPs 88
compliance data, for QPPV 8, 9–10
compliance monitoring, on expedited reports 46
computer systems
  checklist of requirements 24–5
  decision trees for expedited reporting 42
  hybrid with paper-based systems 25–6
  laptop computers, security 117
  pharmacovigilance data handling 20, 23–5
  see also electronic documentation; electronic reporting
concerned investigators, reporting SUSARs to 137
conclusions, PSURs, inconsistent with content 71
confirmation
  consumer reports 74–5
  receipt of pharmacovigilance data 20–1
consistency, RSI 92, 97–8
consultants *see* medical information, contracts for outsourcing
consumer(s), definition 191
consumer reports of adverse drug reactions
  follow-up 34, 74–5, 77
  in PSURs 65
  validity 19
  when expedited 45
contact details
  follow-up 36–7
  Qualified Persons for Pharmacovigilance 3

'Contact us' web forms 30
continuous safety monitoring 11–13, 73–4
  in non-interventional studies 132
  written procedures *100*
contract(s), for transferred pharmacovigilance tasks 8, 119–26
contract QPPV 2–3
contract research organisations, definition 191
contracting out
  literature searches 58–9
  management of registries 146–7
  pharmacovigilance inspections and 151
  quality assurance for 103–4
  written procedures 100
  see also outsourcing
contractual partners
  adverse drug reactions in PSURs 65
  Individual Case Safety Reports from 32–3
control of documents, written procedures for 101
controls *see* comparator drugs
Corrective Action, Preventive Action (CAPA) plan *152*
counterfeiting 82–3
  detection from review of cumulative data 75
covering letters, with PSURs
  of delegation 10
  on RSI versions 69
critical deficiencies 154
critical safety concerns 115
cross-references, in Periodic Safety Update Reports 67
cumulative data
  in PSURs 69–70
  systematic review 75–7, 83
curricula vitae, QPPV 3
customer-facing personnel, training 108

D

data lock points (DLP)
  Annual Safety Reports 142
  PSURs 63
data packages, on potential signals 80
data safety monitoring boards (DSMB) 143
databases
  access for QPPV 7
  within company 117
  decision trees for expedited reporting 42
  epidemiological, adverse drug reactions in PSURs 65

databases—*cont.*
   of medical literature 49, 52
   outside EU 7
   outsourcing, contracts for 122
   for safety data analysis 76
   searches 52–5, 79
date(s)
   ranges, database searches 55
   of receipt, Individual Case Safety Reports 33
   submission of PSURs 63
   see also birth dates
dating, Summaries of Product Characteristics
   97
day zero
   awareness of adverse drug reactions in the
      literature 57, 59
   expedited reporting 34, 45
   upgrading of case assessments 40
deactivation, case reports 41
deadlines
   responses to inspection findings 155
   see also frequency; periodicity
death during clinical trial, legislation 169,
   177
decision trees, expediting of reports 42, *43*
defence of due diligence 168, 171
deficiencies
   adverse drug reaction reporting 47–8
      contracts 125–6
   data management 26–7
   grading of 154–5
   literature searching 59–60
   Periodic Safety Update Reports 70–1
   Qualified Persons for Pharmacovigilance
      14–15
   quality management systems 105–6
   Reference Safety Information 96–7
   signal management 83
   solicited reports 147–8
delegation
   letters of, with PSURs 10
   by QPPV 5
      re PSURs 62
deletion, case reports 41
detailed description of pharmacovigilance
   system (DDPS) 4
   for inspections 153
   with marketing authorisation applications
      114
   offences connected with 164–5
   Risk Management Plans, discrepancies 89

Development Core Data Sheets (DCDS), with
   investigator brochures 135
"Development Safety Update Report" (DSUR),
   CIOMS VII working group 142–3
Developmental Core Safety Information
   (DCSI) 91
   with investigator brochures 135
diagnoses, for adverse drug reaction reports 35
diaries, medical representatives, as source
   documents 31
Direct Healthcare Professional
   Communications (DHPCs) 81
Directives
   2001/20/EC 159
      clinical trials, definition 127–8
      electronic reporting of SUSARs 140
      interventional studies, event reporting
         177–9
      on NIMPs 138, *139, 176*
      on non-interventional studies 176
      (Table)
   2001/28/EC, on investigator brochures
      135
   2001/83/EC 1, 159
      Article 24, 'Sunset Clauses' 113
      Article 93 110
      Article 98 109
      Article 104 46
      Article 111 149–50
      non-interventional studies, safety
         reporting 131–2
      Paragraph 40 109
   2004/24/EC 1, 96, 159
   2004/27/EC 159
      Article 1(23) 113
      on pharmacovigilance inspections
         149–50
      Commission Directive 2003/63/EC 159
directors *see* senior management
disaster recovery plans for information
   technology 24, 117
disease-defining events, clinical trials 136
disease registries 130
disposal of outdated documents, RSIs 94
disputes, on inspection findings 155
distribution of products, by third parties 123
documentation
   of follow-up 36–7
   harmonisation of RSI documents 92
   inspections 153, 154
   labelling committees and 93

of management of contracts 121
on requests for information from
    Competent Authorities 11
on signal detection 74, 80, 83
storage of 105, 106
see also written procedures
double blinding, definition 190
downgrading, case assessments 41
drug registries 130
due diligence, defence of 168, 171
duplicate reports 22, 188
    deactivation 41
    from the literature 58–9

E

early-phase trials, Annual Safety Reports and
    142
efficacy, lack of
    complaints 31
    data in PSURs 66
    expedited case reporting 45
elderly patients, PSURs 67
electronic documentation, conversion from
    paper 105
electronic Medicines Compendium (eMC)
    website 94, 97
electronic reporting
    expedited reports 46
    SUSARs 140
email
    delivery notifications 21
    fitness for purpose 25
Embase 52
emerging safety concerns, role of QPPV 14
end-points, clinical trials 136
enforcement provisions, legislation 164–74
enquiries, to medical information departments
    30
'ENTR/CT' guidance documents 137–8
epidemiology
    databases, adverse drug reactions in PSURs
        65
    safety specifications in Risk Management
        Plans 86, 89
ethics committees
    ASR copies to 144
    independent, definition 192
    reporting reactions to NIMPs 138
    reporting SUSARs to 137, 144
    urgent communications from DSMB 143

EudraVigilance system
    electronic reporting 140
    expedited reporting to 136
    registration of QPPV 4
European Commission Strategy for
    Pharmacovigilance 188
European Medicines Agency (EMEA)
    CHMP-requested inspections 150
    guideline documents 162
    on herbal products 96
    information required 12, 165
European Union
    legislation 159–60
        see also Directives; Regulations
    Risk Management Plans 85, 86–8
events
    cases *vs*, expectedness of adverse drug
        reaction 40
    see also adverse events
Excerpta Medica 52
expectedness
    assessment
    spontaneous cases 39–40, 48
    interventional trials 134–5, 136
    RSIs for 91
expedited reporting 41–6
    from blinded trials 140
    from Competent Authorities 32
    day zero 34, 45
    deficiencies 48
    expectedness and 40
    Individual Case Safety Reports 29
    from interventional trials, to EudraVigilance
        system 136
    from non-interventional studies 131
    product technical complaints 31
    requirements 37–8
exposure registries 130
extensions, PSUR submission dates 63

F

false information, offences 167–8
false representation, fraud by 172–3
final study reports, non-interventional studies
    and 132, *179–81*
follow-up
    adverse drug reactions 34–7
        by Marketing Authorisation Holders 35
    Individual Case Safety Reports (ICSRs) 23
    in Periodic Safety Update Reports 71

follow-up—*cont.*
    potential signals 79–80
    reports in literature 57
'for cause' national inspections 150, 153
forms
    standard, for follow-up 37
    web forms 30
formulations, PSURs for 67
fraud, legislation 172–3
frequency
    reporting SUSARs from clinical trials 137
    submission of PSURs 62–3
        paediatrics 68
    see also periodicity

G

generic products
    review of cumulative data 75
    timing of PSURs 62
geriatrics, PSURs 67
global systems *see* worldwide systems
guidelines
    guidance documents 161–2
    see also written procedures

H

Hampton Review 151
harmonisation
    birth dates (HBD), PSURs and 63
    CIOMS VII proposal on safety documents
        142–3
    RSI documents 92
    see also International Conference on
        Harmonisation
health care professionals (HCPs)
    adverse drug reaction follow-up 34
    clinical trials led by 145–6
    definition 191–2
    medical representatives and 110–11
Healthcare Professional Communications,
    Direct (DHPCs) 81
healthy patients, risk-benefit profiles and 80
herbal medicines
    PSURs and 63
    Updating RSI 95–6
holiday periods, safety information
    management 148
hotline, reporting of counterfeits 82–3
human resources departments 116

hybrid computer- and paper-based systems 25–6

I

impact assessment, changes to computer
        systems 25
independence, data safety monitoring boards
        143
independent ethics committees, definition 192
indexing, database searches 53
Individual Case Safety Reports (ICSRs) 23,
        29–48
    definition 192
    literature search outputs as 56
    literature searching for 49–50
    time allowed 45
infants, definition 68
infectious agents, transmission 45, 79, 195
information technology
    departments 117–18
    electronic documentation, conversion from
        paper 105
    programmers 7
    see also computer systems; electronic
        reporting
infringement procedure, Commission
        Regulation 658/2007 173–4
inspections 149–58
    responding to findings 155–6
    metrics, MHRA website 27
    role of QPPV 13
    see also deficiencies
inspectors, rights 149–50
intensive monitoring, products subject to 42, 97
international birth dates
    Annual Safety Reports 142
    definition 192
International Conference on Harmonisation
        (ICH), documents 161
    E2D, on follow-up 36
    E2E, on Risk Management Plans 85
    E2F, periodic reporting during clinical trials
        143
interventional trials 130–1, 132–44
    definition 128
    PASS 144
    safety reporting 176–85
    SUSARs 133, 135–6, 137–8
        legislation 170, 176
interviews, inspection planning 153
invented names, definition 192

investigational medicinal products (IMPs)
   definitions 129, 193
   reporting requirements 136–8
investigator-led studies 145–6
investigator's brochures (IB) 91, 134–5
   consistency with SPC 97–8
   definition 193

J

job descriptions, QPPV 3

L

labelling
   regulation of 113
   updating 95
labelling committees 93, 97
laboratory parameters, clinical trials 136
language, database searches 55
laptop computers, security 117
legal departments 115–16
   contracts and 120
legislation 159–60
   changes 147–8
   enforcement provisions 164–74
   see also specific instruments
letters, covering PSURs
   of delegation 10
   on RSI versions 69
life-threatening drug reactions, definition 38, 195
limits, to database searches 54–5
listed adverse reactions, definition 193
lists of products, Risk Management Plans and 87
lists of terms, for seriousness assessment 39
literature searching 49–60
   adverse drug reactions in PSURs 50, 65
   outsourcing, contracts 122
   reports of adverse reactions found 58
   results 55–8, 59
literature services, BROMI 187
local affiliates, agreements with 124–5
local publications, Individual Case Safety Reports 49, 50

M

Macrory administrative fines 157
mailboxes (email), fitness for purpose 25
major deficiencies 154

management responsibilities, of QPPV 9
managers see senior management
manufacturing, by third parties 123
marketing applications, requirements on QPPV 4, 6
Marketing Authorisation Holders
   causality assessment 39
   Competent Authorities, duties re reports from 32
   expansion 8
   follow-up of adverse drug reactions 35
   inspections, preparation for 158
   investigator-led studies, role in 145–6
   medical literature, duties re 49
   QPPV, duties re 1–3, 11–12, 13–15
   registry data, duties re 146–7
   reporting reactions to NIMPs to 139
   risk-benefit profile changes, duties re 80
   RSI changes 93
   scientific meetings and 52
   standard operating procedures 6–7
   take-overs 8
marketing authorisations
   Annual Safety Reports and 142
   dates see birth dates
   failure to comply with conditions 164
   rejection 157
   renewal and PSURs 64
   transfer to other companies 125
   worldwide status 113–14, 130–1
marketing departments 111
   signals from 78
   see also medical sales representatives
master cases, duplicate report management 22
medical information 109–10
   contracts for outsourcing 122
   evaluation of adverse drug reactions 35
medical information departments 30
medical meetings
   communications from, literature searching 52
   Individual Case Safety Reports from 50
medical sales representatives 31, 110–11
medically qualified persons
   clinical trials led by 145–6
   pharmacovigilance 5
medicinal products
   definition 193
   risks related to use, definition 195

Medicines Act 1968 160
    inspectors' rights 149
    penalties 168, 171, 172
Medicines and Healthcare products Regulatory
        Agency (MHRA)
    follow-up of reports from 23
    herbal products 96
    Pharmacovigilance Inspectorate 149–58
    website, inspection metrics 27
Medline 52
meetings
    inspections 153, 154
    safety committees 12
    see also medical meetings
misleading information, offences 166, 167–8,
        171
missing facts, adverse drug reaction reports
        18–19
misuse of drugs, reports 36
monitoring see continuous safety monitoring
monographs
    herbal medicines 96
    products 91
multi-item gamma Poisson shrinker 76

N

named-patient use, adverse drug reactions in
        PSURs 65
National Health Service, investigator-led
        studies 145, 146
national inspections 150, 153
national QPPV 2
    PASS protocols and 12
National Research Ethics Service, SUSAR
        reporting 178–9
newborn infants, definition 68
non-clinical staff 114–15
non-interventional studies 130–1
    definition 128, 193
    PASS 144–5
    safety reporting 131–2, 176–85
    using registry data 146
non-investigational medicinal products
        (NIMPs) 133
    definition 129
    reporting requirements 138–9, 176–84
non-serious adverse drug reactions
    delays in transfer to other companies 125
    literature searching 59
norelgestromin 78

Norway 1
note-taking, inspection meetings 154
notepads, medical representatives, as source
        documents 31
notification
    changes, RSI 93–4
    details, QPPV 3–5
    email delivery 21
    end of clinical trials 142
nullification case reports 41
numbering
    cases, duplicate report management 22
    inspection findings 155

O

offences 163–74
    obstruction of inspectors 149
off-label 18, 51, 67
ongoing safety monitoring see continuous
        safety monitoring
ongoing studies, pharmacovigilance plans in
        RMPs 88
organisational charts, QPPV in 4
out-of-hours periods
    contracts on 122
    database access 7
    receipt of adverse drug reaction reports 109
    staff training for 108
outcomes, terms for 54
outdated documents, disposal, RSIs 94
outsourcing
    contracts 121–3
    quality assurance for 103–4
    see also contracting out
over-reporting 45, 136, 147
    see also duplicate reports
overdoses, reports 36
ownership of products, literature search results
        and 56–7, 59

P

paediatrics,
    definitions 68
    PSURs 67–8, 184–5
paper systems 25–6
    computer systems with 25
    conversion to electronic 105
partners see contractual partners
PASS see post-authorisation safety studies

patient information leaflets (PIL) 91
    updating 95
patients
    reports from *see* consumer reports
    special populations
        adverse drug reactions, reports in PSURs
            68
        contraindications in 114
        paediatrics, PSURs 67–8, *184*
    see also registries
penalties
    Medicines Act 1968 168, 171, 172
    see also enforcement provisions
Periodic Safety Update Reports (PSURs) 9–10,
        61–71
    adverse drug reaction reports in preparing
        19
    Annual Safety Reports and 147
    BROMI working group on 188
    deficiencies in management 26
    definition 194
    formulations (pharmaceutical), separate for
        each 67
    legislation *181–5*
    literature monitoring for 50, 52
    non-clinical studies 115
    non-interventional studies 132
    outsourcing of production, contracts
        122–3
    regulatory affairs departments and 113
    review of 77
    when to be submitted 62–3
periodicity
    pharmacovigilance inspections 151
    RSI updating 94–5
    refresher training 108
    review of cumulative data 75, 83
    updates to Risk Management Plans 87
    see also frequency
Pharmaceutical Information and
        Pharmacovigilance Association, website
        110
pharmacovigilance data
    definition 17–18
    management 17–27
    selection for PSURs 64–5
    see also databases
Pharmacovigilance Inspection Action Group
        (PIAG) *152*, 156–7
Pharmacovigilance Inspectorate, MHRA
        149–58

pharmacovigilance plans, European Union
        Risk Management Plan 86, 88, 89
pharmacovigilance systems (MAHs), QPPV
        responsibilities 6–9
placebos
    reporting reactions to 140
    see also comparator drugs
planning of inspections 153
poison control centres, adverse drug reactions
        in PSURs 65
post-authorisation data, in Risk Management
        Plans 87
post-authorisation safety studies (PASS) 130–1,
        144–5, *181–2*
    definition 129, 194
    medical information personnel and 109
    protocols 12
    in PSURs 65
    reports 12–13
    signal validation 80
post-authorisation studies 130–1
    definition 129, 194
post-marketing commitments 112
posters, literature searching 52
potential signals 78–81
precision, database searches 53
pregnancy 35, 48
    database search deficiencies 54
    expedited case reporting 45
prescribing information, changes to 69
prioritization by importance, follow-up 36
product monographs 91
product quality 115
product technical complaints 30–1, 115
    legal departments and 115–16
profile-raising, of QPPV 9
programmers, IT 7
progress reports, from PASS 145, *179*
promotional activities, Risk Management Plans
        and 89
proportional reporting ratio (PRR) 76
PSURs *see* Periodic Safety Update Reports

Q

qualifications
    Qualified Persons for Pharmacovigilance 5
    for searching literature 56
Qualified Persons for Pharmacovigilance
        (QPPV) 1–15
    changes of 4

Qualified Persons for Pharmacovigilance
    (QPPV)—*cont.*
  failure to appoint 166
  Competent Authority lists of 5
  offences of 166
  outsourced, contracts 122
  Periodic Safety Update Reports 61–2
      quality control 70
  potential signals and 79
  responsibilities 6–13
  risk-benefit profile changes, duties re 80
quality assurance 7–8, 103–5, 194
quality control (QC) 7–8, 194
    checks on expedited reports 44, 48
    of PSURs 70
quality management 194
    systems 99–106, 194

R

randomness, pharmacovigilance data sample
    checking 21
re-inspections 156, 157
reassessment of cases 37–8
recall, database searches 53
receipt of ADR reports, out-of-hours 109
receipt of Individual Case Safety Reports, dates
    of 33
receipt of pharmacovigilance data,
    confirmation 20–1
reclassification
  duplicate reports 22
  valid adverse drug reactions 18–19, 22
reconciliation, pharmacovigilance data transfer
    20, 21
  deficiencies 26
record keeping
  for literature searches 55
  offences connected with 166
recording
  Individual Case Safety Reports 33
  of self-learning 102
reference numbers, cases, duplicate report
    management 22
Reference Safety Information (RSIs) 91–8
  consistency 92, 97–8
  in PSURs 69, 71
refresher training 108
registration
  herbal products 96
  QPPV, with EudraVigilance system 4

registries
  data used in studies 146–7
  definition 130
regression tests, changes to computer systems
    25
Regulations (EU)
  658/2007 6
  726/2004 1, 159
      Article 19, on inspections 150
      Article 23(b) 10
      Article 24 46
  1901/2006 68–9, 159–60
  1902/2006 68–9, 160
regulatory affairs departments 111–14
renewals of marketing authorisations, PSURs
    and 64
reportable adverse drug reactions 19
reporters, definition 194
representatives, medical sales 31, 110–11
requests for information, Competent
    Authorities 10–11, 23
requests for inspections, CHMP 150
residence, place of, QPPV 5
results of inspections, MHRA website 27
results of literature searching 55–8, 59
retrospective cohort studies 145
retrospective reviews, pharmacovigilance data
    transfer failures 21
review
  adverse drug reaction reports 74–5
  cumulative data 75–7, 83
  literature search outputs 56–7
  pharmacovigilance data transfer failures
    21
  RSI 94–5
review publications, database searches 55
risk
  minimisation
      after potential signals 79
      Risk Management Plans 86–7, 88
  related to use of medicinal product,
      definition 195
risk–benefit assessment *see* benefits and risks
risk–benefit balance, definition 195
Risk Management Plans (RMPs) 13–14,
    85–9
  data in PSURs 66
  medical information personnel in 109
  signal detection commitments 74
risk management systems, definition 197
RiskMAP (US) 85

S

safety
  concerns
    critical 115
    emerging, role of QPPV 14
    leading to delayed submission of PSURs
      63
    reactions to NIMPs 138–9
  continuous monitoring 11–13, 73–4
    in non-interventional studies 132
    written procedures *100*
  information (data) 109–10
    evaluation 73–83
    holiday periods 148
    in literature 50, 52
    sharing 120, 125
  reporting
    clinical trials 175–88
    legislation enforcement provisions
      169–71
    non-interventional studies 131–2,
      176–85
  restrictions *see* urgent safety restrictions
  specifications, Risk Management Plans 86,
    87–8
  variations of 112
  see also post-authorisation safety studies
safety committee meetings 12
safety monitoring boards, for data (DSMB) 143
sales departments, signals from 78
sales representatives, medical 31, 110–11
sampling
  pharmacovigilance data checking 21
  quality control (QC) checks, expedited
    reports 44
scientific meetings
  Individual Case Safety Reports from 50
  Marketing Authorisation Holders and 52
scientific services 109
  legislation 172
searches
  of databases 52–5, 79
  see also literature searching
security, information technology 117
self-audits 104
self-learning, recording of 102
senior management 116–17
  liability under Medicines Act 168
serious adverse drug reactions (SARs)
  definition 195

investigational medicinal products 136
  to NIMPs 138–9
  from non-interventional studies 131
  overdose and misuse 36
  in PSURs 66
  see also suspected unexpected serious
    adverse drug reactions
seriousness
  assessment for 38–9, 48
severity of adverse effects, detection of change
  77
signals
  deficiencies in management 83
  detection 73–4
    documentation 74, 83
    methods 75–8
    outsourcing 123
  from non-clinical studies 115
  potential 78–81
single blinding, definition 192
solicited reports 127–48
  definition 128
  registry reports as 146
solicited sources of individual case safety
  reports, definition 196
source data, pharmacovigilance data 20
sources of reports
  adverse events 107
  suspected adverse drug reactions
    29–33
special populations *see* patients, special
  populations
'specials' (unlicensed medicines) 46–7
  NIMPs 139, *178*
specificity, expectedness and 40
sponsors, definition 196
spontaneous reporting 29–48
  definition 196
  in PSURs 65
Standardised MedDRA queries (SMQs) 79
standard forms, for follow-up 37
standard operating procedures (SOPs)
  adequacy 104
  Marketing Authorisation Holders 6–7
statistics
  signal detection 76
  special patient populations 68
Statutory Instrument 1994/3144, definition of
  'specials' 47
storage, of documentation 105, 106
submission dates, PSURs 63

Summary of Pharmacovigilance Systems (SPS) *152*, *153*
Summaries of Product Characteristics (SPC) 91
    amendment, PSURs and 71
    communication to sales representatives 111
    consistency with IBs 97
    dating 97
    expectedness assessment against 39, 40
    in interventional trials 134, 135
    unexpected adverse reactions and 197
summary tabulations, in PSURs 69–70
'Sunset Clauses' 113–14
superseded documents, RSI 94
suspected adverse drug reactions 18
    sources of reports 29–33
suspected unexpected serious adverse drug
        reactions (SUSARs)
    blinded 147
    electronic reporting 140
    ethics committees, reporting to 144
    interventional trials 133, 135–6, 137–8
        legislation 170, 176
    National Research Ethics Service *179–80*
    in non-interventional studies 131
    non-investigational products *177–8*, 179
    outside EU 137
    in PSURs 66
synchronisation initiative, timing of PSURs
        62–3
systems-based inspections 150

tabulations, in PSURs 69–70
take-overs, Marketing Authorisation Holders 8
technical complaints *see* product technical
        complaints
templates, Summary of Pharmacovigilance
        Systems (SPS) 153
term selection, database searches 53–4
third parties *see* contract(s)
time allowed
    expedited reporting 45–6
    training 99
timelines
    updating RSI 94–5
    see also frequency; periodicity
toddlers, definition 68
tracking, pharmacovigilance data transfer 20–1
training
    in computer systems 24

of and by medical information personnel
        110
    personnel responsible for 116
    in pharmacovigilance 9, 101–3, 106, 108
    time allowed 99
transfer
    failure of, pharmacovigilance data 21
    marketing authorisations, to other
        companies 125
    pharmacovigilance data 20–1
        deficiencies 26
translations, articles in the literature 57
transmission of infectious agents 45, 79, 195

unauthorised indications, signals from use for
        78
unblinding, for reporting 140–1, 143
unexpected adverse reactions
    definition 196–7
    see also suspected unexpected serious
        adverse drug reactions
United Kingdom legislation 160
    enforcement provisions 164–8
universities, clinical trials led by *see*
        investigator-led studies
unlicensed medicines ('specials') 46–7
    NIMPs 139, *178*
unlisted adverse reactions, definition 197
updating
    algorithms for expedited reporting 42
    computer systems 25
    product information
        dissemination 110
        to sales representatives 111
    RSI 93–5, 96–7
        herbal medicines 95–6
    Risk Management Plans 87
upgrading, case assessments 40, 41
urgent communications from DSMB 143
urgent safety restrictions 112
    definition 197
    failure to implement 164

valid adverse drug reactions 34
    reclassification 18–19, 22
validation of signals, post-authorisation safety
        studies 80

Venn diagrams
   adverse drug reactions *18*
   types of trial or study *130, 131*
versions,
   Reference Safety Information (RSIs) 94
      in PSURs 69
   Procedures, 101

web forms, 'Contact us' 30
websites
   ABPI, on medical sales representatives
      111
   electronic Medicines Compendium (eMC)
      94, 97
   on Medical Dictionary for Regulatory
      Activities 33

MHRA, inspection results 27
Pharmaceutical Information and
      Pharmacovigilance Association 110
withdrawal from market, literature search after
      51
worldwide experience, literature on 51
worldwide marketing authorisation status
      113–14, 130–1
worldwide systems
   pharmacovigilance data collection 20
   quality assurance 103
written procedures 99–101
   on QPPV 4
   for written procedures 101

Yellow Card Scheme 32, *176–7*